DAUGHTERS *of* IRELAND

DEBBIE BLAKE

DAUGHTERS of IRELAND

PIONEERING

IRISH WOMEN

The
History
Press
Ireland

First published 2015

The History Press Ireland
50 City Quay
Dublin 2
Ireland
www.thehistorypress.ie

British Library Cataloguing in Publication Data.
A catalogue record for this book is available from the British Library.

ISBN 978 1 84588 881 7

Typesetting and origination by The History Press
Printed and bound by TJ International Ltd, Padstow, Cornwall

CONTENTS

INTRODUCTION

'It is not easy to be a pioneer – but oh, it is fascinating!
I would not trade one moment, even the worst moment,
for all the riches in the world.'

Elizabeth Blackwell

It was whilst I was researching women in aviation that I came across the remarkable Lilian Bland from County Antrim, who was the first woman in the world to not only design, but to build and successfully fly her own aircraft, which she aptly named the *Mayfly*. Reading her fascinating story of sheer guts and determination led me to explore other women who had pushed and broken the boundaries of their gender to become the first in their field. I soon discovered that there were a number from Ireland, who although they were well known in their day, sadly had been long forgotten or overshadowed by their male counterparts.

Daughters of Ireland is a glimpse into the fascinating lives of a selection of some of the most innovative women in Irish history, women who were ahead of their time, paving the way for future generations to follow. They came from all walks of life, from impoverished to more affluent backgrounds, and some left their homeland and familiarity, either by necessity or choice. Whatever their circumstances they all had total commitment to their passion or cause, which they bravely followed, taking

risks and facing any challenges head on. As the American businessman
Alfred P. Sloan once said, 'There has to be this pioneer, the individual
who has the courage, the ambition to overcome the obstacles that always
develop when one tries to do something worthwhile, especially when it is
new and different.'

The lengths that the women were prepared to go in order to fulfil their
goals is highly admirable. Dr James Barry (born Margaret Anne Bulkley)
went to the extreme of masquerading as a man throughout her adult life in
order to pursue a career as a military surgeon in the British Army. She qualified many years before women were officially recognised as medical
doctors and as early as 1826 performed the world's first recorded successful
caesarean section. Nellie Cashman, intrepid pioneer of the American west,
often risked her life wandering the mining camps of Arizona and Alaska
during the gold rush in search of the 'Big Bonanza'.

The women that I have chosen to include in this book each followed
a different path, from Anne Jellicoe in education to Ninette de Valois
in the performing arts and Eileen Gray in architecture. Whichever trail
they took, these ground-breaking women provided opportunities for
future generations which otherwise may not have been possible. They are
truly inspirational.

Dr James Miranda Barry

1799?–1865

'There was a certain effeminacy in his manner
which he was always striving to overcome.'

Lord Albemarle on James Barry

The life of Dr James Barry is surrounded by mystery and intrigue. Born Margaret Ann Bulkley, she lived the majority of her life as a masquerade, to pursue a career she loved and to succeed in a man's world. She was way ahead of her time regarding health and sanitation and her pioneering surgery and innovative medical treatments saved countless lives.

Little is known of Dr Barry's early life and as it was not mandatory to register births until later in the nineteenth century, there are several assumptions as to the details of her background and exact year of birth. Even Dr Barry herself was very noncommittal when it came to any official documentation, stating her birth date to be 'about 1799' although some sources approximate earlier dates of 1789 and 1795. Details of her parentage were very furtive, with speculation that she may have been illegitimate or orphaned and adopted by notable gentry. However, she did stress in correspondence to a friend that she was the nephew of the most prominent romantic artist of the eighteenth century, the infamous James Barry from Cork. It is believed that Dr Barry was one of two daughters of Jeremiah

Bulkley, who ran a grocery shop at Merchant's Quay, Cork city and that her mother was his wife, Mary Anne Bulkley, the sister of James Barry RA. However, Margaret always referred to and insisted that Mary Anne was her aunt.

Dr James Barry. (Courtesy of the Wellcome Library, London)

Jeremiah Bulkley had accumulated debts which led to his bankruptcy, causing friction within the marriage, so in 1805 Mary Anne left Cork and travelled to London with Margaret in the hope of receiving help from her estranged brother, James Barry, with whom there had been no contact for many years. Unfortunately, her brother had also fallen into financial difficulty, having been dismissed from his position as Professor of Painting at the Royal Academy of Arts, and was living in hardship. However, the introduction into the circle of his closest and very influential liberal-minded friends, three in particular, was to prove imperative for Margaret's future. The most influential was the romantic idealist General Francisco de Miranda, the Venezuelan revolutionary, who allowed Margaret the use of his library in which his extensive collection of books satisfied her appetite for knowledge and her interest in medicine, where she found 'a list of tomes to form a tolerably complete medical library for a private gentleman who is not of the profession'. Her promising aptitude and absorbing mind didn't go unnoticed by the General, who saw a future for her in the medical profession, which required an education at university level. Unfortunately for Margaret she was the wrong sex, as women were not allowed admittance into university, the highest progression they could hope to obtain would be the position of a governess. It was to be around another sixty years before Elizabeth Garrett Anderson, the first female doctor in Britain, graduated in 1865. Mary Anne Bulkley was keen for Margaret to have an education and enter a profession, in order to 'put her in a way to get decent bread for herself' but with the additional hindrance of no financial means, it remained impossible.

In February 1806, James Barry RA died and although he had lived in poverty, his funeral was a grand affair at St Paul's Cathedral in London. David Stewart Erskine, 11th Earl of Buchan, had been a close friend of James Barry and was a passionate patron of the arts and had helped James financially in the latter part of his life. He was also an avid campaigner for female education, declaring that 'the whole female code of education must be changed'. He recognised Margaret's potential as a medical student, along with General Miranda and Dr Edward Fryer, the scholar and physician who had tutored Margaret. The three men became her benefactors, who worked together compiling a publication of James Barry's essays and drawings on art, in which the *Gentleman's Magazine* in 1806, reported that Lord Buchan's intention was 'to publish them for the advantage of some indigent relatives of the departed artist'. *The Works of James Barry* was published in 1809 and with the proceeds of the sale of both the book and some of James Barry's paintings, Margaret was a little closer to entering university. The prestigious Edinburgh University, notably one of the best in the world, was deemed the most appropriate choice for Margaret and with the influence of Lord Buchan's aristocratic position and his connections with the university, Margaret was accepted, but only after a major decision and transformation had taken place.

It is unclear whose idea or decision it was to completely change not just Margaret's name but her whole persona, but in November 1809 she became James Miranda Barry, adopting her late uncle's name and the middle name of her much-admired mentor General Miranda, whom she aspired to imitate. She was to enter university life as a male, a façade that she would continue for the rest of her life. She travelled with Mary Anne to Edinburgh where they found lodgings at 6 Lothian Street, and during the three years of her studying she was prudent in her deception, leading a very discreet lifestyle. On her arrival at university James had stated that she was younger than she was, as she was conscious that her smooth complexion would not pass as a young male. She threw herself into her studies, at which she excelled, but avoided any social jovialities with the other students, keeping her friends to a minimum. Although there was one exception, fellow student John Jobson, who was a similar height to James, being around five feet, but was more athletic. He tried to encourage James to box, but found that 'he would never strike out, but kept his arms over his chest, to protect it from blows'. John appears to have gained James's trust, as he was invited to her lodgings, where she referred to Mrs Bulkley as her mother, rather than her usual term of aunt. In later years John recollected James as being 'remarkable by the persistency with which he avoided his fellow students' and remembered with amusement her 'long surtout' or man's frock coat which she wore, comically standing out amongst the other students in their 'shooting-coats'. He was never suspicious nor did he question James's gender, and was genuinely shocked when it was revealed after her death.

Mrs Bulkley left Edinburgh in the summer of 1810, and arrangements were made by Lord Buchan for James to lodge with a former medical doctor, Dr Robert Anderson, now a scholar, editor and biographer. Highly acclaimed for his radical publications and promotion for new writers, his home was the nucleus for literary life in Edinburgh, regularly attracting poets and writers, and was far livelier than the lodgings that James had shared with Mary Anne. James's life had now become less secluded; she was mixing with other men socially and was able to observe their deportment and attitudes, which enabled her to master her disguise. Dr Anderson seemed convinced, as in a letter to Lord Buchan he described James as a 'well-disposed young man'. Despite the activity in her new lodgings, James remained attentive to her studies and proved to be an outstanding student. In addition to the obligatory anatomy and surgery, she studied gynaecology and midwifery, subjects that were not practiced by male physicians at the time. Nonetheless, they were to prove invaluable further into her career. When the time came for her to take her final exams she was refused due to her 'extreme youth' but Lord Buchan interceded that there was no minimum age regulated for degree candidates and so, in the summer of 1812, James was permitted to sit her exams, which she passed with ease. She was awarded the Diploma of Doctor of Medicine, making history as the first woman in Britain to graduate in medicine, although it was not known at the time.

James left Edinburgh shortly after her exams in the autumn of 1812, and travelled to London where she registered at the United Hospitals of Guy's and St Thomas's, as pupil dresser to Sir Astley Cooper, the country's highly respected and leading surgeon. James was extremely honoured to be taught by the best teacher in the medical profession, as tuition given by Sir Astley was held in high esteem and was the ultimate goal for any medical student. His expertise and skill as a surgeon would be demonstrated to his students, who would watch with fascination his delicacy in performing the most intricate procedures, informing his students that 'A surgeon should have an eagle's eye, a lady's hand and a lion's heart.' Initially the role of the dresser was to hand the instruments and dressings to the surgeon during the operation, but through time they had been given more responsibility and their position had progressed to an assistant surgeon. They frequently had to conduct operations in anatomy theatres, under the watchful eyes of an often knowledgeable and disparaging audience. A letter written by one of James's colleagues clarifies the role of the assistant surgeon as 'a foremost character in the presence of numerous spectators, by which he must acquire confidence and courage'. In these situations the ability to act was also required to some extent in order to instil trust in the nervous public, a beneficial practice for James's charade.

It was not unusual for students to succumb to illness from attending the surgical lectures held in the unhealthy atmosphere of the operating theatres. The death of the young poet John Keats in 1821 from tuberculosis was thought to have been caused by his catching the disease during his time as a medical student. James Barry was conscious of her own health, adopting a code of cleanliness and nutrition, and she drank very little alcohol, unlike her contemporaries who were known to be wild and excessive outside their medical school hours. She would much rather drink milk, recognising its nutritional value, and was also a vegetarian. James may not have had an interest in hard living, but her obsession with fashion was obvious, as she embraced with relish the immaculate and elegant attire of dandyism, the fashion trend of the day. A dandy's clothes were very snug fitting and seamless, with tight-fitting breeches worn with riding boots or silk stockings with pumps. Short, square-cut waistcoats were worn with the upper buttons undone to show the frill of the shirt, of which the upright collar was kept in place usually by a cravat, over which a wasp-waisted padded jacket with a high collar was worn. The hair was dyed, powdered and cut short under a top hat. James was in her element with this effeminate fashion and dyed her hair red to match the red stacked heels on her boots. The clean-shaven face of a dandy finished the look perfectly for her, as Charles Dickens later referred to her as 'unique in appearance, and eccentric in manner'.

Britain's involvement in the Napoleonic Wars had brought a demand for doctors in the British Army, with preference to men educated to university level, to replace the barber-surgeons. The army was a good career, offering a good wage and the opportunity to travel, and James was keen to enlist. She successfully passed her exams at the Royal College of Surgeons, and qualified as a Regimental Surgeon in January 1813, and in June the same year, passed the Army Medical Board Examination. Although a physical examination was required to enlist in the army and it's not clear how James managed to avoid it, in the following month she was stationed at the General Hospital in the Plymouth garrison as a hospital assistant, where she stayed until she was posted to Cape Town, South Africa in the summer of 1816.

Lord Buchan had maintained an interest in James and may have had some bearing on her position at Plymouth Hospital. He had given James a letter of introduction to General Lord Charles Somerset, governor of the Cape Colony, a widower grieving for the loss of his wife Elizabeth only a year earlier. He carried an anger and bitterness towards his physician, who had insisted a few days before his wife's death that 'there was not the slightest cause for apprehension'. Lord Buchan had presented Lord Somerset with a highly favourable character and professional reference of James as a potential successor for his inept physician. James's amusing wit, charm and intellect, combined with her youthful exuberance and excellent medical knowledge appealed to Lord Somerset, who came from a long line of aristocracy and held a position of utmost power within the colony. Although he could be very domineering and pig-headed, Lord Somerset could also be hospitable, kind and full of fun and was a great lover of the outdoors. Both he and James were animal lovers and had a passion for fine horses and a love of horse racing, with both being very adept riders. Shortly after her arrival in Cape Town, James was presented with a poodle called Psyche, which was believed to be a present from Lord Somerset. James made a good impression with the governor and also his two daughters who lived with him, and soon became a regular figure amongst the household.

James was becoming highly respected as a physician and her advanced medical skills were welcomed by the people of Cape Town. However, they regarded her odd effeminate mannerisms and high-pitched voice with suspicion and nicknamed her 'Kapok Doctor' when it became apparent that she was padding the shoulders and upper arms of her clothes with cotton. Doubt had arisen as to the young doctor's gender shortly after her arrival in Cape Town and gossip was spreading rapidly. Captain William Dillon, a patient James had treated, wrote that 'from the awkwardness of his gait and the shape of his person, it was the prevailing opinion that he was a female'. Nonetheless, whether James was aware of the gossip or not, she made no attempt to tone down her flamboyant appearance, and took great delight in the vibrant social life of Cape Town, attending the theatre, balls and various parties. She became very popular with the women, who were attentive to her charm and wit, much to the disgruntlement of their male companions, and earned a reputation as a flirt. It was later thought that this behaviour may have been an intentional diversion from suspicion on her part. Lord Albemarle, after meeting James at a regimental dinner, remarked that 'he was the most skilful of physicians and most wayward of men.'

In September 1818 James was confronted with the ultimate test to her medical proficiency, when Lord Somerset fell very ill with typhoid fever. James remained constantly at his bedside, caring for him and administering his treatment. At one point it looked as though the governor wouldn't survive and the Inspector General of Hospitals wanted to inform the government in England to prepare for the worst, but James was adamant that he would recover and managed to convince the colonial secretary, Colonel Bird, to wait for another two days. On 1 October the governor's fever passed and Colonel Bird was able to announce that the governor was now recovering well, which he attributed to the expertise of Dr Barry. Later that year, in December, James was officially appointed personal physician to the governor, a position which gave her a pay rise and apartments at Government House, where she took on a black slave servant called Dantzen, who, along with a succession of poodle dogs, would remain with James throughout her life. She still stayed with the army, where she remained a junior officer.

James was introducing a radical preventive practice of medicine in Cape Town, and seeing the need for reform in the prisons and hospitals, endeavoured to improve the sanitary conditions and campaigned against inadequate drainage, poor ventilation and overcrowding. Her insistence on scrupulous cleanliness, both in her patients' homes and in the sickbays, was regarded by some as intrusive, but Lord Somerset acknowledged the importance of her methods and took every opportunity to promote her skills. Referring to James as a 'prodigy', he urged any friends that were unwell to avail of 'Dr Barry's very extraordinary skill', as someone who had 'attested wonders since he has been here'. Unlike the local doctors, she showed no discrimination against any patients, whether they were lepers or prisoners and did not go along with the colony's racial prejudices. Her concern for the nutrition and hygiene of black prisoners irritated the prison authorities, as they questioned, 'Why do you ask blacks questions, while Christians are present to answer?'

Although she was known to have a firm but very kind and gentle manner with her ailing patients, James could be quite feisty and was known to fly into a rage at any critical reference to her height or masculinity, and was more than capable of standing her ground in an argument. She knew that she always had Lord Somerset's constant support and backing, even in her acts of insubordination, which according to Lord Albemarle were often, as he later recalled: 'He was frequently guilty of flagrant breaches of discipline. And on more than one occasion was sent home under arrest, but somehow or other his offences were always condoned at headquarters.' By now, a mutual attraction had developed between the middle-aged Lord and the young doctor. At first rumours circulated of a romantic liaison between James and the governor's eldest daughter, Georgina Somerset, but the attention would soon turn to Lord Somerset himself, with whom James was a constant companion.

An incident with Captain Cloete, aide-de-camp to Lord Somerset, added further fuel to the gossip and put James at risk of exposure. It wasn't unusual for men of Lord Somerset's social stature to accept the favours of prostitutes and on one occasion James was told by Captain Cloete, that 'a buxom lady called to see him [Lord Somerset] on business of a private nature, and they were closeted for some time'. Evidently James was furiously jealous and, knowing Cloete's Dutch background, made a derogatory remark about the prostitute being 'a nice Dutch filly'. When James refused to 'retract his vile expression' a duel was fought, in which it appears that Cloete, with whom James was no match, being a complete amateur, may have purposely missed James, although he did recall later that James had boasted that 'he'd shot off the peak of the Captain's cap'. The duel was talked about for many years later and as a result of it, a life-long friendship formed between the captain and the doctor.

Lord Somerset left Cape Town in 1819 and returned to England, with the intention of finding a wife. There is some speculation as to James's whereabouts at this time, as she also left the colony. It's possible that she attended the sick during a cholera outbreak in Mauritius, but due to the inaccuracy of records relating to her life, it remains a mystery. However, she had returned to Cape Town when Lord Somerset arrived in November 1821 with his new wife, Lady Mary Poulett, daughter of the 4th Earl of Poulett.

In March 1822, following the resignation of Dr Robb, James accepted the post of Colonial Medical Inspector, which came with a large salary, huge responsibilities and considerable authority. However, she also chose to remain with the army as an assistant surgeon on half-pay. Her new position enabled her to tackle and bring reforms to the health issues in the colony that had been troubling her. She was extremely determined and left no stone unturned when she inspected every public institution of Cape Town, diligently carrying out her duties above and beyond her position as an inspector. She became a force to be reckoned with, accepting no excuses for the neglect and inadequacies she found in the leper hospitals, prisons and lunatic asylums. People from all social backgrounds were treated by Dr James Barry. She showed no discrimination against black people, slaves or the poor, frequently subsidizing them from her own income.

During one particular inspection visit to the inaptly named 'Heaven and Earth' leper colony, seventy miles from Cape Town, she witnessed the neglect and terrible conditions in the hospital where the lepers were supposed to have been nursed. They were dirty, starved and left untreated, and were made to labour in the grounds, a far cry from what the name of the colony implied. James wrote with horror that 'nothing could excel the misery of the 120 lepers squalid and wretched beyond description ... The doctor seemed to take not the slightest interest in the poor people entrusted in his care'. Through the backing of Lord Somerset, James was able to restructure the hospital and raise the standards to her expectations.

Throughout the 1820s James continued her crusade across the colony, determined to make drastic changes in the lives of those who were disregarded and ostracised, campaigning for their human rights, particularly in the lunatic asylums and prisons. She probed and scrutinised and constantly wrote formal complaints about the deplorable conditions in the lunatic hospital where she found 'the whole establishment void of cleanliness, order or professional care'. Her concern didn't stop at public institutions, she also promoted the importance of hygiene and diet to the public and distributed written publications on advice for the recognition and treatment of certain illnesses. However, her radical improvements to Cape Town were not always met with approval, as she had become known to be obstinate on certain issues and her lack of tact wasn't always well received. She was against cruelty towards the slaves and her support for the rights of black people clashed with some of the colony's official policies and gained her some enemies. This didn't help the rumours that were rapidly spreading of a suspected relationship between the doctor and the governor.

Meanwhile the Cape Government had come under scrutiny, and Lord Somerset found himself in the centre of an inquiry investigating the alleged embezzlement of funds and excessive expenditure. A Commission of Inquiry was sent over from England to investigate. Although some accusations in the press were exaggerated and not completely true, the tense feeling of unrest grew amongst the public. The political attack on the governor was soon to strike at his private life.

On the morning of 1 June 1824, news spread of a placard that had been placed on a bridge at Table Bay, containing serious accusations towards Lord Somerset and Dr Barry. It had been read by several people by the time it was ripped down later in the morning, and the nature of its contents had rapidly spread across the colony. Captain John Findley, who later gave evidence in court, stated that it read:

> A person living in Newlands (Government House), takes this method of making it known, to the public authorities of this Colony that on the 5th instant he detected Lord Charles buggering Dr Barry. Lady Charles had her suspicions, or saw something that led to her suspicion, which has caused a general quarrel ... The person is ready to come and make oaths to the above.

At the time homosexuality was an offence punishable by death. A reward was offered by Lord Somerset, for any information on the perpetrator who he claimed was intending 'to disgrace my character and honour and that of one of the officers of the Government'. The culprits were caught within a few weeks, but the person 'living at Newlands' was never disclosed, perhaps he or she was fictitious or Lord Somerset dealt with them privately.

Sir Richard Plasket, Secretary to the Government, had already informed Parliament in London that the government of the Cape was in a 'state of total incompetence' and the suspected scandalous affair with Dr Barry had made the situation a lot worse. On the morning of 5 March 1826, Lord Somerset set sail for England with his wife and daughter, intending to face the accusations against him and clear his name. He never returned to Cape Town and was later cleared of any charges in 1827. After his resignation as governor, he left politics and retired to a life of horse racing and socializing. James remained in Cape Town and although she was demoted to assistant staff surgeon, she was about to make history for the second time and restore her reputation in the colony.

On 25 July 1826 James was urgently called to the home of Thomas Munnik, where his wife, Wilhelmina, was having a difficult labour with her first child. After examining her James could see that both mother and baby's life were in danger, so she made a quick and dangerous decision to perform a Caesarean section. She had only read about the procedure, and had no practical experience of the operation. Although there had previously been several attempts by other surgeons it had been at the sacrifice of either mother or baby or both. Fortunately, James had made the right decision and delivered a healthy baby boy by the first known successful Caesarean section, with both mother and baby surviving. James' reputation was restored, as not only was the operation a success, which became known worldwide, but the Munnik family were highly influential and were extremely grateful to James. James refused the generous fee offered to her, but asked for the baby to be named after her. She also became young James Barry Munnik's godfather and for many years her name was carried down through the family in the first-born sons.

Two years later, in October 1828, James was posted to the island of Mauritius, and took Dantzen with her. Shortly after her arrival, James received news that Lord Somerset was very ill and immediately left Mauritius for England, without applying for leave of absence. Although Lord Somerset was gravely ill, he perked up at the sight of James, who cared for him for fourteen months until he died of a seizure in February 1831 at the age of sixty-three. The funeral was held at St Andrew's church, Hove in Brighton. Though he was a colourful character in life, Lord Somerset had surprisingly left instructions for a modest burial, 'with the least possible expense'.

Shortly after the funeral James was posted to Jamaica, where she successfully controlled an epidemic outbreak of yellow fever at Stony Hill barracks and by the time she had left in 1834 she had considerably reduced the mortality rate. After a brief period back in England on leave, she was posted to St Helena, as principal medical officer, where her continuing persistence in seeking sanitation improvements and hospital reforms, particularly for women and the mentally ill, landed her in hot water again with the authorities and ultimately a court martial. In 1845 she was sent to the West Indies where, for the first time in her medical career, she became the patient, catching yellow fever. Her refusal to have any visitors other than the doctor attending her and one single friend, aroused suspicion and James travelled home to England, where she would spend the next year recovering.

The remaining years of James's army career were spent in Malta, Corfu and briefly serving in the Crimean War, saving the lives of many soldiers. However, Florence Nightingale was less impressed by Dr Barry's opinions, describing her as 'a brute' and 'the most hardened creature I ever met'. Her last post was as an Inspector General of Hospitals in Canada, a complete contrast to the heat of the tropics which she had been used to. But after catching bronchitis in 1859, she had to return to England, and through recurrent health problems she was forced by the military medical board to retire from the army on half pay.

Apart from a trip back to Jamaica, James spent her last years in London, where she lodged in a dentist's house in Cavendish Square with her constant companions, her black manservant and her poodle. The heat, combined with poor sanitation in the hot summer of 1865 found London in the grip of an outbreak of chronic diarrhoea, which was rapidly claiming lives. In July, James fell ill to the disease from which she had nursed many patients, and which she had spent the majority of her life trying to prevent, but it was one she couldn't recover from herself. On the morning of 25 July 1865, Dr James Barry died. It was also the birthday of her godson, James Barry Munnik, whom she had delivered with her pioneering Caesarean operation, thirty-nine years earlier. She was buried at Kensal Green cemetery, her grave marked with a simple headstone.

James had always insisted that in the event of her death her body should not be examined, but be wrapped and buried in her bed sheets. However, Sophie Bishop, the woman who had laid out Dr Barry prior to her burial, exposed a shocking revelation. She claimed that the doctor was in fact a woman and she had shown evident signs of having carried a child. The epidemic of dysentery that had been the cause of James's death had meant that she had been buried quickly and so no post mortem had been carried out on her body. She was denied a military funeral and to avoid a major scandal the British Army concealed any records relating to her life for many years afterwards. The question of her pregnancy and birth still remains a mystery today, although it's assumed that it may be the explanation of her time spent in Mauritius. Regardless of the ambiguity surrounding the life of Dr James Barry, her high medical standards and skills as a doctor remain unquestionable.

Margaret Louisa Aylward

1810–1889

'It is a glorious and inestimable privilege to
labour for the preservation of the faith.'

Margaret Louisa Aylward

Margaret Aylward's story is of a middle-class woman's faith, courage
and determination, a woman whose passion and philanthropic work
brought about dramatic social changes and improvements amongst
Dublin's poor. Her pioneering fosterage system and her formation of the
city's poor schools are an exceptional contribution to Ireland's history.

Born on 23 November 1810 in Waterford to a wealthy Catholic merchant family, Margaret Aylward was the fifth child of William and Ellen
Aylward, who had ten children. She also had a half-brother, Maurice
Mullowney, from her mother's previous marriage, from which she had
been widowed. The family's wealth was centred on the profitable provisions trade of pork, the most lucrative being the export trade. They had
accumulated land, tenements, ships, as well as property that had been
sold to them by Margaret's two unmarried aunts, Mary and Margaret
Murphy, who also owned extensive properties until their deaths in 1858,
after which Ellen inherited their wealth.

Coming from a background where both men and women were substantial property owners and managers, Margaret had developed excellent

business expertise and knowledge of property management, which would be a huge asset and contribute to her becoming a powerful businesswoman and entrepreneur. A distinguished family in both business and political life in Waterford, they supported several charities including the Christian Brothers and the Irish Sisters of Charity. William Aylward had been in favour of the Act of Union and the Young Ireland movement and their home was regularly visited by political activists Daniel O'Connell and Thomas Francis Meagher.

In 1815 Margaret attended the local Quaker school on the Quays in the city. On her journey to and from school she witnessed the terrible poverty and hardship of the poor and destitute people of Waterford. Barefoot and emaciated children, with their outstretched hands and desperate faces, begging in the streets, and public whippings for crimes that would be considered trivial today, such as stealing a bag of coal, would be a regular occurrence. These images were fundamental to her future work and devotion to impoverished children. At the age of ten, Margaret was sent as a boarder to the Ursuline Convent in Thurles, a Catholic boarding school for 'young ladies' and the only one of its kind in Ireland at the time. In addition to the usual subjects in the curriculum the school also focused on drawing, painting, music, elementary astronomy, botany, French, Latin and Irish. Margaret became fluent in French, the main language of the school, and a talented artist, as can be seen by her existing watercolours preserved at Glasnevin Convent. After extending her schooling to study sacred scripture, classics, art, Latin and embroidery, Margaret returned home in 1830.

Margaret was close to her uncle, Brother Joseph Murphy or 'Uncle Murphy', her mother's brother, who belonged to the Christian Brothers, the Catholic lay teaching order founded by Edmund Rice, who had opened their first school for poor boys in Waterford in 1802. He lived near Margaret and was a great influence on her piousness as she was growing up. She also had family connections with the Presentation Sisters, through her mother's sister-in-law from her first marriage, Teresa Mullowney, who had established the first Presentation poor school for girls in Waterford. Margaret worked with her sisters in several charities in the city and volunteered to teach at the Presentation Convent, where she taught the children to sing hymns and frequently set exams with religious gifts as prizes. She also visited the houses of the local Catholic gentry, seeking their support for the convent schools, and worked in the charitable pawnshop Mont de Piété, which offered poor families lower rates than the extortionate rates that were being charged in the usual pawnshops.

Waterford in the mid-nineteenth century was at the centre of the Catholic heartland and many middle-class women chose a religious life rather than marriage. In 1835 Margaret joined her older sister, Catherine, at the Irish Sisters of Charity in Stanhope Street, Dublin. As with her sister before her, she also received her father's blessing, as he fondly wrote, 'You know not the feelings of a fond parent on an occasion of this kind. But if you feel it is for your happiness most cheerfully I will bear it'. She received the name of Sister Mary Alphonsus Liguori and taught as a novice in King's Inn Street. However, her ambitions differed to what the convent had in mind for her and, also due to her fragile health, she left a year later, in 1836. She returned to Waterford and resumed her work with the Presentation schools and the poor. Margaret's father, whom she was very close to, had also devoted much of his time and money to helping the poor, and when he died in 1840, he was remembered in the obitu-ary notice in the *Mail* on 12 March as, 'very highly respected, William Aylward, Esq, one of the most judicious, most spirited and most success-ful of our merchants'. In the *Chronicle* on the same date it read:

> As a merchant Mr. Aylward's conduct was marked by honourable integrity, as a friend he was steady and unbending, whilst in the domestic relations, he was the kind and affectionate father of a numerous family, whom he had the gratification of leaving after him, not only in the inheritance of his unsullied name, but in the best esteem of the people.

In 1842, with the help of Father Tim Dowley, Margaret founded the first Penitents' Home in Waterford and later, in 1845, she decided to follow her calling again and joined the Ursuline Convent in St Mary's, Waterford. After a short time she found life in the convent too suppressive and much to the disapproval of her family at her second failure in religious life, she left after two months and moved to Dublin, where as well as distancing herself from the gossip of her 'failure' in Waterford, she was also able to seek expert medical advice from consultants regarding her erysipelas, (an infection causing inflammation of the face, across the cheeks and nose). Initially she briefly stayed with her brother John in Clontarf before moving into lodgings in Gardiner Street. Margaret's arrival in Dublin followed the aftermath of the Great Famine of 1845-7, where it had become a city of sanctuary for the poor and destitute arriving from other counties, greatly adding to already existing poverty on the streets. Many desperate people would stop in Dublin, en route for Britain, America and Australia, where they hoped they would find a better life. The majority of those leaving were men, hoping to find employment in England, while the women and children were left behind, destitute, in the already over-crowded city.

Margaret was deeply concerned by the extreme poverty she wit-nessed in the Dublin slums and began her philanthropic work at the Ladies Association of Charity of St Vincent de Paul for the Spiritual and Temporal Relief of the Sick Poor. Founded by St Vincent de Paul in 1617, its first branch in Ireland was opened in 1843 at Kingstown. Margaret went on to establish another branch of the charity in the Metropolitan Parish of Dublin, of which she became secretary and after several moves within the district, the offices were even-tually located at 42 Eccles Street, within the two Catholic parishes that the association ministered. In stark contrast to the grand Georgian town houses within the elegant squares and malls, the rows of dilapidated tenement houses and shacks consumed the back lanes and alleyways, incor-porating some of the worst slum housing in Europe.

St Brigid's House, 46 Eccles Street (originally 42 Eccles Street, prior to renumbering). (Courtesy of Vivienne Keely)

Through the Ladies Association, Margaret wanted to encourage other sympathetic women to join in her quest to alleviate what she could of the merciless poverty she had seen in Dublin. The offices provided a centre for committee meetings and management and a 'house of rest' for the members to live in a semi-religious manner, devoting their time to the charities. The members visited the homes of the poor to advise on parenting, provide assistance and 'to insist, as far as they can, upon cleanliness, order, industry and regularity being perceptible in their homes'. They also aspired to uphold the religious faith and 'to induce all to frequent the sacraments, to hear Mass on Sundays and Holidays, to urge upon the parents the necessity of making their children attend catechism'.

Annual reports were produced in which Margaret described the work of the ladies and the conditions of the poor, documenting the details meticulously with direct quotes from the impoverished men and women. At the public meetings, Margaret distributed the reports and told of the accounts of the sick laying 'on a damp, earthen floor' with a handful of straw as a bed, with no fire and very little food, with often only dry bread to eat. In the year of 1852 the report stated that 3,591 visits to the sick were made by the Ladies and over 200 families received relief. Margaret noted in numerous reports that the work was 'never ending' and claimed that the 'number of poor who occasionally require relief is calculated at 7,000 to 8,000'. In the same year, Margaret appointed Fr John Gowan as her spiritual director, who, apart from his public role in the charity, was to become a significant figure throughout Margaret's career, in his support and as her confidant.

The Ladies Association strived to convince the Catholic poor to retain their faith, as Protestant charities were persistently pressurising Roman Catholics to convert. They urged parents to send their children to Catholic schools and provided 'tickets for free admission, and premiums for regular attendance' as incentives to the poor to send their children to 'approved Catholic schools'. Once registered with a school, children were monitored on their development and the parents of any child who had lapsed from their schooling were reproached. The Ladies worked tirelessly in their mission to keep the Catholic faith amongst the poor and remained insistent in their visits to anyone who had lapsed from their faith, persevering until they complied.

Under the Poor Law Act of 1838, assistance for the poor in Ireland at the time was restricted to the confinement of the workhouse, which the association opposed. Margaret knew that unemployment, especially among women, was the major contributing factor to the poverty and the sickness that was widespread in the slums, which impeded the ability to work, and with no State assistance outside the workhouse, this would be catastrophic for a poor family. From donations, the charity provided food, fuel, clothing and bedding and assisted with securing employment, releasing clothes from pawnbrokers to 'make an appearance' for a position. Many of the Ladies were wives and daughters of doctors and barristers, wine merchants and business men, particularly those in the provisions trade, and in less than five years the association had 148 working visitors. Margaret's business skills also proved invaluable to the accounts and fundraising of the charity. Money was raised from annual bazaars, raffles and charity sermons and clerical support contributed largely to the success of the association. Through the Ladies Association of Charity, Margaret addressed the problem of lack of work for poverty-stricken women and in 1853 she opened St Mary's Industrial Institute, situated in an empty coach factory at 5 Upper Dorset Street. It offered training and employment, mainly in needlework and embroidery. Contributions from St Vincent de Paul and other sources helped with the founding of the institution, but unfortunately, the institute's expenses outweighed its income and funds, so it closed in 1855.

The plight of the children being neglected, abandoned and orphaned distressed Margaret intensely and she strongly believed that a 'family environment' was the best place to rear children and she disliked the institutionalised system of the traditional orphanage. She proposed through a committee within the Ladies of Charity that a 'boarding out' system be implemented. Despite opposition from Archbishop Cullen, Margaret gained support and backing from the Catholic Church and St Brigid's Orphanage opened its doors to the first child on 1 January 1857, through which Margaret became the pioneer of the fosterage system.

The main purpose of St Brigid's was not to provide a permanent residence for children, but to find long-term foster homes for them. The local clergy recommended foster mothers or 'nurses', who in turn would recommend others that had met Margaret's standards. It was run entirely on a voluntary basis and depended heavily on donations and volunteers, making regular heartfelt public appeals where 'there is not one paid officer or collector in the organisation' and 'every shilling goes to the orphan'. A substantial amount of funding came from the clergy, where Margaret, with her pleas, had gained the support of 'Nine Archbishops and Bishops' and a number of priests and annual subscribers. She pledged to support the children until they reached sixteen years of age, and disabled children longer.

Children were accepted not just from Dublin, but from all over Ireland, and sometimes even from Britain. Only those who could not be cared for by a relative would be received, as the charity believed that 'the separation of parent and child is one of the greatest social evils, and that in all cases where it is possible, the parent ought to support and bring up his own child'. Unhealthy or disabled children were never refused, even though 'some have come to us all covered with sores and filth; a great many were weak and sickly' or even 'in a dying state'. The majority of the children came from mothers who had been widowed or deserted or had been left behind when their husbands had left the city in search of work. Unable to work themselves, through illness or deprivation, the women received some solace in knowing that they would eventually be reunited with their children through St Brigid's fosterage system and many of the orphaned children were adopted by their foster families.

Margaret urged that the foster parents would treat St Brigid's children like members of the family and hoped that they would love them as their own so that they might 'enjoy a mother's affection'. She knew that the environment in the city was unhealthy for the children, so she sought to find foster homes in the surrounding rural counties of Dublin, where 'there is the least amount of vice, and the least amount of danger of contamination'. After receiving written recommendation from the local priest the children were sent to small farms where they were employed, along with the other children of the family, to work on the farm and in the home, on the condition that, 'no person shall, however attempt to put labour upon any child above its strength, or to treat it cruelly'. Sadly, some children were exploited in their labour and although twice-yearly inspections and impromptu visits were in place to help guard against neglect and ill-treatment of the children, unfortunately it was not entirely effective.

Margaret wanted to devote all her time to the welfare and education of poor children, so whilst the work of the Ladies Association of Charity continued, she stepped down as their secretary. As with the Ladies of Charity, she wanted to pursue the Catholic faith and teachings, so a child in the care of foster parents was expected to be taught prayers and catechism with their general education. Margaret strongly believed that religious teachings would help if, in the future, the orphan fell into hardship, so that their faith would comfort them and avert any temptation to sin. Payments were granted during the inspection visits to ensure that the children were being properly cared for and educated, and if a child was neglected in any way then he or she was removed and the payment was withheld. As the amount was quite generous, it was considered 'worth striving for' and 'a solid incentive to exertion'.

In a bid to oppose the poor law union and to keep children out of the workhouse, Margaret persistently publicised the comparison between the two systems, affirming that the mortality rate amongst children was significantly higher in the workhouse than those of St Brigid's foster-age system. Children in the workhouse, particularly those under seven years of age, were 'spiritless, dwarfed and prematurely old' whereas children from St Brigid's were, 'playing and bounding in the green fields, the limbs lithe, the chest expanded and the rose of the cheek'. Margaret adamantly continued with her 'family system of rearing children' and in 1862 the Poor Law Amendment Act did allow orphaned or deserted workhouse children to be boarded out until the age of five, but it wasn't until 1869 that the age was increased to ten. The debate over the foster-age system versus institutional rearing continued through to the 1890s, by which time St Brigid's had been established for over twenty years and was held in high regard not just in Ireland, but in England as well.

In April 1858, four years after St Brigid's was established, Margaret faced a dilemma that would nearly cause the ruin of the orphanage, when four-year-old Mary Matthews was brought to St Brigid's. Mary's mother, Maria Matthews, originally a Protestant, had converted to Catholicism when she married Mary's father, Henry Matthews, who was a Catholic. Henry had taken his wife and three children from Dublin to London to seek employment, where Maria left Henry to work in the Bahamas as a nursemaid, taking their youngest child with her. Henry returned to Dublin, where he fell seriously ill and entrusted his two children to his former employer, Mrs Jordon, to be raised as Catholics. His last words before he died were: 'Oh! Protect the faith of my two children and save them from their mother'. After his death, his son was placed in a Catholic home and Mary was brought to St Brigid's.

Four months later, Maria Matthews was deported from the Bahamas, having 'grossly neglected' the child in her care and having reverted back to Protestantism, she took her son from the Catholic home and placed him in a Protestant orphanage. Mary however, had been placed with a nurse in Saggart, where a Catholic friend of the Orphanage, Mr Heffernan, wanting to protect the child, had sent a forged note to the nurse, claiming to be from Margaret, insisting that Mary be given to the messenger, which the unsuspecting nurse did. After keeping Mary in Dublin for a while, Mr Heffernan took her to France, then on to Germany, where she later entered into a Belgian convent and became a nun. Meanwhile, Margaret had been unaware of Mary's abduction until several days later when the nurse had visited Margaret in Dublin and expressed her regret at losing Mary. Maria Matthews had gone to collect Mary from the nurse and having found her gone had informed the police, and Margaret was summoned to court, where a writ of Habeas Corpus was served to her, commanding that Margaret present Mary Matthews in court, and also inform them of the day that she was taken and for what reason. Mary had been known as 'Mary Farrell' in her foster home and that, along with Margaret's failure to inform the police that Mary was missing, immediately went against her and she was accused of deliberately hindering any attempts of relatives attempting to find Mary. Despite Margaret's insistence that she had no idea of Mary's whereabouts she was relentlessly interrogated by the court for two years until 7 November 1860, when she was eventually charged with contempt of court for not producing Mary, but acquitted of a charge of kidnapping. She was sentenced to six months at Grangegorman Female Penitentiary and ordered to pay costs.

Margaret's time at Grangegorman was very grim. She was locked in a partitioned room, hardly more than a cubicle, adjacent to one of the wards, where she was 'compelled to breathe the miasma of the sick and dying'. There were no windows, no fire and she was not allowed exercise for the first three months. As well as being convicts, many of the inmates were mentally ill, insane and epileptic and Margaret would have witnessed and heard their pitiful screams and wails of distress, as they struggled with the hospital nurses and assistants who were trying to restrain them. The terrible traumas that the maternity patients experienced, through lack of skill during and after childbirth, where many babies died, distressed Margaret deeply, as Father Gowan affirmed, 'Besides other poor patients were moaning and lamenting, these sounds – heartbreaking moans, cries, and lamentations – pierced Miss Aylward's soul.' As writing materials were not restricted, Margaret was allowed to receive and send letters, so she continued with her management of St Brigid's while in prison. She received numerous letters of support and compassionate speeches of sympathy were given by several bishops, attracting considerable national media attention. The *Morning News* reported, 'Her sole crime consists in the fact that she is Honorary Secretary to a Catholic institution devoted to deeds of charity and mercy' and even the Protestant press stated that 'Miss Aylward is suffering vicariously for an alleged offence which nobody attributes to her'.

During her incarceration, Margaret's already delicate health declined further with the terrible hardships that she endured. She suffered from varicose ulcers, her teeth fell out and her hands became so numb that she had to have another prisoner cut her bread. Although two doctors recommended her release and Margaret wrote a letter of appeal, proclaiming that her health was 'fast failing' and that she had paid all the court costs, no early release was permitted and she left prison, after serving her full sentence on 5 May 1861.

Following her release from Grangegorman Margaret continued with her work at St Brigid's, but she also wanted to educate 'the more abandoned, more destitute children' and proceeded to open schools for poor children in the slums of Dublin. Within five months, and with Father Gowan's support, the first Catholic School of St Brigid was opened at

Palm Walk, Glasnevin Convent, where Margaret Aylward loved to sit in her wheelchair. (Courtesy of Vivienne Keely)

10 Crow Street in Dublin in October 1861, where fifty pupils were taught in one room. Gradually, more schools were established in Dublin and the surrounding villages and counties, where each school operated on an outdoor relief system. Books, clothes and food were provided for the children, which they could take home to their families. Religious instruction was foremost in the teaching at St Brigid's schools, so that the children in danger of losing their faith would be 'made strong in Faith'.

In 1865 Margaret and fifteen companions formed a religious congregation known as the Sisters of the Holy Faith. They purchased Glasnevin House in Dublin, a school that had been owned by the Sacred Heart Sisters, and renamed it St Brigid's. Set in extensive, beautiful grounds, Glasnevin, believed to have been a home of several saints, was the perfect, tranquil setting for Margaret's congregation. As Margaret declared, 'Glasnevin is a Paradise on earth, too lovely for us.' Through Margaret's own private funds, Glasnevin was extended to provide a training school for Catholic teachers, where particular attention was given to the study of the science of teaching. Although Margaret had taken her vows along with her companions, becoming Sister M. Agatha, and was heavily involved with the running of Glasnevin, she chose to wear secular clothes and continued her work with the orphanage, while Father Gowan resided in the convent and was responsible for the spiritual instruction.

Margaret's health never really recovered from her time in Grangegorman and she spent the last two years of her life bedridden from her varicose ulcers. She died on 11 October 1889 at Glasnevin, and was buried in the convent cemetery. There were many mourners at her funeral, including hundreds of Dublin's poor, as well as friends and clerics from all over Ireland. Father Gowan expressed his grief at her passing, 'Her death has left a void in my heart which nothing in this world will ever be able to fill.' Her legacy lives on and her work still continues in the Sisters of the Holy Faith schools and convents around the world today.

JOANNA BRIDGEMAN
1812–1888

'The superiority of an ordered system is beautifully
illustrated in the Sisters of Mercy.'

Sir John Hall

For many years Mother Bridgeman and her Sisters of Mercy were not given official recognition from the British Government for their pioneering nursing and management system in the Crimean War. Largely overshadowed by Florence Nightingale, their invaluable contribution to the development of modern nursing has only been acknowledged internationally in recent years.

Joanna Bridgeman was the eldest daughter of St John Bridgeman and Lucy Redden and was born in Ballagh, Ruan, County Clare in 1813. Her family, a prominent and affluent family with Norman ancestry on her father's side, had owned substantial estates in Limerick and Clare. Unfortunately, due to the effect of the penal laws on Irish Catholic landowners, the family's wealth had decreased quite considerably by the time of Joanna's birth. Nevertheless, St John Bridgeman managed to maintain the extravagant lifestyle and pursuits of an Irish gentleman, in which his wife had little interest, preferring to concentrate on the rearing of her children. During her youth, Joanna regularly visited the home of the Irish political leader, Daniel O'Connell, who was a relative of her mother. He was a huge influence on Joanna's faith and patriotism.

In 1818, shortly after the birth of her fourth child, Joanna's mother died and following her father's subsequent remarriage in 1819, which brought unhappiness into the Bridgeman's home, Joanna and her siblings went to live with their wealthy aunt, Joanna Redden, in Scariff, who only a teenager herself, looked after the children as her own. Shortly after their arrival, Joanna Redden moved the whole family to the city of Limerick, where she became involved in various charitable works. Her philanthropic work with prostitutes and destitute women and girls led her to establish the Magdalene Asylum in Clare Street. Joanna joined her in her humanitarian work and helped her nurse the sick during an epidemic of cholera in 1832, in the hospitals and in their own homes. At the young age of nineteen she proved to be a very efficient and caring nurse, her kind words providing comfort and solace to the sick and dying. The medical doctors said that she was 'Regarded by all as a child of benediction, her kindness earned for her the grateful prayers of those to whom she so unselfishly ministered'. During her time nursing the sick, Joanna carefully observed the symptoms of cholera and developed her own successful system of treating the patients by applying poultices or hot stupes to the patient's stomach to relieve the painful muscle cramps or spasms, one of the most severe symptoms of the illness. This method became renowned and used extensively in the treatment of cholera.

Joanna's friendly and agreeable nature attracted many friends and invitations to social activities. Her aunt, not wanting to stand in the way of her having a social life, sent her to live with relatives in a more respectable part of the city, where Joanna thoroughly enjoyed herself attending the balls and other social engagements of Limerick City. However, the attraction of Limerick's social life soon ran its course and Joanna yearned for a quieter life, so she returned to her charity work with her aunt in Clare Street, where she also taught in a small school attached to an old convent, which was later managed by the Sisters of Mercy in 1838.

The Religious Sisters of Mercy, founded by Catherine McAuley in Dublin in 1831, was a community of Roman Catholic women devoted to helping poor, sick and destitute women and children, who also had little or no education. Although Joanna came from a comfortable background where she would have been expected to continue the role of a middle-class lady, she chose to join them in their convent in Limerick and within a short time she was professed by Catherine McAuley and became known as Sister Jane Francis on 9 December, 1839.

The Sisters of Mercy received many requests from towns across Ireland to help the poor, and in 1844 an appeal came from the parish priest in Kinsale, County Cork. On 19 April, Sister Jane Francis and four other nuns left Limerick and went to help the starving and deprived people in Kinsale. The following year, the sisters founded the Convent of Mercy there and Jane Francis was instated as the mother superior. The convent ran a school which provided children with an education and food. They received some donations from as far afield as America and from the Society of Friends (Quakers). Joanna Redden also joined the Sisters of Mercy and later followed Mother Bridgeman to Kinsale.

During the harsh years of the famine the Sisters were invaluable in helping the most deprived people in the town. Mother Bridgeman opened a dispensary and with the other Sisters provided medical aid and food to the poor and sick. Later, in 1849, she introduced the nuns as nurses to provide relief in the local workhouse, which accommodated 2,000 inmates. In order to help alleviate the severe poverty in the area, she provided some employment for the poor in the form of net-making for the fishermen and knitting, crochet, embroidery and lace-making for the women. She managed to obtain skilled lace-makers from the factories in Limerick and a qualified teacher was sent from the Board of National Education to teach embroidery. In 1848, an industrial school housing 150 girls was established, where they were taught and employed in lace-making and other forms of needlework. Their work was exhibited and became renowned worldwide.

In 1854, the British, French and Turkish were in conflict with Russia, fighting in the Crimean War. The majority of the fighting took place on the Crimean Peninsula on the northern coast of the Black Sea, which is now an independent republic within Ukraine. William Howard Russell, a celebrated war correspondent with *The Times*, had been sent to cover the events in Crimea. His highly descriptive dispatches sent back to England revealed the true horrors of the war, vividly recounting the sufferings and dreadful conditions that the soldiers endured during the harsh winter of 1854-1855. He criticised the mismanagement of the British Army and the serious negligence of the War Office. In a report published in *The Times* in December 1854, he wrote, 'These are hard truths, but the people of England must hear them. They must know that the wretched beggar who wanders about the streets of London in the rain, leads the life of a prince compared with the British soldiers who are fighting out there for their country'. He reported the story of thousands of soldiers suffering and dying of cholera and malaria and of the inadequate medical supplies and care. He reported that 'The worn-out pensioners who were brought as an ambulance corps are totally useless'. He praised the nursing care of the 'superior' French, declaring that 'their medical arrangements are extremely good, their surgeons more numerous, and they have also the help of the Sisters of Charity, who have accompanied the expedition in incredible numbers. These devoted women are excellent nurses'. He asked, 'Are none of the daughters of England, at this extreme hour of need, ready for such a work of mercy? Must we fall so far below the French in self-sacrifice and devotedness?' A letter also published in *The Times* asked angrily, 'Why have we no Sisters of Charity?'

Although W.H. Russell's reports had stirred a scandal in Britain which had led to the resignation of the Prime Minister, the Earl of Aberdeen, it was the dispatches of another reporter from *The Times*' Constantinople correspondent Thomas Chenery, revealing the appalling conditions of the military hospital in Scutari, Turkey, that caused the government to take action. He wrote:

> It is with feelings of surprise and anger that the public will learn that no suf-
> ficient medical preparations have been made for proper care of the wounded.
> Not only are there not sufficient surgeons – that, it might be urged unavoid-
> able – not only are there no dressers and nurses – that might be a defect of
> a system for which no-one is to blame – but what will be said when it is
> known that there is not even linen to make bandages for the wounded?

In reaction to Thomas Chenery's harrowing reports, the enraged public outcry in Britain led the Secretary at War, Sidney Herbert, to write to his close friend Florence Nightingale, asking her to go and take over the management of the military hospital in Scutari with a group of nurses, over which she would have complete authority and full support from the British Government. She was also told that only on her approval would any further nurses be sent to the Crimea. The party of thirty-eight volunteers, including five Sisters of Mercy under their superior Mother Clare Moore, were sent from their convent in Bermondsey, London. They left London in October 1854, led by Florence Nightingale and arrived at the hospital in Turkey to find it in a dreadful state. They found the wounded and dying soldiers unwashed, underfed and without blankets, lying in their uniforms which were 'stiff with gore and covered with filth' and crawling with bugs, fleas and lice. The deplorable sanitary conditions contributed to more deaths caused by diseases such as cholera, dysentery and typhus, than of battle wounds.

As the number of casualties increased so did the demand for more nurses, so a decision was made by the government to send a second group of nurses out to Crimea, without consulting Florence Nightingale. In addition to the nine lady helpers and twenty-two nurses, fifteen Sisters of Mercy volunteered to join the group. Mary Stanley, a friend of Sidney Herbert's and the daughter of the Anglican Bishop of Norwich, was selected to supervise the whole group, while Mother Francis Bridgeman, who was noted for her nursing experience and organisational skills, was nominated to lead the party of nuns. Although they were referred to as the Irish Sisters of Mercy, three of the group were from Liverpool and one was from Chelsea. They set off for Turkey in December 1854, with luggage that included provisions of soap, starch, a medicine chest, and warm clothing. After a long and arduous journey, travelling through storms in the uncomfortable steerage section of the ship, their arrival in Constantinople was met with hostility from Florence Nightingale. She was furious that the nuns had been sent without her knowledge or consent and felt that the War Office had undermined her authority in the arrangements. She took an instant dislike to them, particularly Mother Bridgeman, whom she later referred to as 'Mother Brickbat'. The Sisters were shocked when she told them that there had been a 'gross misunderstanding on the part of the War Office and that they were not needed, nor could she accommodate them due to the lack of space. Mother Bridgeman later wrote of their arrival in her diary, 'We all believed [Scutari] to be the scene of our future labours; and where we hoped that we should at least have a cordial welcome and abundance of the work we had come so far to do, and for which we had already suffered so many hardships and dangers'. Fortunately, shelter for the Sisters came in the form of a nearby schoolroom provided by the Sisters of Charity in Galata, who had previously housed five Sisters from Norwood faced with the same dilemma. It quickly became apparent that there was going to be friction between Florence Nightingale and Mother Bridgeman, with religion and authority being the main issues.

There was much antagonism between Catholics and Protestants during the mid-nineteenth century, which continued throughout the Crimean War. The Catholic Church hoped that the loyalty shown by the Sisters of Mercy in Crimea would inspire positive feelings for Catholics in Britain. Although Mother Moore and Mother Bridgeman had signed a contract to work as nurses under Florence Nightingale, they had received different instructions under their own bishops. In order not to aggravate any further anti-Catholic feelings, it was agreed by Bishop Grant and Mother Moore that she and her nuns would work solely as nurses. Although the government had forbidden the Sisters to proselytise and warned them only to discuss religion with other Catholics, Mother Bridgeman had been given a different agenda by Bishop William Delaney of Cork. He advised her that the spiritual needs of the patients must take precedence over their nursing care, as he emphasised in a letter, 'Your calling is from God, and principally for the salvation of souls'. As Florence Nightingale was a deeply religious woman of the Anglican Church, she feared that Mother Bridgeman had come to Crimea to found a convent, rather than nurse the sick.

Mother Bridgeman had gained enormous respect, admiration and affection from the Sisters, as Sister Mary Stanislaus Heyfron remarked, 'Indeed, anyone would like her, she is so warm-hearted and motherly,' so she was adamant from the start that she would maintain her authority as superior over them, which also irked Florence Nightingale. The tension between the two women soon developed into mistrust, with the Irish

...at Florence Nightingale was 'ever ready to receive ... to imagine them) against the Sisters. Despite their dif- ... women were excellent nurses and administrators and were ... to nurse soldiers of any faith. Though the Sisters had received ... training, they had gained plenty of experience in nursing the ... with typhus and cholera during the epidemics in Ireland, and they ... highly proficient in nursing patients, and keen to get to work in the ... hospital. However, Mother Bridgeman and her Sisters were ignored after their arrival and would have to wait until the following month to use their nursing skills, when they were needed in an outbreak of cholera.

It was in January 1855 that Mother Bridgeman received a message from Mother Moore telling her that Florence Nightingale had agreed that she and four of her Sisters were to go to the Barrack Hospital in Scutari, which held around 4,000 patients and where fatalities were high, with fifty to ninety deaths a day. Mother Moore informed the Sisters that they were to work in the kitchen or stores as 'the wounded were either dead or convalescent' and that most of the patients were 'only suffering from scurvy, dysentery and enteric fever, and therefore needed no nursing!' The Sisters found the hospital in chaos, where Mother Bridgeman observed 'the utter disorder and irregularity which reigned throughout, and which no-one seemed willing or able to control'. Their accommodation comprised of one room which they all shared, which Mother Bridgeman described as being 'unfit for human occupation'. Apart from a bed and very basic eating utensils, they had to eat their meals 'picnic fashion' on the floor as there was neither a table nor chairs, unlike the nurses who 'had luxuries in abundance'.

After a short time in the rat-infested stores sorting the clothes, due to an outbreak of cholera and consequently the loss of medical staff, the Sisters were finally sent to the wards, where conditions were horrendous. They were not readily received in the hospital and the medical officers did not approve of Mother Bridgeman's method of nursing care. The majority of the care given to the patients was carried out by the orderlies or the nurses, which the Sisters noted was conducted in a very detached and inefficient manner. Although the Sisters were restricted to mainly dressing the soldier's wounds, they worked extremely long hours trying to give comfort to the sick and dying, many of whom were affected by the severe winter frost. One of the nuns, Sister Aloysius, wrote of their plight:

> ... their clothes had to be cut off. In most cases the flesh and clothes were frozen together; and as for the feet, the boots had to be cut off bit by bit, the flesh coming off with them, many pieces of the flesh I have seen remain in the boot. Poultices were applied with some oil brushed over them. In the morning when these were removed, oh, can I ever forget? The sinews and bones were seen to be laid bare.

Many of the men were left unaided for days, as one soldier wrote, 'We are lying here like so many pigs – hundreds lying in the passages. Very seldom you see a doctor, they have so much to do cutting off hands and legs'.

Stuping and poultices of mustard were the main remedies used in treating cholera. A stupe was a flannel or cloth soaked and wrung out in hot water and applied to the wounds. Poultices of mustard and turpentine were applied to help relieve the painful cramps. Mother Bridgeman adopted her own method of stuping, of which the doctors approved, allowing her to include a little of the newly introduced chloroform. A spoonful of brandy, followed by a small piece of ice, would be given to the patient to try and settle the stomach. The Sisters diligently worked in rat-infested wards, where the fever was at its peak and where even some of the medical officers would not venture for fear of contamination. They worked relentlessly to try and ease the terrible afflictions of the disease, but the majority of the patients died within hours of admission.

Florence Nightingale and Mother Bridgeman differed in their approach to nursing, which constantly led to disagreements. The Sisters believed that comfort and care were also needed in tending to the sick and were more than willing to sit up with their patients during the night, to which Florence Nightingale objected, not wanting nurses on the wards after 8.30 p.m. She also believed that only the wounded soldiers needed attention, while the nuns wanted to nurse the fever patients too. The doctors also discouraged the Sisters, as Sister Isabella Croke wrote in her diary: 'A doctor said to me. "Sister, you must not listen to the patients when they ask you for anything. It will be impossible to get them out of the hospital, they will be so petted." To which she replied, "Oh Doctor, Sisters of Mercy always listen to their patients".' Religious words of comfort were also appreciated, not just by the Irish Catholics, but also by the English patients in the hospital, giving hope and consolation to dying soldiers. Whilst their pious words were gratefully received by the patients, Florence Nightingale was livid and in a letter of complaint to the authorities regarding the selection of the nurses, Lady Canning wrote, 'The second party of nuns who came out, now wander over the whole hospital out of nursing hours, not confining themselves to their own wards but *instructing* (it is their own word) groups of orderlies and convalescents in the corridors, doing the work of ten chaplains'. Mother Bridgeman was adamant that she and her Sisters would continue to tend to both the spiritual and physical needs of their patients. The solution to this disagreement came from Sidney Herbert, who, not wanting the nuns to return to England, appointed ten of the Sisters of Mercy to work under the sole authority of Mother Bridgeman, at the new hospital opened in Koulali.

Father William Ronan had arrived from Ireland and presented the reluctant Florence Nightingale with a written agreement of the terms and conditions under which the Sisters were to work in the hospital. The Sisters were to be housed as nurses in appropriate accommodation and be provided with a place for private worship. They were to continue their religious instruction to Roman Catholics, not to Protestants, whilst attending to the sick of all denominations. On 27 January, Mother Bridgeman arrived with nine other Sisters at Koulali General Hospital, where they found it in a 'state of utmost confusion' with conditions just as deplorable as Scutari, but with a higher mortality rate. Mary Stanley wrote, 'In Koulali we realised what protracted war was. Some days and scenes are stamped upon one's memory'. The Sisters set to work scrubbing and cleaning the filthy, lice-infested wards and gradually reformations took place throughout the hospital. Mary Stanley had insisted that Mother Bridgeman was to take full responsibility for the administration of the hospital, which within a relatively short time was working under an orderly and efficient system.

At Koulali, Mother Bridgeman was able to run the hospital her way, with fewer restrictions and with the empathy she strongly felt should accompany their nursing care. The patients were nursed with more compassion and their personal needs were dealt with efficiently and promptly. The Sisters sat at the bedside of a sick or dying soldier at any hour of the night, making them as comfortable as possible in their last hours, strongly believing that the soldiers should die peacefully and with as much dignity as possible. They would wash them and comb their hair, and spoon feed the patients that were unable to feed themselves. Their kind words of compassion were gratefully received by the soldiers, and it was noted by one of the Sisters that 'they often cry and seem more grateful for that than anything else'. One tearful soldier exclaimed, 'Oh, it is long since I heard a kind word before' and another asked, 'Sister, is it wrong for me to say, Ma'am, that the way you take care of me reminds me of my mother?'

The running of the hospital was vigilantly organised with meticulous supervision over each patient's dietary needs, medicines and stimulants. No improvements or changes were made without the senior medical officer's consent first, which contributed to the harmonious working relationship between the Sisters and the doctors. Meals were served at regular intervals from the extra-diet kitchen and provision store, which had been set up for the Sisters by the Purveyor, Mr Scott Robertson. The store kept the provisions required for 'invalid cooking', where each patient was given a diet appropriate to his illness. The diets varied from full-diet, half-diet, low-diet or spoon-diet. 'Invalid foods', which included milk, arrowroot, eggs, sago, lemonade or port wine, were given to those on a spoon-diet. Meals that included mutton chops, potatoes, soup, and vegetables were served in appropriate portions according to the patient's needs, and were recorded on a diet sheet. Lemonade or barley water was dispensed on the wards during the afternoons.

The store was supervised by one of the Sisters who also kept detailed accounts of the disbursements, which were presented to the Purveyor at the end of the month. A laundry room was set up and ensured the regular provision of clean clothes and linen for the hospital. The hospital's beautiful flowering garden provided a place of peace and serenity for the patients, where 'Men just able to crawl out of their wards might be seen there just basking in the sun'. Mother Bridgeman and her Sisters had gained respect not just from their patients and medical staff, but even from the Sultan, who openly expressed his admiration for their work. Fellow nurse in Koulali and author of *Eastern Hospitals and English Nurses*, Frances Margaret Taylor wrote that the 'hospital was from the first admirably managed. The medical officers fully appreciated her value and there was a hearty co-operation between them … we used to call it "the model hospital of the east"'. In fact the only complaint that the doctors had regarding the Sisters was that their numbers were too low.

Within two months of the opening of the hospital Mother Bridgeman's system of nursing had succeeded in slowing the grip of the fever and the mortality rate had dropped quite considerably. The medical doctors appreciated and admired the Sisters' work and their new system, but Florence Nightingale expressed her disapproval whenever she found an opportunity to do so. She envied the success of the hospital that was being run by such an efficient system independently of her and completely different to that in Scutari. If she could have had her way, she would have had the Sisters sent home. She complained to Sidney Herbert that the Sisters were proselytising among the Protestant patients, and that they were giving the Catholic patients preferential care, but Mother Bridgeman staunchly protested that in doing so it would be 'a sin against God and a disgrace before man'.

In April 1855 Mary Stanley, satisfied that she had fulfilled her duty in the hospitals, returned home to England. In a letter to Sidney Herbert, Florence Nightingale predicted that with the absence of Mary Stanley the hospital would close, 'Koulali will break up in all probability', she wrote. 'Try and work a civil hospital with ladies and nuns, and you will see what I mean. The ladies all quarrel among themselves; the medical men all laugh at their helplessness, but like to have them about for the sake of a little female society; which is natural but not our object'. Koulali did not close and Mother Bridgeman and her Sisters remained there until October, when they were assigned to take over the General Hospital at Balaclava, at the Crimean front. Mother Bridgeman had requested the move, convinced that despite being in the midst of the battles, it was 'the *only* place for us'. Her alliance with Dr John Hall, Inspector-General of the Hospitals in Crimea, had overridden any objections from Florence Nightingale, who in asking for more nurses had stated clearly that 'it would be very desirable to have more nuns … *just not* the Irish ones'.

At Balaclava, the Sisters were faced with similar problems to those in the other hospitals, including the rats which were everywhere and the additional problem of mud, which made the route from the hospital to their accommodation extremely difficult. The main hospital was a stone building with the addition of wooden huts in which the civilians were nursed and one of which also served as the Sisters' accommodation. Frances Margaret Taylor noted that, 'The huts in which the Sisters lived were so bare and unfurnished that they looked like Indian wigwams, but every hardship seemed but to increase the good Sisters' cheerful zeal, they were so delighted at having plenty of work'. Despite their difficult living conditions, Mother Bridgeman and her Sisters never complained and set to work, making vast improvements to the hospital at Balaclava, as they had in Koulali.

In March 1856, under a General Order from the War Office, Florence Nightingale became Superintendent of the Nursing Staff in the East and gained control of the General Hospital at Balaclava. Seemingly, the order was a result of a complaint from Florence Nightingale regarding the appointing of two nurses by Dr Hall without her knowledge. Subsequently, Mother Bridgeman decided to leave the Crimea and resigned on 28 March, the same date on which peace was declared. An entry in her diary reads, 'the declaration of peace has arrived, the army was very healthy, and all the soldiers then in hospital were convalescing, so there was little nursing for anyone to do'. On 12 April, the Sisters left Balaclava and travelled by steamship home to Ireland. After a short stay in London and Dublin, Mother Bridgeman arrived back in Kinsale on 25 June, 1856, one year and eight months after she had left. Shortly after their departure a column in the *Cork Examiner* of 28 April stated, 'The nuns leave the Crimea, bearing with them the respect and admiration of officers of all ranks of the army, and with the affectionate regards and cordial blessings of the poor soldiers, both Catholic and Protestant. In the departure of Mother Bridgeman and her Sisters they have indeed sustained an irreparable loss'.

Despite her opposition, after the Crimean War, Florence Nightingale adopted Mother Bridgeman's system of nursing in a scheme for military nursing, which she presented to the War Office Committee. Prior to leaving the Crimea and following a meeting with Florence Nightingale, Mother Bridgeman confirmed in her diary that, 'Miss Nightingale took notes of our manner of nursing which I explained to her, as I hoped someone might benefit from it'. The revised edition of Florence Nightingale's impressive *Notes on Nursing* published in 1859, is said to contain in part, suggestions and ideas for nursing taken from these notes.

Mother Bridgeman continued working with the poor and sick, and with the Sisters founded hospitals in Cork and Dublin. Convents were established under her guidance in County Down, County Donegal, County Limerick, Derby in England and as far away as San Francisco and Cincinnati, USA. Around a thousand children continued to receive free education and meals in her school and her textbook, *God in his Works*, was used widely in the Sisters of Mercy primary schools, both in Ireland and abroad.

Mother Bridgeman died peacefully on 11 February 1888 at the Convent of Mercy in Kinsale. In a letter of condolence Father Michael Gleeson wrote, 'I have always had the greatest esteem for her … I shall never forget all that she and her companions had to endure in the Crimea. The sufferings she went through, and all the annoyances she had to put up with during her time there were more than enough for her to win for her a crown of surpassing beauty'.

FRANCES POWER COBBE
1822–1904

'I hope, as Tennyson told me to do,
to 'fight the good fight' quite to the end.'

Frances Power Cobbe

A prominent social reformer and suffragette, Frances Power Cobbe campaigned throughout her life for the rights of both women and animals, believing them to be defenceless under the control of men. She was a pioneer animal rights activist and was also among the few women of the Victorian era to achieve a career in journalism, her many works promoting the causes that she so passionately believed in.

Frances Power Cobbe spent the majority of the first thirty-six years of her life living on the family estate at Newbridge in Dublin, which was built by Charles Cobbe, the Archbishop of Dublin, in 1737. The prominent Anglo-Irish Cobbe family were alleged to have 'direct pedigrees from 1323', descending from a long line of landed gentry producing significant Irish politicians, Oxford graduates, and country squires. Frances's father, also named Charles, was born in 1781 and later joined the army, serving in India. Ill health forced him to return to his mother's family home in Bath, England, where he met and married Frances Conway in 1809 and brought her to Newbridge. They had four sons in six years and in 1822, five years after the birth of their youngest son Henry, Frances

Power Cobbe was born on 4 December. She was named after her mother and her paternal grandmother, Ann Power Trench.

Newbridge House had been abandoned for a number of years and had fallen into disrepair due to the accumulation of family debts and the death of first Charles Cobbe's father, when Charles was sixteen, and then his grandfather, from whom he had inherited the estate. Charles Cobbe carried out the refurbishments with financial help from his wife. He rebuilt the cottages on the estate in stone and slate, transforming buildings that Frances described as 'little better than pig-styes' into homes 'fit for human habitation'. As the annual rents would not cover the expenses, he sold two of the family's most prized paintings and heirlooms to pay for the costs. In her autobiography, Frances recalled 'seeing the tears in his eyes' as the paintings, a Gasper Poussin and a Hobbema, were taken away. Charles was a very fair-minded and generous landlord and according to Frances, 'not a farthing was added to the rent of the tenants who profited by this real act of self-denial'.

Newbridge House, set in 360 acres of walled gardens, pasture and woodland, provided an idyllic environment for Frances to spend her early years, although with her brothers away at boarding school she was left to create her own amusement. Her mother had suffered an injury to her ankle which had been neglected by the doctors and subsequently caused her bouts of lameness, so Frances spent most of her time with her elderly nurse, May Malone. She recalled having had little contact with other children during this time, but described herself as being 'singularly happy' in a nursery which was 'the most charming room for a child's abode I have ever seen'. Although Frances portrayed her childhood as 'almost solitary', she also stated how happy she was at Newbridge, 'walking along the grass walks of that beautiful old garden and feeling as if everything in the world was perfect'. The house was quiet for most of the year until the Christmas and summer holidays, when it became a hive of activity, where aunts, uncles and cousins gathered to enjoy the Cobbe's hospitality. It was also a time when her brothers would return home and she would join them in their boyish pursuits, preferring fishing and cricket to girlish activities.

Frances received her early education from her mother, who taught her letters and numbers and also read from various books including the children's book, *The History of Robins* by Sarah Trimmer published in 1786, which encouraged children to practice kindness to animals. By the age of seven, lessons with her mother ceased and a governess was employed to teach Frances, proposing to prepare her for a life that was expected of a middle-class lady, which she resented from the beginning. At the age of twelve, following the advice of the family doctor, Frances was restricted to morning lessons only. Puberty was considered a critical time for a woman in particular, as it was believed the blood was needed for the development of the reproductive organs, so intellectual activity was discouraged.

Frances Power Cobbe. (Courtesy of the Wellcome Library, London)

This arrangement suited Frances, as she continued to have the freedom in the afternoons to do as she wished, which were spent either roaming the estate or reading and writing poetry in the library of Newbridge House.

In 1836, Charles Cobbe decided to send his daughter to finishing school in Brighton, England, where she would be taught the 'decorum' required of a young lady, as he said that it was 'a necessity ... much to be regretted ... but her welfare required it'. Frances arrived in Brighton in October to begin her two years schooling at the exclusive boarding school at 32 Brunswick Terrace. Around twenty-five pupils attended the school, who were either daughters of country gentlemen or members of parliament. Frances loathed the school and its noisy schoolrooms and resented having to share her bedroom with another pupil. She hated the constant din of girls reciting lessons or four pianos being played at the same time in different rooms. 'The hideous clatter continued the entire day till we went to bed at night,' she recalled. She had no interest in singing, dancing or playing an instrument and found the formal walks along the esplanade 'dismal'. 'Every movement of the body in entering and quitting a room, in taking a seat and rising from it, was duly criticised', she wrote. There was very little time allowed for leisure, 'unless the dreary hour of walking with our teachers (when we recited our verbs), could so be described by a fantastic imagination'. Frances longed to get back to the open spaces and freedom at Newbridge.

When she did eventually return home to Newbridge, shortly before Christmas in 1838, Frances was confident that she knew 'all that it can ever be necessary for a lady to know' and intended to spend her time pursuing her own interests and reading novels, which she did for the first few months, until she became frustrated with her ignorance and decided to educate herself. Finishing school had groomed her for the social circles of the Anglo-Irish gentry, of which she had no interest, only attending the Dublin balls if her parents insisted on it. Instead, she spent the next four years studying history and with the help of the parson of her parish, who was also an ex-tutor from Dublin College, and learning Greek and geometry. Frances also read as many books as were available to her, including all of Milton's poetry, Spencer's *Faery Queen*, and the original Dante's *Divina Commedia* and *Gerusalemme Libata*. She learned about the Greek and Alexandrian philosophers and extended her interests to astronomy, architecture and heraldry.

During this time Frances had been given full responsibility for the housekeeping at Newbridge, mainly to relieve her ailing mother. She thoroughly enjoyed managing the house and its staff and proved to be naturally proficient at carrying out the task of organising servants, the housekeeping budget and the accounts. Her mother's health continued to deteriorate and when Frances was twenty-four, she passed away with the family at her bedside. She remembered her mother's last words to her, telling her that she was 'the pride and joy' of her life. Frances was devastated by her death, defining her as 'the one being in the world whom I truly loved; the only one who really loved me'. As she was now the female head of the family she took on the additional duties of tending to the tenants' needs and teaching the children in the local village school.

Religion had always been prominent in the Cobbe household and as a child Frances had been extremely devout, which she believed may have been partly due to her solitude. She had started to question her belief around the age of eleven, but had kept her doubts private until after her mother's death, when she read Theodore Parker's *Discourse* and announced her conversion to Theism. She later wrote, 'We had five archbishops and a bishop among our near kindred, – Cobbe, Beresfords and Trenchs, and my father's brother was a clergyman. I was the first heretic ever known amongst us'. Her father was so shocked at her 'infidelity' that he refused to speak to her and by way of a written note, told her to leave the house. Frances went to stay with her brother at his remote farm in Donegal, where isolated and devoid of any duties, she wrote her first manuscript on theology, an *Essay on True Religion*. Within the year, an ageing Charles Cobbe summoned his daughter back home to manage Newbridge House. For the remaining eight years of her father's life, Frances dutifully ran the family home, living 'all the time in a sort of moral Coventry'.

Back at Newbridge, Frances continued to write, and produced the first of her many books advocating Theism, *Essay on the Theory of Intuitive Morals*, in 1855, in which she conveyed her religious and moral beliefs. As her father disapproved, the book was published anonymously and was automatically assumed to be written by a man. The *Guardian* wrote, 'His treatment of morals is often both true and beautiful' and the *Caledonian Mercury* said, 'It is a most noble performance, the work of a *masculine* and lofty mind'. However, when it was disclosed that the author was a woman, the critics were not so positive – 'The writer', wrote the *Christian Observer*, 'we are told, is a lady, but there is nothing feeble or even feminine in the tone of the work ... Our dislike is increased when we are told it is a female who has propounded so unfeminine and stoical a theory ... and has contradicted openly the true sayings of the living God!'

Shortly after Charles Cobbe died in November 1857, Frances decided to leave Newbridge House. Her father had presumed that she would stay on in the house as lodger to her eldest brother and his wife, but Frances wanted to lead her life as an independent woman and insisted that, 'Such a plan was entirely contrary to my view of what my life should thenceforth become'. She had been left with an allowance of just over £200 a year, which although was quite a substantial amount at the time, was not much more than her usual pocket money. Despite the amount Frances accepted her 'poverty cheerfully enough' and with her savings decided to travel across Europe and the Middle East. It was a trip which 'in eleven months and at a cost of only £400', Frances travelled alone, visiting France, Italy, Belgium, Switzerland, Greece, Egypt, Lebanon and Palestine. During her travels she encountered several unmarried women who were successfully independent and living intimately together, an arrangement which also appealed to her. In Rome, she met several prominent women, including the actress Charlotte Cushman, who introduced her to the Welsh sculptor Mary Lloyd, who would later become an enduring and prominent figure in her life.

Frances ended her tour in Bristol, England in 1858. Now aged thirty-six, her long 'pilgrimage' had given her the strength and determination to live her life independently. Through the help of her friend Lady Byron, she found voluntary work in the Red Lodge reformatory and ragged school, run by the philanthropist and Unitarian social reformer, Mary Carpenter. The school had been founded by Mary to provide education for young delinquent and poverty-stricken children from the Bristol slums. Initially Frances lodged in Mary's house adjoining Red Lodge, but the strain of the routine and minimal diet affected her health, so she left in 1859 and moved into Belgrave House, Durdham Down, situated on the outskirts of Bristol. She had also wanted more than a friendship with Mary Carpenter, who, it seems, politely declined, but the two women remained on amiable terms.

Frances continued to work at Red Lodge, while gradually expanding her philanthropic work to the workhouses. Margaret Elliot, daughter of the Dean of Bristol and fellow teacher at the reformatory, was involved in several charitable works within the city and had encouraged Frances on her first visit to St Peter's workhouse. She was appalled and sickened by the conditions in which the paupers and the infirm were housed, describing it as 'a huge *omnium gatherum* of human want, vice, folly and disease'. Although they were hampered by restrictions, the two women worked together to try and improve the situation. They provided easy chairs with cushions, to give relief to inmate's frail bodies from the hard benches, and knitted hammock-type bed rests, to be secured behind the patient's back which enabled them to sit up in bed comfortably. Books, magazines and flowers were brought in to lift the inmate's spirits and they hung cheerful pictures on the blank walls, some of children, which particularly pleased the women. Frances later recalled how one patient, 'who had been lying opposite the same blank wall for twenty years ... actually *kissed* the face of the little child in the picture and burst into tears'.

Many of the paupers who were deemed the 'incurable poor' and who had little or no financial means, were denied the comfort and professional care of the hospital, and were instead sent to the workhouse to live the rest of their days in deplorable conditions. Frances wanted them to be put in more comfortable surroundings, separated from the other inmates in the workhouse and receive care from kindly charity workers. Together with Margaret Elliot, she proposed a plan and published several pamphlets to raise awareness of the hardships of the destitute incurables in the workhouse. She wrote an article called 'Workhouse Sketches', which was published in *Macmillan's Magazine*, for which she received £14. She later wrote of her delight:

> It was the first money I had ever earned and when I had cashed the cheque, I held the sovereigns in my hand and tossed them with a sense of pride and satisfaction, which the gold of the Indies, if gained by inheritance, would not give me! Naturally I went straight to St. Peter's and gave the poor old souls such a tea as had not been known before in the memory of the oldest inhabitant.

In her publication *Workhouses & Pauperism*, the philanthropist Louisa Twining (of the Twining's tea family), credited the article as 'giving an admirable picture of the then state of things, and well calculated to arouse attention to the subject'.

The two women gained support from the newspapers and general public and after posting their circulars to the existing 660 Poor Law Unions, around fifteen unions instigated their plan. Frances then turned her attention to the plight of the young girls in the workhouse, whom she was concerned for, who, after leaving the workhouse at sixteen, ended up living on the streets. The poor, deficient training which they received to prepare them for a life of domestic service subsequently led to dismissal from their employer for incompetence, which in turn led to a downward spiral back into poverty. 'It seemed at that time as if they were being trained on purpose to fall into a life of sin; having nothing to keep them out of it, – no friends, no affections, no homes, no training for any kind of useful labour, no habits of self-control of self-guidance', Frances later wrote.

To try and alleviate this problem, Frances and Margaret Elliot devised a support system for the girls after they left the workhouse, where a Sunday school was set up in Margaret's home for the workhouse girls only, to prepare them for a moral rather than sinful life. Frances would gain the permission needed from the girls' employers to attend the classes on a Sunday afternoon, where they would try to direct them away from a path of sin. The classes proved to be very successful, and they all went on to lead respectable lives. This moral plan was later adopted by a voluntary organisation of women in London who formed the Metropolitan Association for Befriending Young Servants (MABYS) in 1875, who supported young girls and prevented them from becoming prostitutes. Frances and Margaret were later called by Louisa Twining as 'The pioneers of all subsequent efforts on their (workhouse girls) behalf'.

In 1862, at the age of forty, Frances's philanthropic work would take a different direction; when travelling back to Bristol after visiting a friend in Bath, she missed her footing stepping down off the train and sprained her ankle. Through the misconduct of a doctor in Bristol, who bound her ankle too tight, restricting the circulation, she found herself lame and only able to walk with the aid of crutches. She spent as she said, 'Guineas I could ill spare' on treatment from various renowned doctors in London, but still she could 'not drop the limb for two minutes without the blood running into it till it became like an ink-bottle, when, if I held it up, it became as white as if dead'. Frances found that her ankle only improved after she ignored the doctors' advice of not walking on it, although it would be four long years before she would be able to walk unaided. During that time of finding herself virtually immobile and unable to continue her work with the workhouse and school, Frances decided to put pen to paper and wrote several articles for *Fraser's Magazine* on her travels across Europe. This would be the start of a long and successful career in journalism.

Around 1861, Frances had become reacquainted with Mary Lloyd whom she had met in Rome, and shortly after went to live with her in her home at 26 Hereford Square, South Kensington, described by Frances as 'our pretty little house'. Frances continued to write religious essays and books on theology, having several published in succession; *Thanksgiving* (1863), *Religious Duty* (1864), *Studies New and Old of Ethical and Social Subjects* (1865) and her most popular *Broken Lights* (1864), which was successful in both England and America. She worked for several news-papers, such as the *Echo* and the *Standard* and made several trips back to Italy, a country which she loved, and on two separate occasions acted as correspondent for the *Daily News*, from Florence and Rome. While she had been working at Red Lodge in Bristol, Frances had been inspired by the American Revd Samuel J. May's opinion regarding women's suf-frage. He had asked, 'Why should you not have a vote? Why should not women be enabled to influence the making of the laws in which they have as great an interest as men?' She became actively involved in the women's movement, tackling issues such as education, domestic violence and married women's property rights, and was determined as she said, to 'do everything in my power to protect the property, the persons and the parental rights of women.'

Her views on feminism became a dominant theme in many of her articles, of which there were hundreds. *Essays on the Pursuits of Women* (1863), was a volume of reprinted articles previously published in *Fraser's* and *Macmillan's* magazines, on the subject of women's rights, particularly single women. In one of her articles, *Celibacy v Marriage*, she argued that education should be available to all women in order for them to gain employment and live independently as a single woman, as opposed to the traditional married life that was expected of them. After reading her articles, women's activists such as Barbara Bodichon, Emily Shirreff and Bessie Rayner Parkes, asked Frances to join the various committees advocating women's suffrage. She became an executive member of the London National Society for Women's Suffrage, and at the National

Association for the Promotion of Social Science Congress in London in 1862, she read her paper *The Education of Women and how it would be affected by University Examinations* in which she made the first public appeal for the granting of university education to women. Through her own experience of being schooled towards a life of domesticity, she particularly sympathised with the difficulties that upper-class women faced in gaining employment. 'At nearly every door they knock in vain,' she implored, 'and what is worse, they are sometimes told that they are unfit for work (even for philanthropic work), because they are not soundly educated, or possessed of steady business habits. Yet when they seek to obtain such education, here again they meet the bolted door!' Her pleas were mocked by the newspapers, and 'for a week or two I was the butt of universal ridicule', she later wrote.

Although a single woman herself, Frances didn't oppose marriage and frequently criticised the common law affecting women in matrimony. In one of her most renowned articles, published in 1869, *Criminals, Idiots, Women and Minors*, she criticised the unfairness of 'The Common Law of England' for denying independent rights to the married woman. Husbands had no legal commitment to support their wives, which often left them helpless and vulnerable. Unless the woman was fortunate enough to have the financial means to cover the legal costs to protect her property against the common law, upon marriage her control over any personal property would automatically be given to her husband, whereby he would be entitled to any income obtained from the property. Frances questioned the law in her article, 'When all that a woman possesses in the present and future is handed over unreservedly by the law to her husband, is there the smallest attempt at obtaining security that he on his part can fulfil that obligation, which is always paraded as the equivalent; namely, the obligation to support her for the rest of her life? She went on to indicate, 'If he spends £10,000 of her fortune in a week in paying his own debts and incapacitate himself for ever from supporting her and her children, the law has not one word to say against him.'

The legal system also ignored women suffering abuse from their husbands, and as divorce was expensive they were trapped in a dangerous marriage with no protection. After reading in a newspaper of several cruel incidents of domestic violence against women, Frances vowed to do something about it. She meticulously gathered detailed information of many accounts of brutality towards women, including statistics which were shockingly high at around 1,500 assaults on wives each year. She noted that most of the victims were not 'drunken viragos (who usually escaped violence or gave as good as they received), but poor, pale, shrinking creatures, who strove to earn bread for their children and to keep together their miserable homes'. Frances wrote of her investigations in her powerful article 'Wife-Torture in England', which was published in the *Contemporary Review* in April 1878. She wrote:

> I desire specially to avoid making this paper more painful than can be helped but it is indispensable that some specimens of the tortures to which I refer should be brought before the reader's eye. Wife-beating in process of time, and in numberless cases, advances to Wife-torture, and the Wife-torture usually ends in Wife-maiming, Wife-blinding, or Wife-murder. A man who has 'thrashed' his wife with his fists half-a-dozen times, becomes satiated with such enjoyment as that performance brings, and next time he is angry he kicks her with his hob-nailed shoes. When he has kicked her a few times standing or sitting, he kicks her down and stamps on her stomach, her breasts, or her face. If he does not wear clogs or hob-nailed shoes, he takes up some other weapon, a knife, a poker, a hammer, a bottle of vitriol, or a lighted lamp, and strikes her with it, sets her on fire; and then, and then only, the hapless creature's sufferings are at an end.

Her exposure of the true cruelty of wife-beating as told in 'Wife-Torture' shocked the public and gained huge support for the campaign.

Frances noted that the assaults suffered by women from the poorer classes were more severe and more frequent than those of the middle and upper classes, but unlike their affluent sisters who could pursue a divorce, they had no hope of escaping such brutality. She saw that the only means of escape for them would be a legal separation. In 'Wife-Torture', she also criticised Parliament for failing to bring measures against domestic violence and worked with the son of an old friend and a Birmingham magistrate, Alfred Hill, to draft a Bill which would grant any woman a

Separation Order from her husband if he had been convicted of assault against her. Both the Bill and the contents of 'Wife-Torture', caught the attention of Lord Penzance, who added Frances's proposals to the Matrimonial Causes Act Amendment Bill under whose influence and without debate, the Act to Amend the Matrimonial Causes Act became law on 27 May 1878. In addition to the Separation Order, several other things were also proposed by Frances; legal custody of children under ten years of age was given to the wife and a weekly sum was paid to the Board of Guardians for the parish by the husband to support his wife. Frances later wrote of her achievement, 'The part of my work for women, to which I look back with most satisfaction was that in which I laboured to obtain protection for unhappy wives, beaten, mangled, mutilated or trampled on by brutal husbands'.

As well as campaigning for women's rights, Frances was also involved in the anti-vivisection campaign. She had always been very fond of animals and was never without the companionship of her favourite breed of dog, the Pomeranian. Her interest in anti-vivisection had started in 1863, when she had read various articles in the newspapers of the terrible cruelties suffered by the animals in the Veterinary Schools at Alfort, near Paris, where operations were performed on live, conscious horses in the course of instruction to their students. English students were gaining the same level of tuition, but on dead animals. Frances was horrified and, hoping to raise public awareness, she wrote as article for *Fraser's Magazine,* entitled 'The Rights of Man and the Claims of Brutes', which she believed to be the first attempt to raise 'the moral questions involved in the torture of animals either for the sake of scientific and therapentic research, or for the acquirement of manipulative skill'.

Later that year, while Frances was staying near Florence in Italy, she heard of other cruel practices of vivisection being carried out by Professor Moritz Schiff in his laboratory at Specola. The reports of the shocking treatment suffered by the animals were confirmed after a visit to the laboratory by Dr Appleton, an American physician, who had witnessed the horrifying state of the animals which included dogs, cats and pigeons. Reports of Professor Schiff being forced to kill a badly tortured cat to relieve it of its suffering infuriated Frances and many other anti-vivisectionists. She drafted a petition which held 783 signatures, including those of the aristocracy of Florence, but the Professor ignored it. However, numerous objections to the sorrowful cries heard from the poor, distressed animals at Specola created negative feeling towards the professor and he later left Florence for Geneva. The Royal Society for the Prevention of Cruelty to Animals had also failed in their attempt to stop these barbaric acts, which was thought to have been due to the influence of Napoleon III, who was rumoured to have been a keen and regular observer during the operations. A few years later a petition was signed by 500 English veterinarians appealing to the French to use dead horses in their students' training, like their English counterparts. This did have some effect and significantly reduced the number of operations performed.

In 1870, Frances attended the British Association for the Advancement of Science meeting in Liverpool, where the committee discussed Physiological Experimentation. The report from the meeting, published in 1871, contained four recommendations regarding vivisection: the compulsory use of anaesthetic during experimentations, experiments carried out for use of teaching purposes to be painless, painful experiments to be performed by skilled persons with appropriate instruments in properly regulated laboratories and that these would not be performed for the mere purpose of physical dexterity. Frances was delighted at the proposals, but as they were only voluntary guidelines she soon found that 'as time passed we were surprised to find that nothing was done to enforce these rules in any way or at any place; and that the particular practice which they most distinctly condemn, namely, the use of vivisections as illustrations of recognised facts, was flourishing more than ever without let or hindrance'. Guy's Hospital and St Thomas's Hospital Medical Schools were openly promoting vivisection in their prospectuses, publicizing 'Demonstrations on living animals'.

At the Medical Congress in Norwich in 1874, Mr Magnan a renowned French physiologist, carried out an experiment in which he injected a dog with absinthe in order to provoke an epileptic fit. On seeing the animal suffer, protestors objected and, following a disruption, the experiment was stopped. The RSPCA's secretary John Colam proceeded to

prosecute Mr Magnan, who narrowly escaped conviction by swiftly returning to France. Nonetheless, it was agreed by the magistrates at the trial that
vivisection was 'scientifically useless'. Although the incident gained considerable publicity, Frances realised that new legislation was needed to put an
end to this unwarranted cruelty and decided that she needed the backing
of the most dominant and influential animal organisation, the RSPCA,
to promote such a Bill. She drafted a memorial to its committee and distributed copies to be signed by numerous prominent people, together with
two accompanying pamphlets entitled, *Reasons for Interference* and *Need of
a Bill*. Frances collected 600 signatures, all of which were either highly significant in the medical profession or were notable peers.

Frances felt extremely hopeful when, shortly afterwards, she was
invited to the first meeting of the sub-committee for vivisection of
the RSPCA, but her optimism was short lived when she arrived at
the meeting and found the members to be 'worthy gentlemen, mostly
elderly, but not one of the more distinguished of the committee or a
single Peer or member of Parliament … they were not the men to take
the lead in such a movement and make a bold stand against the claims of
science'. Although disappointed, Frances was still determined and with
the help of some of her most influential friends, namely Lord Henniker
and Sir William Dyke, a Conservative whip, a Bill for 'Regulating
the Practice of Vivisection' was presented to the House of Lords on
4 May 1875. The Bill proposed that laboratories practising experiments on
live animals were to be inspected annually and all animals be anaesthetised during experiments, except when the animal needed to be cognisant.
A few days later the physiologists, backed by Charles Darwin, presented
their own Bill to the House of Commons, also recommending painless
experiments but with the addition of the granting of licenses to undertake painful experiments without anaesthesia, on certain grounds, for
the development of scientific research. Although both bills were unsuccessful, support was gained from the public, including Queen Victoria,
who strongly opposed vivisection and prompted the government to issue
a Royal Commission of Inquiry into vivisection. Later in January 1876,
this Commission recommended legislation to control vivisection, favouring the use of anaesthetics.

Meanwhile, Frances realised that further action was needed to enforce any positive changes to vivisection, and so together with fellow anti-vivisectionist and friend, Dr George Hoggan, she formed the world's first society to campaign against experiments on animals. Originally named by Dr Hoggan as The Society for Protection of Animals Liable to Vivisection, its aim was 'to obtain the greatest possible protection for animals liable to vivisection'. Shortly after acquiring their offices in Victoria Street, Frances renamed the organisation, The Victoria Street Society, and vowed from the onset to 'never go to bed at night leaving a stone unturned which might help to stop vivisection'. She rallied the support of some of her most prominent and influential friends, including Lord Shaftesbury, who led a designated group of highly significant men to the Home Office to persuade the Home Secretary, Richard Cross, to bring in a Bill following the Royal Commission's recommendations. Initially the Bill was favoured, but just as it was at its final stages in the House of Lords the Home Secretary received a memorial signed by 3,000 doctors requesting that the Bill be amended to protect the physiologists, rather than the animals. Richard Cross relented and on the 15 August 1876, The Cruelty to Animals Act or, as it is more commonly known, The Vivisection Act, was passed.

Frances was bitterly disappointed, as she later wrote, 'The world has never seemed to me quite the same since that dreadful time'. She resolved to fight for total abolition of vivisection and endeavoured to maximise the anti-vivisection campaign by displaying 1,700 handbills and 300 posters of enlarged copies of disturbing illustrations of vivisection taken from the physiological handbooks. The posters made the impact she had intended on the people of London, proving to be 'more effective than as many thousands of speeches and pamphlets'. Although the movement had rapidly gathered momentum, with other anti-vivisection societies emerging across Europe and America, Frances realised that the possibility of a Bill being passed in parliament to abolish vivisection was extremely unlikely.

By 1878, the society had expanded considerably, with highly distinguished members on its committee and it had changed its title to the Society for Protection of Animals from Vivisection. In 1881 they presented another Bill to parliament, but as with their previous Bill, it was unsuccessful. Frances diligently continued in her vigorous campaign against vivisection, but by 1884 her health had declined and being unable to agree with the society's decision to tolerate the legislation allowing vivisection on anaesthetised animals, she resigned from the society and left London with Mary Lloyd to retire in the Welsh mountains.

Two years later her life-long companion, Mary Lloyd, died. Frances wrote during the empty years after her passing, 'God has given me two priceless benedictions in life – in my youth a perfect mother; in my later years, a perfect friend.' Mary's dying wish was for Frances to continue 'working for the cause of the science-tortured brutes' which she upheld until her death in April 1904, corresponding with newspapers and writing pamphlets till the end. Her legacy lives on in the British Union for the Abolition of Vivisection (BUAV), which she founded in 1889 and continues to grow internationally today, campaigning to abolish all experiments on animals.

ANNE JELLICOE

1823–1880

'Mrs Jellicoe was the apostle of employment as a
means of salvation and elevation for women.'

Journal of the Women's Education Union (1880)

T hroughout her life, Anne Jellicoe persisted in her passion of giving
women the opportunity to study in further education and so increase
their career prospects equal to their male counterparts. Her devotion
to her pioneering cause eventually led to the founding of a vocational
college in Dublin, which enabled the women of Ireland to gain 'the glorious privilege of being independent' regardless of their social class.

Anne was born in 1823, in Mountmellick, County Laois, into a wealthy
middle-class Quaker family (see p. 74). Her father, William Mullin, who
died when Anne was three years old, had been a schoolmaster who had
opened a boy's school in Mountmellick in 1820. Although religion was
extremely important and predominated in Quaker schools, subjects which
would be beneficial in adulthood, both for girls as well as boys, were
also taught. William Mullin's school provided training in book-keeping
and business studies, both uncommon subjects at the time. There were a
number of schools in Mountmellick, but education for girls was on a more
rudimentary level. It is likely that Anne received her education from a
private governess, as did the majority of middle-class girls of that time.

Quakers had settled in Mountmellick since the seventeenth century and through them the town had flourished, with the growth of industries such as woollen mills, breweries, glass, cotton and linen manufactures, tanneries, and a distillery. The town's textile industry grew and prospered to a level parallel with Manchester, which was the nucleus of England's industry at the time, and became known as 'the Manchester of Ireland'. The development of a number of large mills established a thriving cottage industry, weaving cotton and wool, enabling many households to earn an extra income in addition to their existing farming income.

Anne grew up with her brother, John William and her mother, who died when she was seventeen years old. Her Quaker background meant that she was involved in philanthropic work in the community from her childhood and was conscious of the lower standard of education for women. She was also concerned with the hardship for women that had resulted from the decline of the weaving industries in the 1830s, and she became very much aware of the difficulties women faced in finding useful employment. In an attempt to alleviate the situation and provide an additional income for those in hardship a fellow friend and Quaker, Johanna Carter, established a small school of fifteen girls, in a thatched cottage, teaching them white embroidery work. This eminent, pioneering high-quality embroidery used a locally sourced and moderately priced white knitting cotton of varying thickness which was sewn on a heavy white satin jean, known as 'white on white'. The motifs were quite large and they were a selection of natural floral designs, inspired by plants found locally along the banks of the Owenass River, such as roses, blackberries, woodbine, wild clematis, acorns, and dog-rose. They were traditionally sewn on christening

Anne Jellicoe, aged approximately 17 years. (Courtesy of the Alexandra College Archive)

gowns, pillow shams, nightdresses, dressing table mats and cushion covers. Towards the latter part of the nineteenth century, Mountmellick embroidery became extremely popular, where a finer type of needlework was used on children's dresses, aprons, pinafores and the panels of ladies costumes. Anne was very much involved with helping Johanna in the school, teaching the girls embroidery and she drew some of the designs used for the embroidery work. Mountmellick embroidery continues to gain popularity around the world today, having been revived in the 1970s by Sister Teresa Margaret McCarthy. Now a 'social' craft, rather than an income for the poor, weekly classes are held in Mountmellick, keeping this tradition of Irish needlework alive. Pieces of this exquisite embroidery are displayed in several museums, including the Victoria and Albert Museum in London and the National Museum of Ireland in Dublin.

In 1846, Anne married John Jellicoe, a Quaker who came from a family of mill owners from Mountmellick, although he had left to work in his father's mill at Flemingstown in Tipperary. The couple moved to Clara, County Offaly in 1848, where John had purchased a flour mill. Employment for women was limited in Clara, as the heavy work in the flour mills, the town's main source of employment, was unsuitable for them. Some were employed in the cottage weaving industry, making jute sacks for the flour mills owned by the Goodbody family, a distinguished local Quaker family, who were also friends of Anne and John. Anne was aware of the problems that women faced and wanted to improve their situation, and so in 1850, using her knowledge and expertise from the embroidery school in Mountmellick, she opened her own embroidery school in Clara, County Offaly, also teaching sewed muslin work. Although the cottage industry of sewed muslin work started in the north of Ireland in 1822, the 1850s saw it rapidly spread across Ireland, providing around 200,000 women with work. Anne had contributed to the growing number of schools teaching the crafts of crochet and lace set up across the country, a progressive movement started by women to help their own sex in impoverished times.

The little employment that was available for women was as domestic servants and needlewomen, both of which were under-paid, particularly for the high-quality skills of the needlewomen. In 1853 Anne closed her embroidery school due to the disapproval of the Catholic Church and with the help of Lewis Goodbody, son of the milling dynasty in Clara, she established a lace crochet school, a skill which offered better pay to the workers. Anne's Quaker background of business expertise turned the school into an enterprising business. She went on to employ a hundred women, whose work was exported to Glasgow, but apart from providing women with work and a skill, Anne wanted to instil in the women a feeling of independence and self-worth. She was also convinced that women needed an education to improve their prospects in employment, a cause that she would pursue after the crochet lace school had closed in 1856 and she and John had gone to live in Harold's Cross in Dublin, where he had secured a flour mill. It was in Dublin that she would meet other prominent social reformers who would share her visions and help her improve the working conditions of all classes of women.

Parts of Dublin in the post-famine Victorian years suffered extreme poverty, and had some of the worst slums in the British Empire. The famine had a devastating effect on both peasantry and the middle-classes alike, leaving countless women destitute following the emigration of many men, whom they had depended upon for financial support. The perception of women in Victorian society as the 'weaker sex' who were to be protected, particularly those of the higher classes, wasn't entirely true. Many women were living in devastating hardship, due to being single, widowed or deserted and the middle-classes were no exception. The reality that more than half the adult female population worked in hard, demanding manual jobs, was often overlooked and women, especially the middle-classes were portrayed as delicate, gentle creatures who were kept safe and secure by their loving husbands or male relatives. Ironically, middle-class women had more difficulty in finding work than the lower classes, frequently facing discrimination, as 'ladies' were deemed to be unskilled and oblivious to the pressures of the job market, and as a result they often succumbed to life on the streets and starvation. Anne witnessed the deprivation and hardship in the Liberties area where John had a corn and flour store, and was determined to relieve the helpless and desperate women from their plight. Firmly believing that education was the best direction out of poverty, Anne started by helping to improve the Quaker-run Cole Alley Infant School for poor children and encouraged mothers to send their children to school.

Work for skilled needlewomen at home was becoming scarce due to the use of modern sewing machines in the factories. Anne became involved with philanthropic work in the slums and looked further into the conditions in the factories and prisons in Dublin. The vulnerability of the women was apparent, as many working in the factories were faced with the uncertainty of the duration of the work, with the possibility of being dismissed without any warning or wages owed to them. She prepared an account of this, along with other observations, such as working conditions, wages and the future prospects in their work, and presented it in August 1861, to the first meeting in Dublin of the National Association for the Promotion of Social Science. Established in England in 1857, the association discussed at their meetings issues of the social difficulties that women frequently encountered and presented proposals of social reform. In her paper, 'The Condition of Young Women Employed in Manufactories in Dublin', Anne stressed how women were vulnerable to corruption in the workplace. The working conditions were unhealthy, with women working 'day and night in stifling rooms, where fresh air was rarely permitted to enter'. She stated the long working hours, particularly in the larger factories, of ten hours a day with only one hour's break and very little food, resulting in the women being very listless. Apprentices from the age of twelve, worked for a whole year without receiving wages. Anne also noted that with the introduction of the sewing machine, there was an increasing demand for skilled machinists and although the girls were 'not required to read and write while occupied in the lower departments, education greatly facilitates their rise in the trade'.

As many of the workers were young teenagers, she suggested that evening school be available for the girls, to advance their education and provide training, such as the correct use of the sewing machines, which would enable them to improve their position in the factory. Her paper also urged the need for accommodation 'where timid and friendless women could receive shelter at moderate cost, where the useful but neglected arts of cooking and mending might be taught and practised'. She also suggested 'the establishment of a registry of the various employments open to young women, and the different institutions available for their aid'. Women needed to be encouraged to be 'thrifty and provident housekeepers' and she recommended an increase in Penny Savings banks. In a bid to create further employment prospects for women and enforce their position in society, Anne also proposed that they be employed as supervisors over female employees, as well as men. In response, *The Englishwoman's Journal* of October 1862, confirmed that in Anne's report, 'she outlines the various forms of factory employment open to women in the city, noting the pay and conditions of work which are applicable. She examines those crafts and trades which were undergoing increased mechanisation, and notes the attendant problems for women. Jellicoe also alludes to the moral implications of women's employment, particularly in regard to the performance of their domestic duties'.

After visiting and observing the conditions in Mountjoy Prison, Anne prepared another paper in 1862, called 'A Visit to the Female Convict Prison at Mountjoy, Dublin,' in which she recorded a new approach to discipline amongst the female convicts which had proved to be very successful. She noted that through the new system, introduced by Captain Crofton and Mr Lentaigne, prisoners could obtain an education, under the authority of assigned female figures such as superintendents, managers and matrons. Classes were held which demonstrated that the women were keen to learn and their morale was lifted, and here 'school becomes daily most prized, and, even when little progress is made, is a relief from moody thoughts and morbid imaginations'. It was evident that the success was largely due to the appointed female matrons and it showed that in the balance of power, 'men and women work harmoniously and helpfully, combining in due proportion the masculine element of power and the feminine prerogative of influence by love'.

Through the NAPSS, another important organization had been formed in 1859, called the Society for Promoting the Employment of Women. Its headquarters were at 19 Langham Place in London, where it set up a reading room and a meeting place for lonely and impoverished ladies, and also more importantly, an employment register which showed the jobs available for women. Initially the society expected a minimal response, but after much publicity, they were inundated with female applicants, many of whom were middle-class. It quickly became evident and shocking that there was a serious problem of female unemployment.

The same problem in Ireland had been intensified by the famine where the gentry, as well as the peasantry, had been forced into destitution. Following the example of the society in Langham Place, Anne and Ada Barbara Corlett, daughter of a local businessman, established the Dublin branch of the first society in Ireland for the employment of women. The committee consisted of both professional and businessmen and some ladies of the aristocracy. Anne was part of the managing committee and Ada was an honorary secretary.

Although, there was a large influx of women who arrived to register, the society's willingness to help the 'distressed gentlewomen' met with the same problems that the society in London had encountered. The main goal of the society was to find employment for middle-class women, but it wasn't easy, as many of the women had little to offer an employer in the way of useful skills and they had limited education. They also looked upon working for money as undignified and considered it unthinkable to accept salaries from those socially lower than themselves. They requested to be paid for their labour in an absurd, secretive way, so as not to be seen openly accepting payment for their work and to hide their identity from their employer to avoid any blemish on their social demeanour. Neither Anne nor Ada had any patience for the women's delusive notions and promptly rebuked them for believing work to be demeaning when they should recognise that 'the faculty of earning' was in itself 'a respectable gift'. Employers conveyed to the society that 'so universal was the ignorance of arithmetic among women, that in establishments in which departments existed where fashion compelled their employment, necessity forced the addition of a male clerk to overlook the bills'.

The solution to this problem came in the start of Anne's fulfilment of her dream of educating women to further their prospects in employment, and give them their independence. Her plan was to form an institute of education for women where technical and vocational training could be offered to improve their prospects. She wanted women to have 'within their reach that privilege of which men are so proud, but of which men ought not to possess the monopoly – the glorious privilege of being independent'. The outcome was the founding of a 'Technical Training

Institution for Women' where classes in arithmetic, book-keeping, dicta-tion and writing were offered, but the women had to be persuaded to undertake any training that would be deemed appropriate for refined Dublin ladies. To coax them into joining any classes, members of the committee and their daughters enrolled in the first classes, and only then did the women consider the training socially acceptable. From her observations in the textile factories, Anne knew that there were open-ings for overseers and supervisors and so a sewing machine class was set up, to further advance the skills of a seamstress for the promotion to supervisor. She hoped that not only would the women find 'lucrative and honourable posts in this field, but also that they would there find oppor-tunities to introduce reform, where now the worst influences unhappily prevail'. The classes were started in 1861, in two unfurnished rooms at 25 Molesworth Street and were initially funded by the public. Following the patronage of Queen Victoria and Prince Albert, this innovative establishment was named The Queen's Institute for the Training and Employment of Educated Women, and was the first technical college for women. It eventually received support from prominent companies such as Belleek Pottery and the British and Irish Magnetic Telegraph Company and received grants from the Department of Education in South Kensington.

The intentions of the institute were to 'assist the ladies of limited means, by training them to the pursuit of professions and occupations, in which a demand is found to exist for their industry'. Along with the textile classes, a number of other classes were linked to employment, which proved to be the most popular and successful, such as law-writing and telegraph clerk training, which enabled many of the ladies to secure work with the Telegraph Company. Other classes, such as wood and metal engraving, colouring photographs, lithography, art and architec-tural drawing, and engraving on silver and ivory were offered and some women were employed as artists, decorating porcelain at Belleek Pottery. Anne wanted to encourage governesses to come to the institute, so Latin was added to the classes and it was her intention that after their training they would receive a certificate with which they could then insist on a higher salary that was proportionate to their qualifications.

The institute continued to grow, with its intake of pupils increasing yearly, and a large number gaining employment. However, the committee did not share Anne's enthusiasm for the inclusion of governess training and seeing the need for a separate academic college to educate governesses, she decided to pursue her lifelong dream and in 1866, she founded Alexandra College for the Higher Education of Women. The people of Dublin were adverse to a training college for governesses, so funding proved to be difficult to find. Anne approached Dr Richard Trench, the Archbishop of Dublin, whom she knew had an interest in higher education for women. Initially he was reluctant and had reservations concerning the success of such a college in Ireland, but after much persuasion he agreed to assist her with her idea, as he was 'won over by her enthusiasm'. Dr Trench had been a Professor of Divinity at King's College, London and a close friend of Frederick Denison Maurice, the founder of Queen's College, London, which had been established in 1848. He advised Anne to extend the training in the college to a wider and more advanced university type and increase the focus on liberal education, similar to Queen's College in London.

In 1866, the college opened its doors at Earlsfort Terrace, Dublin and was the first institution in Ireland to offer higher education for women. Anne's prevailing desire to improve education for women, which had originated in her childhood in Mountmellick, had finally been accomplished, as she declared in a letter dated from 1867, 'Well, I have carried out one dream, the dream that "pleased my childish thought," the founding of a college'. Sadly Anne's husband, John, who had supported her throughout all her campaigns, didn't get to see her dream fulfilled as he died in December 1862. Although very little is recorded of their marriage, their devotion is confirmed in the *Freeman's Journal* of 1880, which mentioned that Anne 'never ceased to mourn' her late husband.

The college was named after its patron, Alexandra, the Princess of Wales and with the support of the Church of Ireland clergy and professors of Trinity College Dublin it became extremely successful. The intention of the college was 'to afford an education more sound and solid ... and better tested, than is at present easily to be obtained by women of the middle and upper classes in this country', as was specified in its prospectus. Adapting the philosophy of Queen's College in London, the objective of Alexandra College was to prepare and train girls over the age of fifteen years old for careers in teaching. Lectures and examinations were given by the professors from Trinity College Dublin, offering a higher standard of education than the level of contemporary secondary schools. In addition to the usual subjects of English language and literature, history and theology, rudimentary classes in English, geography, history and arithmetic had to be taught, due to the low standard of basic education that the incoming students had received at other schools. Anne established a system to help improve the students that were behind academically, by appointing older students who had studied at the college for a minimum of three terms to help in the classes as assistant teachers for a small wage. In 1868 Anne introduced lectures in advanced subjects such as Greek literature, astronomy and English poetry, which led on to advanced classes being held on Saturdays at Trinity College, attracting both men and women. The classes proved to be very successful, with over 200 women attending each year until 1877, when they ended.

Anne still had concerns about the inadequate education for women and wanted to show that they could be just as literate as men and achieve a high standard academically. In 1869 she formed the Governess Association of Ireland (GAI), 'to promote the higher education of ladies as teachers'. Its committee consisted of both men and women and included professors of Trinity College. The GAI wanted to increase educational prospects for women and provide information and funding for women to study and train for positions as governesses or teachers. It also set up an employment registry to help them find employment. Anne wanted to raise the standards of education further and give women the opportunity to gain a recognised academic qualification. The GAI and the Council of Alexandra College proposed to the Board of Trinity College Dublin the formation of examinations for women and an examining board, assigning examiners comparable to those at Cambridge. The Board agreed and the first examinations for women were held in 1870. Scholarships for students were introduced by the GAI for entry to Alexandra College to study for the examinations, which broadened possibilities for many young women, especially those in need of financial assistance.

However, there was still the problem of girls entering Alexandra College with a poor academic background. To solve this issue, Anne approached the Council in 1871, to open a collegiate school to prepare the girls for the standard of the college. After much persuasion, the Council and the Committee of Education agreed and adjacent to the college, a 'feeder high school' was opened named Alexandra School in April 1873. The school proved to be a success and a financial asset to the college, as when the admission of pupils decreased during the depression in the early 1880s, the profits from the school supported the upkeep of the college, enabling it to survive through to the present day. Many of the girls from Alexandra College went on to become teachers at the school. One notable pupil was Isabella Mulvany, who after winning a scholarship and studying at the college for two years, became the first headmistress of Alexandra School. Anne deeply believed that in order for women to have a voice in politics or academic debate, they would need to be accepted into the Royal University, which had been founded in 1880. Although university-type lectures were regularly given at Alexandra College by lecturers from Trinity College, and women were educated to degree level and capable of sitting the exams, they were still excluded from the university campus. It wasn't until 1884 that the Royal University awarded degrees to nine female graduates, generally known as 'The Nine Graces'. Six of them had studied at Alexandra College, including Isabella Mulvany. They were the first women in Ireland or Britain to attain degrees.

Anne was never to see the momentous graduation ceremony, as she died suddenly at the age of fifty-seven whilst visiting her brother at his home in Birmingham on 18 October 1880. Her body was returned to Ireland, where she was buried at Rosenallis, the Quaker cemetery in County Laois. In his speech at her funeral, Dr Trench stated that, 'He never knew one in whom there was a more entire absence of self-seeking … It never so much as passed through her thought that one of the purposes for which Alexandra College existed was her glorification.'

Today Alexandra College continues Anne's legacy in the form of an elite, private secondary girl's school in Milltown, Dublin, having moved from the original site at Earlsfort Terrace. It sustains a respectable reputation for high exam results and is one of the most exclusive schools in Ireland.

Anna Maria Haslam

1829–1922

'Equity knows no difference of sex, the law of equal freedom
applies to the whole race – female as well as male.'

Herbert Spencer from *The Women's Advocate*

A nna Haslam's story is not just of a pioneering suffragist, but of a
strong and enduring partnership with her husband, Thomas
Haslam, that lasted for sixty-three years. Together they broke down
social boundaries in Ireland and tackled women's issues that were highly
taboo in their time.

Anna Maria Fisher was born in April 1829, to an affluent, middle-class
Quaker family in Youghal, County Cork. Her father, Abraham Fisher,
a native of Youghal, was a successful corn-miller and came from a genera-
tion of prosperous merchant traders, and her mother, Jane Moore, came
from Neath in South Wales. They had seventeen children, of which Anna
was the second youngest. Both of Anna's parents were from Quaker backgrounds and were consequently involved with philanthropic work and
social reform.

The Society of Friends, or Quakers, are a Christian sect that were
quite radical when they were first introduced to Ireland in 1654 by the
Englishman George Fox. Their fundamental belief was in equality between men and women and they were predominantly known for
their help with the poor and their support for the anti-slavery campaign,

prison reform and temperance. By the 1800s many Quakers had become extremely successful in various commercial enterprises and businesses, with leading pioneers in the milling and textile industries. Their simple and prudent lifestyle, as opposed to the extravagance of the landed gentry, and their honest reputation contributed to maintaining the businesses that are still successful today, such as Bewley's Cafés and Jacob's Biscuits. Anna's upbringing and membership of the Society of Friends would have considerable influence in her life-long commitments to her causes, particularly in the women's movement and education.

Until the age of sixteen Anna was educated at Quaker boarding schools in both Ireland and England, attending Newtown in County Waterford, then Castlegate (The Mount) in York until 1845. She returned to Youghal, where she worked with her parents in the soup kitchens organised by the Society of Friends for relief in the Great Famine of 1845-1849. Members of her family were heavily involved in the Central Relief Committee, which had been set up in Dublin by the Society and worked closely with the Quakers committee in London, from whence many English members came to Ireland to help with relief work. A nationwide network of committees had been established across Ireland, to organise their own subcommittees in their area and the Quakers that were merchants distributed goods throughout the country. Abraham Fisher was one of the representatives from the Society for Youghal and Anna's brother, Peter, who had organised a number of food kitchens in the area, imported corn from India to provide a substitute for the potato.

Anna and her sister Deborah started an industry from their father's kitchen in Youghal, teaching young local girls to crochet and knit. Anna organised the sale of their work, and as the orders increased and the business flourished the girls carried on working from their own homes. The sisters had created much-needed work in the area, ultimately employing over 100 girls, which enabled many of them to emigrate and escape the horrors of the famine. After a number of successful years trading, the nuns of the Presentation Convent eventually took over and introduced lace-making which later established Youghal's renowned lace industry.

Anna's upbringing as a Quaker meant that her parents were involved in several causes, particularly the international peace movement and the anti-slavery movement, with delegates from various campaigns regularly visiting the family home, who she would have met. Following her involvement in the peace movement, Anna went on to help establish and become secretary of the first Olive Leaf Circle of Quaker pacifists in Ireland in 1849. The Circles originated in London and were initiated by an American, Elihu Burritt. They were a gathering of fifteen to twenty women, from various Christian denominations, who held monthly meetings in a member's home to discuss universal peace and correspond with other circles, not just in Britain but also in Europe. They wrote children's pacifist stories and fables, opposing slavery and war, which they published in a journal called *The Olive Leaf* and to raise further awareness of the movement, short messages of peace known as 'Olive Leafs' were sent to foreign newspapers.

By staying on an extra year at The Mount in York, Anna had received apprentice teacher training and along with her structural skills gained in the running of the cottage industries for young girls and her involvement in the Olive Leaf Circles, she was able to obtain an assistant teaching position at Ackworth School in Yorkshire, in 1853. It was there she met fellow teacher and Irish Quaker, Thomas Haslam, who was originally from Mountmellick in County Laois. Already a devoted feminist, Thomas shared Anna's deep belief in equality for women. After returning to Ireland they married in a registry office in Cork in 1854. Thomas had left the Society of Friends and as it was not acceptable to marry a non-member of the society, it was decided at the Cork Monthly Meeting that Anna had 'forfeited her right to membership of our religious society' and so she had to leave the Society of Friends. Although they were no longer Quakers, Anna and Thomas sustained their contacts with members of the society and its values stayed with them throughout their lives.

The Haslams' moved to Dublin, where Thomas left teaching and obtained a position as an accountant at Jameson, Pim & Co. Brewery, in Aughrim Street. They were extremely close and devoted to each other, with friends often referring to their marriage as idyllic. They moved to Rathmines in Dublin in 1862 and in 1866 Thomas suffered ill health which was to afflict him for the rest of his life. He was unable to work so Anna became the breadwinner by running a small stationery business from their

home, which she ran for the next forty years. The couple had been involved
in various campaigns regarding women's rights, which she managed to
pursue despite her other commitments supporting Thomas and the business. One of her main concerns was the need for a good education for
women, by which she hoped to improve the standard of education and consequently provide equal employment opportunities for women.

In 1861, Anna worked with other Irish women activists on several
campaigns. She had been among the reformers led by Anne Jellicoe,
also a Quaker, in the founding of the Irish Society for the Training and
Employment of Educated Women, later called the Queen's Institute,
Dublin. This pioneering technical institute offered training for girls,
including machinists and office clerks, to broaden their employment
prospects. This paved the way for Anne Jellicoe to establish Alexandra
College for the Higher Education of Women in 1866, the first college
in Ireland to provide university-type education for women and then in
1873 Alexandra High School for Girls. Anna persisted in her crusade
for women's further education and contributed in both the Intermediate
Education Act of 1878, which enabled girls to sit public school examinations for the first time, and the Royal University Act of 1879, which
permitted women to study for degrees of the Royal University. Anna
extended this campaign to include women in medical training, and in
1874 she played a significant role in establishing the London School of
Medicine for Women. In 1882 she assisted in initiating the Association of
Schoolmistresses and Other Ladies Interested in Education, an extension
to what had already been accomplished, providing a system that not only
endorsed, but supervised and safeguarded women's educational interests.

Like Thomas Haslam, many other men were active in women's suffrage
at the time, including the notable British philosopher and civil servant,
John Stuart Mill, who organised and presented to the House of Commons
the first petition for women's suffrage in 1866, which Anna signed, along
with twenty-five other Irish women. Despite his poor health, Thomas continued to back Anna in her feminist activities and campaigns, and was able
to make a huge contribution in his writings for women's suffrage, when
in 1874, he published *The Women's Advocate,* the first of three Irish suffrage
pamphlets and the first to be published in Ireland supporting women's

suffrage. They contained invaluable information and advice on the organisation of suffrage activism and debated the vote for women.

In 1876 the first Irish suffrage society was formed by Anna and Thomas, called the Dublin Women's Suffrage Association or DWSA. Anna became secretary, a position she held for thirty-seven years, during which time she never missed a meeting and was considered the 'driving force' of the DWSA, providing constant guidance. The DWSA's membership largely consisted of Quakers, both men and women, and sought for reform for any discrimination against women, on both a legal and social level. They strove to obtain public support, both locally and nationally, through public meetings, demonstrations, parades, and letters to the newspapers and were rigidly non-militant in their approach. They aimed to enfranchise women and regularly sent petitions to the House of Commons and lobbied Irish MPs in a bid to support their purpose. Initially, men were only able to vote based on a property qualification, which was eventually reduced in the Reform Act of 1884. Although the Act increased the number of male voters, including farm labourers, it was not universal and still held restrictions, excluding male lodgers and women. This created much criticism and frustration amongst women and in 1886 Anna stated that 'it is not easy to keep our temper when we see the most illiterate labourer, with no two ideas in his head, exercising the very important function of self-government while educated women capable in every way of giving a rational vote are still debarred.'

In 1864, 1866 and 1869, parliament passed Contagious Diseases Acts where women suspected of prostitution living in specified garrison towns in Britain and Ireland were given a compulsory check for venereal disease. If a woman was found to be infected, she was admitted to a lock hospital or lock ward, where she would be detained for three months initially, but this was increased to one year when the 1869 Act was passed. The Acts were to provide protection for service men who frequented prostitutes and so were vulnerable to infection. As the Acts specified women not men, many feminists opposed the Acts as being discriminative against women and maintaining a sexual double standard and they also felt that prostitution, which was considered a threat to family life, was being acknowledged by the state and therefore accepted.

The Ladies National Association for the Repeal of the Contagious Diseases Act was formed in England in 1869, by Josephine Butler and Elizabeth Wolstenholme, in a campaign against the Acts. Anna and Isabella Tod, a leading feminist from Belfast, were involved in the campaign from the beginning, and by 1871 they had helped to establish branches of the association in Ireland – in Dublin, Cork and Belfast. Although still very much a taboo subject amongst middle-class women, it encouraged them for the first time to speak openly about sexual morality. Thomas Haslam continued writing for women's causes and in 1870 he published a pamphlet entitled, *A Few Words on Prostitution and the Contagious Diseases Acts*, in which he criticised his fellow men and argued that prostitution, 'one of the deadliest evils of our time', made women the prey of reckless men, by luring them and then deserting them. He urged the law to prosecute the men, especially if they were married; and if they enticed a 'virgin girl' they should be made to marry her. He disputed the Contagious Diseases Acts, stating that they should be revoked as they encouraged prostitution by trying to eradicate one of the 'natural penalties', venereal disease. He also stated that the lack of employment for women was the primary cause for their descent into prostitution.

Anna campaigned relentlessly, attending demonstrations in Dublin and Belfast and speaking at many public meetings. She continued to lobby MPs, while Thomas contributed to the campaign in a petition for repeal by collecting signatures from over 100 doctors. The long campaign ended in 1886 when the Acts were finally repealed. Anna later said that the fight and the commitment to the campaign for the repeal of the Contagious Diseases Acts slowed the suffrage movement by ten years. 'We were all so absorbed in it,' she said.

Prior to the repeal of the Contagious Diseases Acts Thomas had published a fifteen-page birth control pamphlet called *The Marriage Problem* in 1868, in which he claimed that regulating family size would reduce the anxiety of providing for additional offspring and so promote a happy domestic life. This was a view that was carried into their own marriage, as they never had children themselves, with Anna later stating, 'we had decided before we were married that we were too poor – had less than £100 a year and [were] unsuitable to be parents.' Thomas stated in his pamphlet that a practical method was urgently needed, 'by means of which mankind can secure the satisfactions of married life without exposure to the miseries resulting from an excessive number of offspring'. He recommended the use of the 'safe period' as a method of birth control and implored married couples 'who couldn't afford to maintain a family… to observe the rule of strict abstinence during a period of about twelve or fourteen days out of every month'. Although similar literature on family planning had been published in England associated with the birth control movement, it is believed that Thomas's pamphlet was the first of its kind in Ireland and as the cover stated, was for 'gratuitous circulation amongst Adult Readers only'.

Following the publication of *The Marriage Problem*, Thomas wrote a longer paper in 1872, called *Duties of Parents*, in which he showed his preference for sexual abstinence as a form of family planning. Their own marriage was one of lifelong devotion and support for each other, which was clearly apparent both publicly and amongst friends and is thought to have been one of happy celibacy. Anna frequently wrote to Marie Stopes, the founder of the first birth control clinic in Britain, and enthusiastically read her books on parenthood and marriage. Birth control was the main concern in her letters, and she wrote openly about the subject within her own marriage, in one particular letter stating, 'we practised what we preached and I do not think there could have been a happier or more united couple'. Although they appear to have been celibate, both Anna and Thomas were quite open and frank in their letters and publications concerning sexual matters and contraception.

As well as her commitment to the Repeal of the Contagious Diseases Act, Anna was also involved in the married women's property rights campaign. The law at the time gave husbands full legal rights and free access to their wives' assets and denied women the rights to control their property, regardless of their social class. Anna was a member of the Dublin support committee and one of the organisers of the Dublin petition. The campaign proved successful when the Married Women's Property Acts of 1870 and 1882 changed the law and gave married women legal rights to own and control their property.

During the 1880s, the women's suffrage movement wanted to improve women's status in local government. The Poor Law system in Ireland was imperative in local government and had been under much criticism since the 1850s, where outdoor relief was preferable to the workhouse system and considered less dispiriting. Boards of Poor Law Guardians were elected by magistrates and ratepayers who governed the functions of the Poor Law Unions in their area. Under the existing Poor Law system introduced to Ireland in 1838, Irish women that were ratepayers could only vote for Poor Law Guardians, whereas in England and Wales women could both elect and become a Poor Law Guardian, although this only applied to the wealthy, due to the high property qualification. Anna wrote, 'that [it] was so commonly carried out upon exclusively party lines, and with so little regard to the well-being of our destitute poor, that we were fairly excusable for taking little interest in it'. Along with Isabella Tod, Anna campaigned for women in Ireland to have the same position as Poor Law Guardians as in England, drawing attention to the stringency of the Irish Poor Law and better treatment for women and children under the poor laws. Anna visited several workhouses in Britain, where she noted the standards to be higher than in Ireland and that the attendance of women as guardians proved to be beneficial. At election meetings she urged the people to vote for women as Poor Law Guardians and also encouraged them to stand for election themselves; however, she did not go forward herself.

After much lobbying and a succession of ineffective bills put to parliament, the DWSA approached William Johnston, the MP for Belfast, and asked him to introduce a Bill which was subsequently passed in 1896 as the Women Poor Law Guardian Act, in which Irish women were finally allowed to act as Poor Law Guardians. There were thirteen women elected in 1897, which increased to twenty-two the following year and by 1899 over eighty women had been elected, opening the doors for women in local government. In the *Englishwoman's Review*, October 1898, Anna wrote, 'backward as Ireland has heretofore been in so many respects, she has never lacked capable women equal to the efficient discharge of whatever public duties lay open to them' and regarding the passing of the 1896 Bill, 'thirteen ladies of the very highest character immediately responded to the call'. Sadly, 1896 also saw the death of Isabella Tod, and as Anna affirmed, 'a serious loss to the cause of women in the northern province'.

Following the success of the 1896 Act, Anna and the DWSA continued campaigning to increase the status of women in Irish local government and lobbied Irish MPs to endorse the proposed amendments to the Bill. Although some MPs thought that if women were in parliament it would be a disaster for the country, in 1898 the Local Government (Ireland) Act established county councils and extended the local government vote to all women over thirty who satisfied the resident qualification, and entitled them to be elected as local councillors, though it wasn't until 1911 that women were entitled to be elected to county councils. The 1896 Act had opened doors for women to partake in political activities and Anna took the opportunity to encourage women to stand for election and along with the DWSA, published pamphlets containing all the necessary guidance needed for qualified women to put themselves forward as candidates. The success of the Act was seen by Anna and the DWSA as a major progression towards the parliamentary vote and, as Anna had predicted, it also enhanced the suffrage movement. The DWSA grew and extended further outside Dublin and throughout Ireland and after several name changes it eventually became the Irishwomen's Suffrage and Local Government Association (IWSLGA) in 1901. Educated women were encouraged to join from any political or religious background and there was an increase in Catholic members. There had been only forty-three members of the DWSA in 1896, but by 1912 new suffrage societies had formed across the country and the numbers in the IWSLGA had increased to 700.

As Anna was a working woman herself, she became actively involved in improving the conditions of working-class women in employment and, along with other feminists, she supported the formation of trade unions for women, to be run by the workers themselves. Following the Trade Union Congress that was held in Dublin in 1880, she gave her support at a public meeting, accompanied by women from the English Weaver's Union, and for many years she continued to support the National Union of Women Workers of Great Britain and Ireland, which was in fact not a trade union, but an organisation of women workers concerned with the general social welfare of women. She was also fervent in her campaign for women to be paid sanitary inspectors and wrote to the chairman of the Public Health Committee in 1898, regarding this issue and by 1900 there were twenty female inspectors in Dublin, which included sanitary officers and school attendance officers. However, there was only one appointed inspector of boarded-out children, a matter which Anna continued to pursue into the twentieth century, along with the appointment of paid female officials in hospitals, reformatories, asylums and gaols.

More suffrage organisations had emerged both in Britain and in Ireland and the international development of the movement brought new methods in its campaigning. The turn of the twentieth century saw a more militant approach, with protestors marching in the streets, carrying banners of their adopted colours and slogans, which led to disrupting public meetings, and the heckling of MPs. Anna disapproved of militant methods and during the street marches in London the IWSLGA kept their conduct peaceful and legitimate. But in 1908, two members of the Association, Hanna Sheehy-Skeffington and Margaret Cousins, grew restless and wanted more positive action and in 1908 formed a new militant suffrage society, the Irish Women's Franchise League (IWFL). Although fundamentally both organisations shared the same purposes, unlike the IWSLGA, the IWFL was prepared to break the law if necessary and they were nationalists in their views as opposed to the IWSLGA being unionists. Although Anna was disappointed with their intentions, Margaret Cousins verified that they 'parted as friends, agreeing to differ on means, though united in aims and ideals'. Hanna Sheehy-Skeffington's admiration for Anna showed in her description of her as a 'Quaker rebel, one of the most consistent and ardent feminists I have known of the old school'.

Thomas continued to be at his wife's side when they frequently visited England, where they were highly respected. Together they regularly gave speeches at meetings and gatherings, where Thomas received the same recognition as Anna, and became known as a suffrage pioneer. A local suffrage society in North Hackney, London, defined him as, 'one of the earliest champions of the cause of Women's Suffrage ... whose chivalrous efforts have not ceased for 53 years'. Prior to a meeting at which the Haslams were to attend, the secretary of the society stated that 'it is an exceptional honour to receive pioneers with such a magnificent record of unselfish work behind them'. The local newspaper coverage of the same meeting was equally admiring, 'The meeting was exceptionally favoured in the presence and speeches of two of the pioneers of women's suffrage'. The couple, both well into their eighties, joined the demonstrations and suffrage marches in London, most notably in June 1911, in which, amongst the 40,000 women, the sixty Irish women were led by the Haslams.

The exclusion of women's suffrage in the Home Rule Bill of 1912 brought more frustration for the suffragists. They resorted to further and more drastic militant action and aggression by damaging government buildings, the first being the Custom House, the GPO and Dublin Castle, where they caused considerable damage by breaking the windows. The consequence was a prison sentence for those responsible. Anna was in London at the time but stressed her disapproval in a letter to the suffrage newspaper the *Irish Citizen*, proclaiming that the IWSLGA, 'has always consistently disapproved of what are called militant methods in the advancement of our cause'. The women from the militant groups became known as 'suffragettes' and by 1914 a further thirty-five women had been convicted of suffrage militancy in Ireland.

Anna resigned as secretary of the IWSLGA in 1913, after thirty-seven years of being at the helm of the movement in Ireland, and became life-president. The onset of the First World War in 1914 brought a lapse of activity in the suffrage movement, with suffrage societies in Britain concentrating more on supporting the war effort. The IWSLGA followed suit in Ireland, but the IWFL refused to assist in war relief work, and urged women to maintain the suffrage campaign, with the headline in the *Irish Citizen* declaring, 'Votes for Women Now – Damn Your War'. Despite her age, Anna remained active in women's issues and in 1915 she established the voluntary women's police patrols, which operated in conjunction with the police to prevent young girls from walking the streets. As part of her feminist campaign, Anna had wanted women police officers for a long time and it was reported in that same year by the Patrol Committee, of which Anna was joint president, that there were twenty patrols in Dublin. The following year two female patrollers were appointed as police officers, with the view to taking further recruits following training.

At the age of ninety, in 1916, Thomas Haslam published his last pamphlet, *Some Last Words on Women's Suffrage*, where he continued to implore the government for full adult suffrage for both men and women, regardless of whether they owned property or not and for women to be able to stand for parliament. Sadly, he died a year later of influenza and did not live to see Anna finally vote in the 1918 election. The Representation of the People Act of that year had allowed suffrage to women over thirty, providing they or their husbands were householders. At aged ninety, Anna voted on election day, where women from all organisations, not just suffrage, cheered her and presented her with a bouquet of flowers in suffrage colours. Although victorious, the IWSLGA persisted in their campaign for universal suffrage and in the same year changed its name to the Irish Women Citizens and Local Government Association (IWCLGA). They endeavoured to promote political education for women and election of women in parliament and continued to be foremost in feminist campaigns, surviving long after Ireland gained its independence in 1922.

Anna died in November 1922, the same year that the Irish Free State Constitution granted full adult suffrage to all women over the age of twenty-one. Her huge contribution and involvement in the women's movement was unprecedented, with her contemporaries perfectly defining her as 'one of the giants of the women's cause'. For many years the IWCLGA continued to be active in feminist issues and gender equality, particularly in the civil service and in 1947 they merged with the Irish Housewives Association which campaigned to improve the lives of women in the home and any relating women's issues such as consumerism, family planning and education. Its work continues today in Ireland in the form of the National Women's Council of Ireland.

ELLEN (NELLIE) CASHMAN

1845–1925

'I'm mighty apt to make a million or two before
I leave this romantic business of mining.'

Nellie Cashman

Described by one biographer as, 'Pretty as a Victorian cameo, and when necessary, tougher than two-penny nails', Nellie Cashman became known throughout the American and Canadian west for her immense courage and determination. An intrepid, pioneering prospector, entrepreneur and philanthropist, she was a true trailblazer in every sense of the word, caught up in the 'Gold Fever' of the late 1800s, and spent most of her life wandering the frontier mining camps of Arizona and Alaska, seeking her fortune and helping others.

As information regarding Nellie Cashman's early life is very limited, the exact date of her birth seems to be unknown, but her biographer, Don Chaput, states that she was baptised on 15 October 1845 in Midleton, County Cork. She had been born into desperate times at the start of the Great Famine, the severe and devastating consequences of which led to disease, starvation and mass emigration. As much as one-third of the Irish population was dependant on the potato crop, and when the potato blight caused the crop to fail in the autumn of 1845 more than a million people left the Irish shores in search of a better life in the

United States, Canada, Australia and England. Nellie's parents, Patrick Cashman (anglicised from O'Kissane) and Fanny Cronin, were poor farmers whose situation would have been dreadful. County Cork was one of the most severely affected areas and thousands flocked to the nearby port of Queenstown (now Cobh), to make the long and arduous journey to America, hoping to build a new life. By around 1850, at the height of the famine, Nellie's mother had become widowed and she left Ireland with Nellie and her younger sister, Fanny, and headed for Boston, Massachusetts.

During the famine years Boston received over 100,000 Irish immigrants. Many would have had no choice but to travel the cheapest way on board ships that were unseaworthy, enduring appalling conditions with little food, water and sanitation, for up to ten weeks. A large number of the passengers were already in a very poor state of health, suffering from malnutrition which left them more susceptible to fever and fatal illnesses. Typhus and dysentery rapidly spread throughout the overcrowded ships, claiming hundreds of lives during the voyages, consequently they soon became known as 'coffin ships'. Canada and America were overwhelmed by the thousands of Irish immigrants arriving at their ports, many of whom were barely alive. Temporary wooden hospital sheds and tents were set up, but they were inadequate and understaffed, so many people were left to die along the roadside.

Boston was swarming with impoverished Irish immigrants and in the summer of 1847 the *Boston Transcript* reported: 'Groups of poor wretches were to be seen in every part of the city, resting their weary and emaciated limbs at the corners of the streets and in the doorways of both private and public houses'. When Nellie arrived in 1850 there were 46,000 Irish immigrants living in Boston, around one-third of the city's total population. Very little is known of the family's time in Boston, except that as a teenager Nellie worked as a bellhop in a prominent Boston hotel. The decrease in available manpower following enlistment in the American Civil War in 1861 meant that women were employed in what were usually considered to be male occupations. Nellie's job brought her into contact with a variety of different people, and on one occasion, she met General Ulysses S. Grant, the future president, to whom she apparently mentioned that she 'wanted

Nellie Cashman. (Courtesy of Alaska State Library, ASL-P01-4024)

to do things'. Horace Greeley, editor of the *New York Tribune*, was urging young men to go west at the time, where there were more opportunities, and the general advised the restless Nellie to do the same. 'The West needs people like you,' he said.

Nellie had no intention of staying in Boston and 'being a bellhop or an Irish servant girl' and after saving for the fare of around $40 per ticket, in 1866 the Cashmans made their way to San Francisco, California on the newly constructed Panama railroad. California had become a magnet for Irish immigrants, with numbers rapidly increasing from the start of the gold rush in 1848. Many had used their wealth gained from the gold rush to buy land and businesses, and played a significant part in the early commercial growth of San Francisco. By 1859 the Irish population had grown to 30,000, and Irish names would soon become associated with prominent architecture, art, politics, finance and even streets bore the names of O'Farrell, Phelan, Hayes and O'Shaughnessy.

A few months after the Cashmans arrived in San Francisco Nellie's sister Fanny met and married Tom Cunningham, a fellow Irish immigrant and boot maker, and they soon started a family. By 1874 Tom had worked his way up to become superintendent in the United Workingmen's Cooperative Boot & Shoe Company of San Francisco, the leading manufacturer of hard-wearing boots worn by the miners in the west. Thousands of people flocked to California during the gold rush years and as a result San Francisco's population and economy grew substantially. A San Francisco newspaper reported, 'The whole country … resounds to the sordid cry of gold! Gold! Gold! While the field is left half planted, the house half built, and everything neglected but the manufacture of shovels and pick axes'. Prospectors had discovered gold, silver, copper and other minerals in Northern California and Sierra Nevada, resulting in the development of mining towns in some of the most remote areas. Unlike her sister, Nellie had no interest in marriage, she was far too adventurous, and she later told the *Arizona Star*, that she 'preferred being pals with men to being cook for one man'. At barely five feet tall and weighing less than 100 pounds, her small stature wasn't going to stand in the way of her great ambition. She wanted to follow the prospectors and seek her fortune, so in the summer of 1872 Nellie and her mother headed to the mining camp of Pioche, Nevada.

Pioche had become one of the most important silver-mining towns in Nevada in the 1870s, and also one of the roughest in the west. At the time, it had seventy-two saloons and thirty-two brothels. It was dirty and had a reputation for violence and gunfights, mostly instigated by bitter lawsuits over mining claims, and its murder rate was high. After working as a cook in several Nevada mining camps, Nellie used her savings to open the Miner's Boarding House at Panaca Flat, which she ran with her mother and, as a devout Catholic, she joined the Irish community in various fundraising events for Church causes. Due to the increased production of the mills and mines Panaca Flat had grown rapidly and businesses, including Nellie's boarding house, were booming. Her highly regarded culinary skills and 'Good Board at Low Rates' gained her the reputation for being the 'No. 1 board'. However, by 1873, due to rising unemployment as a result of the decreasing supply of quality ores, many people left Pioche to seek their fortune in the silver mines of the Panamint Mountains of California. Nellie and her mother decided to sell their boarding house and returned to San Francisco to her sister and her family.

The following year gold was discovered in the Cassiar Mountains in British Colombia, and Nellie, having caught the mining bug, was keen to join the gold stampede and set off with six other male prospectors to Canada. According to her friend, Fred Lockley, the group had been undecided whether to go to South Africa or British Colombia and the latter had been chosen by a flip of a coin. Nellie braved the long and arduous journey as well as the men, arriving in Dease Lake in the early summer of 1874, where she opened a boarding house combined with a saloon. She also purchased mining claims and provided the miners with money or supplies in return for a promised share of the profits, otherwise known as grubstaking. In a later account of her early prospecting days, she told the *Daily British Colonist*, 'At that time, we penetrated a practically unknown country. When the party settled down in what was then a very rich region, I alternately mined and kept a boarding house for the miners.' Due to the severe weather in the winter of 1874-75, many of the miners had been left stranded at the mining camp without supplies and an outbreak of scurvy had seriously aggravated their situation. Without hesitation, Nellie and six other men gathered provisions, including vitamin C-enriched foods such as fruits and vegetables, to aid the miners' recovery, and set off into the treacherous weather.

Nellie and her party trailed over rocky terrain and through snow so deep that they could not use dogs and had to pull the heavily laden sleds themselves. Despite major challenges faced throughout the trek, Nellie remained completely undaunted by it all, persisting fearlessly in her mission to reach the miners. One particular night, after a heavy snowfall, she and her tent and bedding were carried a quarter of a mile down a hill by a snow slide and, by the time her companions found her the next morning, to their amazement, she had managed to dig herself out. A columnist with the *Daily British Colonist* stated that fifty inches of snow had fallen and the temperature was about forty-two degrees below zero. On meeting the 'famous Miss Cashman' the astonished reporter commented, 'The woman was on snowshoes and was as jolly as a sand-buoy. At the Boundary Post she lost the trail and was twenty-eight hours exposed to the pitiless pelting of a storm, without shelter or blankets'. At one point, a search party of soldiers was sent out to look for Nellie after a white woman's death had been reported by an Indian to the Commander at Fort Wrangel. They found her happily sitting next to a campfire, casually drinking a cup of tea. Eventually, after several months, Nellie's group arrived at the remote miners' camp to find some of the men 'half-dead for want of proper supplies'. She diligently fed and cared for the miners, and through her selfless endeavours the men's lives were saved. For many years after prospectors would speak of Nellie with respect and admiration and thereafter she would be known as 'The Angel of the Cassiar'.

For the next few years Nellie stayed at Dease Lake and continued to successfully mine and run her boarding house. Her finances grew and she was able to send her mother $500 in gold. She raised much-needed funds for churches, schools, hospitals and religious groups in the west, including the Salvation Army, and collected money from various mining camps, with which she donated $543 to the construction of the new St Joseph's hospital in Victoria. But by 1876 gold production was dwindling and Nellie, who was by now an astute businesswoman, saw that the time was right, as she had done in Pioche, to sell her boarding house, and returned again to San Francisco to her mother and sister. After a while Nellie grew restless and by the following year she was on the move again, this time towards Tucson, Arizona. Although a small, sleepy Mexican pueblo, the construction of the Southern Pacific Railroad in the late 1870s would make Tucson more accessible and, as predicted by the *Daily Arizona Star* in May 1879, would also bring 'wealth and prosperity'.

Shortly after arriving in Tucson, in the summer of 1879, Nellie opened Delmonico Restaurant, which she advertised in the newly established newspaper, the *Daily Arizona Citizen*, as serving 'the best meals in town'. She was greatly admired by the owner of the newspaper, John P. Clum, who many years later in his tribute to Nellie published in 1931, stated that at the time very few white women lived in Tucson and 'Nellie was the first of her sex to embark solo in a business enterprise'. He also added that 'Her frank manner, her self-reliant spirit and her emphatic and fascinating Celtic brogue impressed me very much, and indicated that she was a woman of strong character and marked individuality, who was well qualified to undertake and achieve along lines that would be regarded as difficult and daring by a majority of the weaker sex'. Nellie was known to be a fairly strict employer, particularly regarding hygiene and cleanliness, but as she was also kind and compassionate. She developed a good working relationship with her employees, who held her in high esteem. She not only became known for her good food, where a small fee bought the many miners and prospectors who had flocked to Tucson, 'a chuck that would stick to a man's ribs' but also for her kindness towards anyone who was down on their luck, often providing their meals and lodgings for free.

Despite Nellie's generosity her business was a success, but news was spreading of the discovery of silver by a prospector called Ed Schieffelin, in a place he had named Tombstone, about seventy miles south-east of Tucson. Nellie was keen to join the thousands of businessmen and prospectors flocking towards the newly booming mining camp, so in 1880 she sold her restaurant and joined the stampede heading for Tombstone. Her departure was reported in the *Arizona Star* on 3 June 1880; 'While Miss Nellie Cashman's many friends will regret her leaving the city, Tombstone will have cause to rejoice, as she makes a business stir wherever she goes'. Nellie wasted no time in starting another enterprise in Tombstone and opened 'The Nevada Boot and Shoe Store', which she ran briefly with business partner, Kate O'Hara. She sold boots from her brother-in-law, Thomas Cunningham's Boot & Shoe Co., and used her previous mining experience in Pioche to promote her business to the many miners in the area. However, Nellie and Kate soon parted and Nellie went on to open several more businesses, including the Nevada Cash Store, which sold groceries, boots and shoes, the Arcade Restaurant, and the Russ House Restaurant, which she later renamed The American Hotel, which also gained the reputation of having 'the best food this side of the Pecos'.

In addition to running her enterprises and investing in mining claims, Nellie was active in raising funds for various charities from any source available. She organised Tombstone's first amateur theatre production, a musical comedy called *The Irish Diamond* and she was responsible for raising enough money to build the town's first hospital and Roman Catholic church, where she collected donations from every street in Tombstone, including the red-light district. Contributions were readily given for the miners or anyone in need of support and no one was refused help, regardless of their creed and sect. Whether they were prisoners or prostitutes, she treated everyone with equal compassion. The population of Tombstone was growing rapidly, and so were the numbers of illnesses and accidents amongst the miners and, as a result, many had fallen on hard times. Nellie's generosity was boundless in helping the miners in any way she could and through her constant selfless actions she became extremely popular and respected in the town. On one occasion

Doc Holliday, the famous gunfighter, drew his gun on a customer at Russ House who had complained about Nellie's food. When Doc asked him to repeat what he had said, the customer quickly replied, 'Food's delicious. Good as I've ever tasted.'

John Clum had also relocated from Tucson to Tombstone and in 1880 had launched another newspaper called the *Tombstone Epitaph*, which was primarily a mining journal. He later recalled:

> Nellie was prompt and persistent and effective with plans for relief. It might be a simple contribution, or an entertainment of some sort, but whatever it might be, Nellie's plan met with immediate and substantial support. If she asked for a contribution – we contributed. If she had tickets to sell – we bought tickets. If she needed actors for a play – we volunteered to act. And, although Nellie's pleas were frequent, none ever refused her.

One particular incident is noted in which Nellie wasted no time in collecting $500 to help towards expenses and care for a miner who had fallen down a shaft and broken both of his legs.

On 20 February 1881 Thomas Cunningham died of tuberculosis at the age of thirty-nine and Nellie's sister Fanny, who was also weak and in poor health, was left to bring up their five children on her own. Nellie immediately moved her sister and her children to live with her at Russ House, where Fanny helped Nellie as much as she could. The gold and silver rush had increased Tombstone's population to around 15,000, and like other frontier towns it had numerous saloons, gambling halls and brothels, attracting thieves, murderers and outlaws. In this lawless community, conflicts were frequently settled by a shootout, the most famous being the gunfight at the O.K. Corral, which took place on 26 October 1881, between the McLaury brothers and Ike Clanton against the Earp brothers and Doc Holliday. Nellie was unfazed by the dangers and continued to live in Tombstone. Even after narrowly dodging an Apache raid, she later declared, 'I was never afraid of anything. There was no need to be. I am still here to tell the story, and I have too much to do to be afraid.'

Following the news of a gold strike in the summer of 1883, Nellie organised a group of twenty-one prospectors and headed towards Baja

California. But this was one trip that would prove to be not only unsuccessful, but also extremely dangerous. After travelling by train and ship for six days, the party had to cover the remainder of the journey on foot across the barren desert in the blistering heat. Their search for gold was futile and very soon they realised that their situation was becoming desperate, as their water supply was rapidly running low, and after a few days the group was weakening due to heat exhaustion and dehydration. According to John Clum Nellie appeared to be the strongest of the group at that time and after assuring them that all would be well, she set off in search of water. She returned a day later from an old Catholic mission she had discovered tucked away in a nearby valley, accompanied by several Mexicans leading pack mules carrying goatskin containers full of water. As there was no gold to be found, the group returned to Tombstone. But despite the trip being a failure, Nellie was praised for her resourcefulness and her organisation of the expedition, with the newspapers hailing her as 'an energetic and plucky woman'. The news that the highly acclaimed Nellie Cashman had returned empty-handed discouraged other miners and so the Baja California gold rush came to an end.

Back in Tombstone, Nellie bought and sold numerous mining claims, including one named Nellie near Tombstone and another named Cashman by the Alpha Mine. Not forgetting her Irish roots, she also named one in the Chiricahua Mountains the Parnell Mine, in honour of Charles Stewart Parnell, the great Irish nationalist political leader. Others included the Big Blue claim in the Huachucha Mountains, the Last Chance in the Turquoise Mining District, the Littlefield and the New Year in the Cochise District, and part of the Big Comet near Tombstone. Nellie's mining and business enterprises would often be in partnership, but her name would appear at the front, as she would usually be the initiator of any such ventures.

On 8 December 1883 a robbery took place in the Goldwater and Castenada General store in the nearby town of Bisbee. During the raid five outlaws killed four people, including a pregnant woman. There was a public outcry at what has become known as the Bisbee Massacre and after the men were caught and tried they were sentenced to be hanged on 8 March 1884. Their execution was to be public, with tickets being sold by

Sheriff Ward for spectator's seats with an unhindered view. Nellie objected to the planned exposition, feeling that no death should be 'celebrated'. She frequently visited convicts in prison, as Frank Cullen Brophy in his article 'Frontier Angel' recalled, 'She knew the outlaws better than anyone in the community, and she knew how guilty they were. In the absence of a chaplain, she had actually baptised two of them while she helped the killers make their peace and prepare to meet their Maker'. On the night before the execution, Nellie and several other miners, equipped with crowbars, sledgehammers, picks and saws, demolished the grandstand prepared for the hanging, until it was no more than kindling wood. Triumphant Nellie said 'There'll be no Roman holiday in Tombstone for *this* hanging anyway.' The executions were carried out without an audience. Rumours followed of the convicts' bodies being exhumed and used for medical research, but Nellie had two prospectors keep a vigil over the bodies at Boot Hill cemetery for the next ten nights and they were left untouched.

By 1884 Fanny's health had deteriorated rapidly and in July of that year she died from tuberculosis, leaving Nellie as sole provider for her sister's five children, ranging from 4 to 12 years old. The mining boom in Tombstone was also starting to decline, mainly due to the decreasing market value of silver and the continual problem of rising underground waters that were flooding the mines, making them too costly to control. People were leaving Tombstone as quickly as they had arrived and, as her customers dwindled, Nellie decided to take her sister's children and travel across Arizona. Her first stop was at Kingston, New Mexico, where in 1887, she opened a boarding house called the Cashman House. She employed Edward J. Doheny to the wash dishes, who later, having had little success in mining, went on to become a prominent oil tycoon. In November 1888 prospectors Mike Sullivan, Henry Watton and Bob Stein struck gold in the Harqua Hala Mountains, which became known as the Bonanza mine. The following month Nellie set off with provisions to the new camp. By now Nellie was well known throughout the mining towns of Arizona as a 'mining expert', as the *Tombstone Epitaph* reported, 'her judgement is so good, that the oldest and most experienced mining experts are governed by it'. A column printed in a later edition of the *Western Liberal* on 22 February 1899 read:

Miss Cashman gave some good advice about where to dig for ore. Some of the best in the Contention was found by following her advice about running a drift. Mines that were bought by her advice after she had examined and reported favourably on them are now good paying properties … She is adventurous in pushing forward to a new region as any man miner with a fresh stake, and she no sooner hears of a new and promising camp then she starts for it.

According to the *Western Liberal* Nellie was the first woman to arrive at the Harqua Hala camp of 1,500 men, but that didn't deter her; she had and would spend her life in the company of men. John Clum later wrote in his tribute:

She was inclined to associate more generally with men than with members of her own sex, and on several occasions she joined in stampedes with men, tramping with them over rugged trails and sharing the vicissitudes and discomforts of their rude camps. Nevertheless, she maintained an unimpeachable reputation, and her character and conduct commanded the universal respect and admiration of every community in which she lived.

Nellie may have found love in the Harqua Hala mining camp, as on 23 February 1889, the *Phoenix Daily Herald* reported: 'Mike Sullivan, one of the owners of the Bonanza mine at the Harqua Hala camp, left there yesterday in company with Miss Nellie Cashman, on their way to the nearest station where a minister could be obtained, in order to be made man and wife'. However, a marriage doesn't appear to have materialised as, according to one biographer, Don Chaput, 'Sullivan sold off his interests in July and headed back East, probably never to return'. Although Nellie also left Harqua Hala a few months later, while she was there she wrote an informative article for the *Arizona Daily Star*, which demonstrated her knowledge of mining geology, providing details of the mines, their prospects and, in her opinion, the rudiments to a prosperous mining community.

Nellie spent the next few years wandering the various mining camps of Arizona, including Nogales, Jerome, Prescott, Globe and Yuma, prospecting and opening new businesses, mainly boarding houses and restaurants. Later she moved on to other mining camps in Wyoming, Montana and New Mexico, always accompanied by her sister's children. Her nephew, Mike Cunningham, later recalled their prospecting days, 'We were always on the move, looking for gold and silver'. Despite their constant roaming, all five children received Nellie's full support and a good education in various Catholic schools, sometimes as boarders. Mike Cunningham went on to become one of the most influential citizens of Cochise County as President of the Bank of Bisbee and the Bank of Lowell. He is said to have attributed his success to the 'care, counsel and encouragement' he had received from his 'Aunt Nell'.

In August 1896 gold was discovered by American prospector, George Carmack, and his Canadian brother-in-law, Skookum Jim Mason, in the Yukon River Basin, Canada. It is believed that they found a gold nugget the size of a dime in a small tributary of the Klondike River called Rabbit Creek, later renamed the world-famous Bonanza Creek. Due to the extreme weather and the remoteness of the area, it would be another year before the news would spread, which subsequently led to a stampede of thousands of would-be prospectors, not just from the United States but from all over the world. When the news of the gold rush reached Nellie she immediately started making plans to go to Klondike. News of Nellie's forthcoming trip was published in several newspapers. The *Tombstone Prospector* reported that the 'only woman mining expert in the United States' had remarked, 'Going to Alaska! Well I should say I am.' The *Mohave County Miner* wrote on 1 January 1898:

> Miss Nellie Cashman left last Wednesday for Klondike ... Miss Cashman is the best known woman in Arizona, having made two or three fortunes in mining speculations in the early days, and has watched the rise and fall of more mining camps than any other woman in the west. The land of the eternal glaciers has no terrors for her, and the good wishes of her many friends in Arizona go with her. Success to the honest, fearless little woman.

When she was asked by a reporter for the *Daily Colonist* what she might wear for such an expedition she replied, '... long heavy trousers and rubber boots. Of course, when associating with strangers, I wear a long rubber coat. Skirts are out of the question up north as many women will find out before they reach the gold fields.'

Nellie originally planned for her nephew, Tom Cunningham, and a male companion to accompany her on her trip, but after they failed to meet her in San Francisco she set off alone on the long, arduous journey to Alaska. Following what would have been an extremely challenging and difficult voyage heading north along the Pacific Coast from Victoria to the port of Skagway, Nellie and thousands of other prospectors took the most famous and difficult gold rush trek; the Chilkoot trail heading towards the Chilkoot Pass. This mountainous route had very few paths, with meandering, turbulent rivers which were often impossible to cross. The stampeders would have endured extremely harsh conditions on their ascent to the pass, climbing the steep and treacherous 1,500 steps of the 'golden stairs' which had been cut into the thick snow and ice. They would have trudged thirty miles through storms of sleet and rain, and many lost their lives in the frequent avalanches. At the summit of the pass the North West Mounted Police Station enforced the regulation stating that anyone entering or crossing the British Columbian border had to have enough food supplies to last them a year. As it was too steep for animals, miners had to haul their provisions in numerous trips over the pass by hand, which could have taken several weeks or even months. Due to the difficulties of the journey and the extreme temperatures, only around 30,000 of the estimated 100,000 prospectors that joined the gold rush completed the trip. However, Nellie, who by now was middle-aged, trudged on and eventually made it across the pass to Bennett Lake, where she and the other prospectors travelled the final part of the journey in hand-built boats, 500 miles down the perilous Yukon River through dangerous rapids and canyons to Dawson City, the heart of the Klondike gold rush. Nellie later told the *Daily Colonist*, 'We built boats and went down the Yukon to Dawson, going through the White Horse rapids, Five Finger rapids and all the others. Believe me, it's some journey, all right, to go through those rapids. I never want to travel any faster than I did there.'

By the time Nellie finally reached Dawson in April 1898 it was already a bustling boomtown which had rapidly expanded into a city of 40,000 people. Nellie settled in Dawson for the next seven years, where she

Chilkhoot Pass, 1898. (Courtesy of Alaska State Library, ASL.- P289-218)

ran several restaurants and stores and staked mining claims. One of her richest claims was made whilst she was in Dawson, which she had bought as a shareholder with five others. No. 19 Below Bonanza, made her over $100,000, which she invested in further claims. As she had always done previously, she contributed and raised funds for the Church and the much-needed expansion of Dawson's first hospital. She opened the Can-Can restaurant and another 'Delmonico' restaurant, which she later claimed made very little profit partly because 'if a young fellow was broke and hungry I would give him a meal for nothing.' Many miners who were lonely spent their evenings in the gambling halls and saloons just for the company, so Nellie adapted part of her store into a quieter social area for them to go for a chat and a free cup of coffee, as well as cigars and tobacco. This became popularly known as 'The Prospector's Haven of Retreat'. John Clum, who met up with Nellie again in Dawson City recalled, 'She was generous to a fault, always helping some worthy – but hard-up miners'. Her generosity would often leave her broke, but her kindness was never forgotten by her fellow prospectors. Alex McDonald or Jim McNamee, who had made their fortunes in the Klondike would, 'supply her with sufficient gold dust to put her back on easy street' which Nellie would invariably put back into a charitable cause, rendering her broke again.

In 1902 Felix Pedro, an Italian immigrant, discovered gold in Fairbanks, Alaska, which triggered a gold rush. By 1904 Dawson was in decline and Nellie headed to Fairbanks, where she opened a grocery store and toured the gold camps by dog sled, collecting funds from the miners for St Matthew's Hospital, apparently telling them, 'Okay, boys! This is for the hospital. If you've got money to throw away at poker, you can give it to them hard-workin' Christian women that's takin' care of the sick.' In 1907 Nellie embarked on her final stampede, travelling several hundred miles further north to the Koyukuk District. She settled in a remote camp called Coldfoot, sixty miles north of the Arctic Circle, and worked claims around Nolan Creek. Due to the remoteness of the region, transportation costs were high and to enable productive mining the ground needed to be thawed, so Nellie purchased expensive steam boilers and piping for herself and the other miners. She formed the Midnight Sun Mining Company and sold shares of stock to help cover the costs of the mining.

Nellie spent the remaining twenty years of her life in Alaska, staking claims and periodically travelling, mostly by sled, hundreds of miles to visit friends and relatives, particularly her nephew, Mike Cunningham in Bisbee. She ignored Mike's pleas for her to give up her wandering life-style and despite her advancing years, in 1922, at the age of seventy-seven, she set a record as champion woman musher of the world when she travelled 750 miles in seventeen days, from Nolan Creek to Anchorage by dog sled. In a letter to Mike confirming her safe arrival, she wrote, 'The sled only turned over once. I had a little roll in the snow'. Nellie had become a mining legend, with newspapers regularly reporting of her whereabouts. When the subject of marriage was approached in an interview with the *Arizona Star*, she told the reporter, 'Men are a nuisance anyhow, now aren't they? They're just boys grown up. I've nursed them, embalmed them, fed and scolded them, acted as mother confessor and fought my own with them and you have to treat them just like boys.'

In 1924, whilst on a trip to Fairbanks, Nellie became very ill with pneumonia. After spending six weeks in the hospital her wish was to go to 'her friends, the Sisters of St. Ann at St. Joseph's Hospital' in Victoria, British Colombia, the very one which her donations had helped build many years before. She arrived in October, barely able to walk. She refused a wheelchair, but declared she was 'all in' and was 'coming home to die'. The Sisters cared for her until she died of pneumonia on 4 January 1925. Famous throughout the west, newspapers as far away as New York published tributes to Nellie. *The Arizona State Miner* described her as 'one of Arizona's most picturesque pioneers'. John Clum wrote in his tribute that Nellie was 'a noble woman, whose energetic, courageous, self-sacrificing life was an inspiration on a wide frontier during half a century'. In 2006 Nellie was honoured by the Alaska Mining Hall of Fame and today this remarkable woman is remembered and celebrated in Tombstone on 'Nellie Cashman Day'. Meals are still served at Tombstone's oldest restaurant, the Nellie Cashman Restaurant.

ALEEN CUST

1868–1937

'We can understand women educating themselves
to tend women – but horses! Heavens!'

Ballinasloe Western News

Towards the end of her life Aleen Cust wrote, 'I have the inestimable privilege of attaining my life's ambition '. To fulfil her ambition, this remarkable woman's determination and love of animals surmounted the many challenges and strong opposition encountered by a woman in what was predominantly a male profession. She was 'a champion and role model', making it possible for future women to follow a career in veterinary medicine.

Aleen Isabel Cust was the fourth child of Sir Leopold Cust and his wife, Charlotte Bridgeman, the daughter of Vice-Admiral Charles Bridgeman. Leopold Cust was employed as a land agent by the very unpopular landowner, Arthur Smith-Barry, and the family lived at Cordangan Manor in County Tipperary, where Aleen was born on 7 February 1868. According to her biographer, Connie M. Ford, she was registered 'Aileen' at birth, but she always preferred to sign herself as 'Aleen'. She described her as 'a big girl with good strong features, red hair, and the strong will and temper that often goes with it. She was warm-hearted and plucky, with an impish sense of humour'. Her childhood

Aleen Cust. (Courtesy of the Royal College of Veterinary Surgeons)

was idyllic on the estate of the beautiful stately home, where she and her
three brothers would roam with the horses and dogs in the woods and
meadows within the spacious grounds. Another brother was born when
Aleen was two and a sister when she was nine.

In 1878, when Aleen was ten, her grandfather Sir Edward Cust died at
his home in London and her father, Leopold, inherited the baronetcy and
around £18,000. Soon afterwards, Sir Leopold who suffered from gout,
died suddenly, throwing the family into turmoil and effectively ending
Aleen's tranquil and untroubled childhood at Cordangan. Unfortunately,
Sir Leopold was unpopular amongst the people of Tipperary, as the
Tipperary Free Press reported:

> Immediately after his death became known, the Tipperary Brass Band
> turned out and paraded the streets, playing airs of rejoiceful character.
> The hills around blazed with bonfires, and there was quite a demonstration
> of an extraordinary character because of the event. It is understood that the
> deceased was very unpopular in the capacity of agent to A.H. Smith-Barry
> esq, which was the cause of this demonstration … Very severe comments
> were made on the deceased gentleman's character as a land agent.

Although Sir Leopold had left instructions in his will to be buried
near the place of his death and for the funeral to be a discreet affair
with little cost, Aleen's mother, wanting to escape the humiliation and
gossip, took the children to live with her mother in Shropshire, England.
Sir Leopold's body was shipped with them and he was buried in Leaton
churchyard. Sir Leopold had stipulated in his will that in addition to
his wife, his good friend Major Shallcross Fitzherbert Widdrington
of Newton Hall, Northumberland, be appointed guardian of his children. Aleen and her siblings became very close to the Widdringtons and
often stayed at Newton Hall, where Aleen was able to pursue her love of
horse riding and wander in the beautiful grounds. She became particularly close to the Widdrington's eldest child Dorothy and they formed a
loyal and steadfast friendship that lasted until Dorothy's death in 1906.
Aleen described her as 'the greatest friend of my life' and in her memory
donated money to the British Trust for Ornithology.

Unlike Aleen's own family, the Widdringtons were very open-minded and encouraged her aspirations to pursue a career, rather than lead the conventional life of a Victorian middle-class lady that was expected of her. Following a private education at home, Aleen started training as a nurse in the London Hospital, but as she felt more empathy towards animals she decided to leave nursing and pursue a career as a veterinary surgeon. Her family, especially her mother, disapproved of her daughter's radical career choice that was deemed unacceptable for a respectable woman of that time and it may not have been possible for her to pursue it had it not been for the unexpected tragic death of her elder brother, Orlando, from meningitis in 1893. Aleen's small share of his estate enabled her to live independently and in 1894, determined to become a veterinarian, but receiving little support from her own family, she travelled to Edinburgh, accompanied by Major Widdrington, to study at the university. However, not wanting to provoke further humiliation for her family, Aleen adopted the surname Custance, which Connie M. Ford believed may have been inspired by the renowned three-times Derby winning jockey, Henry Custance, who was very much admired by horse-loving Aleen.

Aleen spent the next five years self-supporting and prudently living as a student. Years later, in 1934, she recounted her penurious student days in a letter to *Veterinary Record*, proclaiming that she had been:

> … half starving on six shillings and sixpence a week, eating only one solid meal a day at a cost of five pence in company with the newspaper boys of Edinburgh, my only other meal being of raw oatmeal with hot water poured over it … I was living in an attic in winter with no fire, and when too cold to work anymore, I used to go out after dark into the quiet back streets and run to get warm enough to sleep.

After gaining the necessary qualifications, Aleen was accepted into the New Veterinary College Edinburgh, founded by William Williams in 1873. Veterinary college in the late nineteenth century had a reputation for being raucous and chaotic. The dissection room was often a place of complete bedlam, where students would engage in the rowdy activity of 'meat fights'. The more diligent students would try to study amidst the surreptitious battles, in which the missiles were the rejected meat or limbs of the dissected animal. Aleen was a very conscientious student and being out-numbered by the male students must have found this disruptive pastime very intimidating. Fellow student Major F.J. Taylor later remarked how she 'carried out her arduous studies under very great difficulties'. She was mocked by some of the male students who were of the opinion that she was deluded in thinking she could succeed in what was principally a male profession, and was shown little regard. However, despite her challenging circumstances, she excelled in her studies during her college years, coming first in her classes and winning several medals, including a Gold for Zoology.

Although Aleen had passed through the four-year curriculum with distinction at the Edinburgh Veterinary College, she was refused by the Council of the Royal Veterinary Surgeons the right to sit her first profes- sional examinations in May 1897, on the grounds that she was a woman. At a meeting on 14 April, a month before the examinations, it was con- cluded that they did not have sufficient authority to allow a woman to sit the examination, though they were divided in their opinion and a debate had ensued. Professor Williams of the New Edinburgh College affirmed that 'a good many members of the Council knew a year ago that Miss Custance was going up for the examination' to which Mr Mulvey, chairman of the Examination Committee interjected, 'I had no idea whatsoever that the name of "Custance" was a woman.' The *Veterinary Record* on 24 April published the minutes of the meeting and was conse- quently inundated with correspondence from fellow veterinary surgeons.

The views were mixed, with some in favour of a qualified female vet, but also strong opposition: 'The medical schools may open their doors, but let us pray to the gods for strength to keep ours closed', signed W.B. Junior, and an anonymous reader wrote, 'Certainly there are many callings from which women have been excluded that they can and should completely fill, but that of a veterinary surgeon is out of the question entirely and no true womanly nature would tolerate such an idea'. The Counsel stated that the admission of women should be authorised by a court of law and advised the Council to 'refuse to admit the lady [Aleen], and invite her to *mandamus* them'.

Aleen's intention was to avoid any publicity in London, especially as her mother was a Woman of the Bed-chamber to Queen Victoria, so she proposed that the proceedings be held in the Scottish Courts, but the College's solicitor, Mr George Thatcher, refused due to the lengthy process and cost involved. After much deliberation Aleen decided to drop the proceedings and continued to concentrate on her studies. Meanwhile, despite all her efforts to protect her family from any embarrassment, they were outraged at her actions and eventually any communication with them ceased altogether. In contrast, her friendship became stronger with the Widdringtons, who incessantly gave her the encouragement and support that was deficient in her own family.

After completing her studies in 1900, Aleen left college and Edinburgh altogether. Equipped with a reference of competence and recommendation from Professor Williams, she returned to Ireland to start her position as an assistant to William Augustine Byrne, MRCVS, at his practice in County Roscommon. William had qualified at the Royal Veterinary College, London, in 1899 and a year later had set up his own private practice at Castlestrange, a castle in Athleague, which he had inherited from his wealthy uncle. He was also a founder member of the Irish Central Veterinary Society formed in 1897 and had openly voiced his approval of women entering the veterinary profession in his paper entitled 'Veterinary Ethics' stating how he couldn't 'comprehend the mental attitude of those who insist that there is no work for a woman veterinary surgeon except castration and obstetrics'. Yet, despite the difficulties women faced he had no doubt that they would 'get there in the end'.

Aleen had been highly commended by Professor Williams and her lack of qualification and her gender held little concern for William. His appointment as president of the Irish Central Veterinary Council in 1899 had presented him with additional duties away from his practice, so he gave Aleen the extra responsibility of managing his business in his absence. William's unusual choice of employing a female assistant was initially met with trepidation within the community, particularly with the priest, who William led to believe that he had no knowledge of the sex of his new assistant prior to her arrival. However, Aleen proved to be very competent in her work and her kind and sympathetic nature gradually gained her popularity and respect, both from fellow veterinary surgeons and within the rural community.

William was highly respected professionally and extremely popular socially, due to his good looks, charm and wit. Both he and Aleen were attractive and unattached, sharing many interests, particularly their passion for horses, and their friendship soon sparked speculation of their relationship being more than professional. Rumours quickly circulated of the couple living together as man and wife, but Aleen's lodgings were several miles away, and as both were regarded highly in their profession, any gossip was largely overlooked. She did, however, share a brief engagement with Major Widdrington's son Bertram, who was a young army officer serving in India, but for unknown reasons the engagement was broken off and Aleen stayed single all her life. Her friendship with William Byrne remained steadfast and he played a huge part in Aleen's acceptance into the veterinary profession, discreetly introducing her as a 'visitor' at veterinary meetings and associations. In 1905, following his recommendation, Aleen was appointed part-time as the official veterinary inspector under the Diseases of Animals Act by Galway County Council.

In September of the same year, Aleen attended the 8th International Veterinary Congress in Budapest, where she was in the company of some of the most prominent veterinary surgeons, including Professor John McFadyean, who was the principle of the Royal Veterinary College, London. The Professor was at the top of his profession, being qualified in both human and veterinary medicine and had made pioneering discoveries in understanding and controlling animal diseases. He was also against women entering the veterinary profession. However, during her trip, Aleen met and formed a lifelong friendship with Professor Frederick Hobday, a renowned equine surgeon who developed a pioneering surgical procedure known as 'Hobdaying' used in the treatment of horses suffering from laryngeal hemiplegia or 'roaring'.

Immediately after the Congress, Aleen visited and took photographs at several horse-breeding studs and Royal Estates in Hungary, some of which were published in the *Veterinary Record* and *Veterinary Journal*. They were also used by Professor Hobday in his report on the Budapest Congress to the Central Veterinary Society of London. Aleen was gradually gaining acceptance and recognition for her veterinary expertise and in February 1906, the Irish Central Veterinary Association invited her to talk at their meeting, where she read a paper accompanied by her own lantern slides entitled 'A Trip to the Imperial Horse-Breeding Studs and Large Herds of Hungary and Serbia'. The general reaction to Aleen's talk was positive and she was praised for her 'instructive and graphic lecture'. A favourable report was also published in *The Irish Times*.

Meanwhile Aleen's position as veterinary inspector wasn't as well received by the Royal College of Veterinary Surgeons. They were not happy that she had been chosen over two other males in the profession who were registered veterinary surgeons. An article in the *Veterinary Record* read; 'The Galway County Council has appointed a person who is not a MRCVS, but a lady … We do not dispute Miss Cust's intelligence or acquirements for the post, but as she does not possess the licence to practice granted by the diploma of the RCVS, her appointment is obviously a trespass on their domain'. The Veterinary Surgeons Act passed in 1881, imposed certain procedures and registration requirements, preventing anyone from falsely taking the title of a veterinary surgeon, without having received instruction at a veterinary college and passed an examination of the Royal College of Veterinary Surgeons. However, this did not apply in Ireland, where it was left to the discretion of the Lord Lieutenant regarding the qualifications of veterinary inspectors. The article went on to urge the Department of Agriculture to refuse this 'improper' appointment, stating that 'It would be strange indeed if we were to be undone by the appointment of a lady who has no diploma, simply because she is a lady. No man, even in Galway, could have driven through our Act, but if once the breach is made men without diplomas will follow'.

The strong opposition from the RCVS and the Department of Agriculture led to the post being re-advertised, but the county council persisted in Aleen's favour and it was agreed that as she lacked the relevant qualification she would be appointed on a provisional arrangement as an 'inspector' not a 'veterinary inspector'. Aleen's position with Galway County Council had publicised the subject of admitting women into the profession and prominent veterinarians were starting to address the issue, both in Ireland and Britain, with pressure mounting against the RCVS. Many members of the Veterinary Medical Association of Ireland were in favour of Aleen, referring to her as 'a member of my profession' and of the opposition as 'old fogies'. Also, members from Veterinary Associations in Britain approved of the inclusion of women in the proposed new Veterinary Surgeons' Bill, and saw no reason why they couldn't follow the example of Europe, America and Australia, where women were allowed to train as veterinary surgeons. Aleen had come a long way since her last conflict with the RCVS. She had become highly respected in her profession, with skills equating to some of the most proficient in her field and was now earning a good living. In contrast, the RCVS was gradually losing its power and descending into bankruptcy.

In 1910 William Byrne died suddenly at the aged of 46. Aleen had lost a very dear and loyal friend who had been her protector and instructor and who had instigated her career. His funeral was the largest seen in the town for many years, with the cortège stretching for two miles. As he was still a bachelor his estate was left to his two brothers in America, and Aleen took over his practice. She bought a large house in Athleague known as Fort Lyster, where she had four domestic servants and kept goats, Jersey and Kerry cattle, cats and cocker spaniels. She would often make her visits riding sidesaddle on a white Arabian stallion, or driving a back-to-back gig when she needed to take equipment. The wealthy would be charged for her visits, but not the poor – instead they would often receive money from *her*. Often on her visits to horse owners there would be a succession of horses waiting to be castrated, a practice that some felt should not be performed by a woman. The *Ballinasloe Western News* described it as 'disgusting, if not absolutely indecent!' The local priest boycotted Aleen and tried to encourage others to do so, but he eventually relented when his own cow became ill and Aleen was called to treat it.

In 1914, with the outbreak of the First World War, there came a demand for horses initially from Britain and Ireland and, later in the war, from Europe and North America. Britain still depended heavily on horsepower to transport goods and people, and in many places the horse was more common on the roads than the motor car. The War Office estimated that at least 100,000 horses would be needed and as the British Army didn't keep large numbers during peacetime, purchasing officers and veterinary surgeons were hastily dispatched around Britain to buy horses for the British Army. A census had been previously set up, documenting the whereabouts of every horse in the country and within as little as two weeks 165,000 horses had been requisitioned from businesses and farms and shipped over to France. In addition to being used in cavalry battles, horses were used to pull heavy artillery and supplies through the deep mud and rough ground, a task they performed more efficiently than a mechanised vehicle. The army depended heavily on them and without them the Great War could not have been fought.

The conditions on the Western Front were extremely harsh and the animals suffered terribly. On a daily basis horses suffered from foot injuries, particularly from nails, mud fever, shrapnel and bullet wounds, mange, malnutrition and dehydration. A total of twenty horse hospitals were set up behind the lines, where the Veterinary Corps tended the sick and wounded animals. Aleen was keen to offer her veterinary skills in the Great War, but as she was still unqualified on paper, she could not work officially with the army. But she was determined one way or the other, and so in 1915 she left Ireland and drove her own car to Abbeville in France, where she volunteered for the Young Men's Christian Association (YMCA). The YMCA was founded in London in 1844 by George Williams, who was concerned about the welfare of the young men migrating from the rural areas to find work in the cities. He primarily started a prayer and bible study group, which grew to the development of education classes, public lectures, reading rooms and refreshment areas, providing a safe haven away from the dangers of the streets.

During the First World War, the YMCA was invaluable in supporting the moral welfare of the troops in France. Their huts or canteens provided soldiers with a place to rest, eat, drink, and use free writing paper and envelopes. Aleen was based at Remount Hut, near Abbeville, where she unofficially helped with the crucial work of the veterinary surgeons in the field veterinary hospital, tending to the huge numbers of ailing and injured horses. The role of the veterinary corps in maintaining the health and fitness of the horses was absolutely vital and, during the course of the war, 2.5 million animals were treated and over 80 per cent recovered and were returned to duty.

In 1917, Major General Sir John Moore, Director of Veterinary Services in France, proposed to the War Office that assistants were needed to help Captain E.A. Watson, a bacteriologist, in a larger laboratory, to carry out research and prepare vaccines. Surprisingly, he suggested that 'much of the routine work could be carried out as well, if not better, by women than by men'. He recommended Aleen to sign up for the Queen Mary's Army Auxiliary Corps, which she did in January 1918. She served as a bacteriologist, researching the diseases responsible for the deaths of many of the war horses, during which time she became a unit administrator, a rank given to women equivalent to that of a captain. Aleen left France in October, a month before Armistice Day and went to stay with her cousin, Kathleen Skipwith in London. The terrible conditions she had endured in France may have been detrimental to her health, as shortly afterwards she developed pneumonia and nearly died. Thereafter she suffered from a weak chest and in later years was advised by doctors to retreat to a warmer climate in the winter months.

Aleen returned to Athleague in Ireland, but found that it had undergone significant changes since she had left for France. Ireland was in the midst of a civil war, which had followed the Irish War of Independence and the establishment of the Irish Free State, and like many other Irish returning from the Western Front, her arrival was not welcomed. Connie M. Ford writes of her house being besieged by the Irish Liberation Army, 'and on at least one occasion she is said to have held them off with a shotgun'. Also during her absence there had been advancing progress in Britain for women pursuing professional careers. Universities were increasingly admitting women and allowing them to gain degrees in professions such as law and medicine, and the RCVS was starting to look dated in their reluctance to accept women as veterinary surgeons. The demand for veterinary surgeons during the First World War greatly outnumbered the number of those registered, and the RCVS's resistance was being questioned. An article published in *The Times* on 22 April 1915 stated: 'In view of the recognition of women in the medical services, and the rank of Major bestowed on Dr Garrett-Anderson for her work at the military hospital which she and Dr Flora Murray are opening in Endall Street, it is curious to find that the RCVS still refuse to admit women'. It wasn't until the passing of The Sex Disqualification (Removal) Act in 1919, which prohibited the exclusion of women from any occupation because of their gender, that the Royal College of Veterinary Surgeons had to lift their restrictions regarding women and so in October 1922, after having moved to London, Aleen applied to the RCVS examinations committee to sit the final examinations in December. Due to her service in the war she was granted a concession whereby she was only required to sit the oral examination. The *Veterinary Record* welcomed the decision 'as a matter of plain justice'.

On 21 December 1922, Aleen received her Diploma, along with seven other men, twenty-two years after completing her training. She was at last given the official recognition that she deserved, and the event was acknowledged by the president of the RCVS, Henry Sumner, as an 'epoch in the history of the RCVS'. Various newspapers and medical publications printed tributes to Britain's first qualified female veterinarian, and the Central Veterinary Society welcomed her membership. The *British Medical Journal* acknowledged that:

> The Veterinary profession has been rather a long time following the example of the medical profession in admitting women, but we have no doubt that there is a considerable opening for them, both in practice and in research. The importance of the scientific investigation of diseases of animals, and the light that the study of disease in animals can throw on pathology in general, are now far more fully appreciated than ever before.

Although a milestone for women had been reached there was still a certain reluctance to employ female veterinarians and it would be a number of years before women were able to gain employment as easily as men.

Although she was now a registered veterinary surgeon Aleen decided not to open a practice, as her health was declining. She sold her home in Ireland in 1924 and retired to the village of Plaitford in the New Forest, Hampshire. She retreated into a quieter, country life, where she bred pomeranians and cocker spaniels and kept a few horses. Though retired, Aleen still kept a hand in her profession, attending meetings of the Southern Counties Veterinary Association, and was always on hand to help with any animal emergencies, often assisting in the work of the Royal Society for the Prevention of Cruelty to Animals.

By the winter of 1936 her health had deteriorated further and she was rapidly losing the energy and vigour that she had held throughout most of her life. Following the advice of her doctor, she travelled to the warmer climate of Jamaica, a place she had visited previously whilst working for the RSPCA. She arrived in Jamaica in January 1937, intending to stay for four months in the home of Frank Cundall, a veterinary surgeon she had befriended on her last visit. Hours after her arrival, she suffered a heart attack from which she recovered, but later in the month, just a few days before her sixty-ninth birthday, she had just finished tending to a wound of the Cundalls family dog, when she collapsed and died. An obituary published in the *Veterinary Record* on 6 February 1937 stated that she 'will be specifically mourned by the women who, already numbering sixty, have taken the road thus courageously opened up for them'.

9

MARGARET MARY EDITH [MAY] TENNANT

1869-1946

'I doubt very much whether the office of
Factory Inspector is one suitable for women.'

Alexandra Redgrave, Chief Factory Inspector, 1879

May Tennant worked tirelessly for women's working rights and health throughout her adult life. She became a pioneering advocate for reforms in industrial working conditions for women, which consequently led to her being the first female factory inspector in Britain and Ireland.

Born on 5 April 1869, in Rathgar, Dublin, May Abraham was the daughter of Margaret Curtin and Dr G.W. Abraham, a prominent Irish lawyer. She was educated privately at home, largely by her father, and so, lacking in consistent education, gained no qualifications. However, the development of her temperament and character, helped by her father's home tuition, would form the basis of the social worker that she became later on in life, an attribute that could never be achieved with any certificate.

After the death of her beloved father in 1887, and with the family in financial ruin, May, aged eighteen, left Dublin and moved to London to seek a better life for herself, where she found accommodation in a boarding house in Bloomsbury. May had taken very little with her to London, but she did have a letter of introduction to an associate of her father's, Lady Emilia Dilke, who gave her employment as her secretary. May's lack of qualifications had been overlooked by Lady Dilke as she had perceived other qualities in May's mind and character that showed far more promise than any certificates. May would meet the high standards which Lady Dilke required from her secretary, and her association with her would prove to be imperative to her career progression.

Lady Dilke was a renowned feminist and trade unionist who cared passionately about the difficulties that working women faced. Although she was an art historian and an author, having had numerous essays and articles published in journals in Britain and France, she devoted much of her time to the women's labour movement and was president of the Women's Trade Union League (WTUL). Formed in 1889, the WTUL originated from the first Women's Protective and Provident League, which was founded by Mrs Emma Paterson in 1874. This trade union was established for women of all classes and aimed to support the rights of women in the workplace and improve the standard of their working conditions, eradicating the sweatshop or sweat factory environment. After Mrs Paterson's death in 1886, Lady Dilke became the leader of the organisation, and intended to improve relations between the women's and men's trade union movements, hoping to gain stronger support in their disputes for equality for women in the workforce. Initially the male trade unionists were doubtful and mistrustful of the WTUL, and were afraid of being under-cut by the women, but eventually they relented. Her other main concern was the health hazards that some women in industrial work faced. Exposure to phosphorous and white lead was a major health risk to the women, but an issue of which the public was generally unaware. Lady Dilke's worry was apparent when she wrote, 'It is impossible to sit idly by whilst the anguish of our working sisters and their little ones lifts its voice to heaven. They are crying to us for their redemption. The seal of death is on their lips'.

Lady Dilke's niece, Gertrude Tuckwell, was the administrator of the Women's Trade Union League and eight years older than May, but they formed a solid friendship and May moved out of the boarding house in Bloomsbury and into a house in Oakley Street in Chelsea with Gertrude. Gertrude's fondness for May was later expressed when she wrote that, 'Her enthusiasm and wit were endearing … she was a perfect friend'. The two women shared the same principles on social issues and reform and spent much of their time at the Dilke's London home at 76 Sloane Street, where May's mind was broadened by the non-conformist views and ideas of Lady Dilke and her husband, Sir Charles Dilke, the reformist politician and Liberal MP. Their home was a hub for eminent politicians and people from an arts and literature background, an environment in which May flourished.

May had arrived in London with no knowledge of the trade union movement, but very soon after being introduced to Lady Dilke she became involved in the WTUL and almost immediately found herself sharing Emilia's passion for her causes. She immersed herself in the labour movement and worked closely with Emilia in her campaign to organise female workers, which was thought to be the answer in alleviating the poor working conditions of industrial workers. The increasing rise of the employment of women in factories, and the criticism over the efficiency of male inspectors led the WTUL and other women's organizations to put pressure on the government to appoint female factory inspectors. They believed that the female inspectors, who should be working women with experience in their trade, would be more methodical, and the female workers would be more comfortable approaching another woman with their problems or grievances, so resulting in more collaboration within the workforce. This was to be a long battle, as the proposal was opposed by Alexander Redgrave, the Chief Inspector of Factories and Workshops, as he confirmed in his 1879 annual report, 'The general and multifarious duties of an inspector of factories would really be incompatible with the gentle and home-loving character of a woman'.

The poor pay the women received for working long hours and in dreadful conditions were publicised at every opportunity by the WTUL. May joined Lady Dilke on her public speaking trips, where her observations and quality as an attentive listener proved invaluable, as was her efficiency in dealing with any difficulties that arose, which in a short time led to her appointment as treasurer of the league. May became more prominently active during 1888-89, when the Dilke's were away in India. She became particularly concerned with the protection of female laundry workers, who were not included in the legislation of the Factory Acts. May was determined to change their situation, and organised demonstrations and meetings in Hyde Park, showing her natural ability as an organiser. She lobbied the House of Commons and attended numerous meetings with employers and attracted the attention of the newspapers, which disclosed her battle to improve the conditions of the workers to the public. May and Gertrude had moved to a larger flat in Tite Street, which was accessed by 104 steps. However, the long ascent didn't deter visitors, and the flat soon became a hub for notable socialists, leaders and supporters of the trade union movement, including Beatrice Webb, Margaret Llewellyn-Davis and Keir Hardie. Benjamin Tillett and Tom Mann, two of the leading figures in the London Dock Strike in August 1889, also visited the flat regularly. In Lady Dilke's absence, May continued touring the country and speaking to crowds of workers, vowing to improve the working conditions of industrial female workers. She proved to be a persuasive and credible speaker, expressing her passion and dedication to her cause.

The public exposure resulted in an extensive enquiry across Britain by the Royal Commission on Labour in 1891, appointed by Lord Salisbury's government, with the Duke of Devonshire as its chairman and Sir Geoffrey Drage as its secretary. Although hundreds of people, including factory inspectors and trade unionists, confirmed the conditions to the commission, it soon became evident that further investigations were needed to provide facts regarding the female workers. The Commission decided that the enquiries should be undertaken by four Women Assistant Commissioners, so at a meeting held on 7 March 1892, at 44 Parliament Street, Clara Colet, May Abraham and two fellow trade unionists, Margaret Irwin and Eliza Orme were appointed. Their task was to visit industrial workplaces, collecting information from the employers and the workers themselves regarding the women's wages and conditions, and the resulting consequences on their health and domestic life.

The investigation was carried out across Britain over the course of a year, in which time May threw herself fervently into her job. She was horrified by the conditions she found and meticulously noted every detail to use as evidence to support her cause. She predominantly covered the Midlands and northern counties of Lancashire and Yorkshire, where she visited numerous textile mills and factories. The unhealthy and inadequate sanitary conditions were recorded, as due to the low numbers of local sanitary inspectors appointed, the proficiency of their work was hampered. Harmful levels of dust, fumes and extreme heat, with inadequate ventilation, added to the unhealthy working environment and May was especially concerned for women with regards to the dangers of exposure to lead, which was widely used in factories. The risk of lead poisoning was extremely high and May was shocked and disgusted at the recorded numbers of illnesses and mortalities. She gathered medical evidence directly from the employees themselves, either visiting them in their own homes or in hospital. May also found that female workers unduly faced a penalty for talking and laughing at work and for arriving late. Various costs were deducted from their wages, including a charge for hot water and oil for the looms in textile mills. May didn't just restrict her reports to the large industrial mills and factories but also extended her enquiries to the home workers and small workshops of the confectionary, cycle, watch, and hosiery trades.

May followed the same procedure in Ireland, where she found the conditions just as appalling. She involved the Medical Officer of Belfast, who confirmed that a high number of fatalities in the city was largely due to the unhealthy working environment in the linen mills. The Assistant Commissioners left no stone unturned and produced an honest and accurate report, painstakingly disclosing every possible detail of the working conditions and wages of women in the industries. This first authorised inquiry, documented and carried out by female investigators into women's work, was published a year later in the *Blue Book*, which was a shocking revelation to many people, at a time when industry was largely the core of Britain's wealth.

Although it was clearly apparent that women continued to feel uneasy talking to a male inspector or official over such issues as inadequate sanitary conditions, and despite growing pressure from women's trade unions and various women's associations, the battle for female inspectors continued. In their argument against the appeals, the Home Office presented numerous hazards which female inspectors would encounter, one objection being that women's clothing was deemed unsuitable in the factories, for fear of getting caught in the machinery. This was specified in their memorandum in July 1891, which stated that 'unless Female Inspectors wore garments properly arranged, as those of the operatives are, they would run a great danger to which men Inspectors are not liable'. The inspection of the small workshops late at night, 'after 10p.m' in the city slums, also presented a problem for the lady inspectors, as the memorandum questioned, 'Could they – as inspectors are now doing – pass an hour or more after that time of night in the purlieus of Shoreditch and Whitechapel?' This did not deter the activists and the public became increasingly in favour of female inspectors.

In the summer of 1893 Herbert Henry Asquith was appointed Home Secretary in William Gladstone's Liberal government and, favouring the recommendations made by the assistant commissioners, agreed with their perception of female inspectors, stating, 'that there could not be free and frank communication between female operatives on the one side and the male inspector on the other. In addition to that there was the peculiar knowledge, the intuitive and instinctive knowledge which, without complaint and without inquiry a woman necessarily had as to the wants of her own sex.' Despite continuing opposition within the civil service, H.H. Asquith appointed two women to the Inspectorate of the Factory Department of the Home Office. He was keen, as he said, 'to extend the area of female employment' and he had noted the benefits gained through the women who had worked on the board of guardians and school boards. He later recollected, 'It was considered by state officials at the time to be a terrible proposition, they shook their heads and they did not sleep at night.' Through her work as assistant commissioner May's reputation had received a boost and her enthralling and engaging nature had gained her a great deal of popularity with the public. She had shown that a woman was more than capable of fulfilling the role of this new and dangerous position, and with her determination and the invaluable experience and knowledge gained from Lady Dilke, May Abraham made the obvious choice to be appointed the first Woman Factory Inspector in England, along with Mary Paterson of Glasgow, for Scotland.

The two women started their new positions in May 1893, with Mary covering Scotland and May travelling the length and breadth of Britain and parts of Ireland, where in some remote areas she was the first inspector they had seen. Back in her native homeland May carried out her visits on horseback, despite the objections from some officials in Britain. It also became apparent during the first year of their inspections that many of the male inspectors, having a background in engineering, had appeared to be more interested in the mechanical workings of the machinery and had overlooked the dreadful working conditions in the factories. Alexander Redgrave had retired from his post as Chief Inspector of Factories, and his successor was R.E. Sprague Oram who had been appointed by H.H. Asquith in October 1892. Fortunately, in contrast to his predecessor, Sprague Oram had faith in the abilities of women, supporting and trusting them in their work. His loyalty and praise for the women was evident in his first report when he stated, 'that there is no field in which they could be more fruitfully employed than in looking after the health and industrial conditions under which their fellow women labour in factories and workshops, you appointed two ladies as inspectors whose labours have already been found to be most useful'. Despite opposition from the male inspectors, from the start Sprague Oram gave the women the same authority as their male colleagues, where they were 'to promote and enforce the uniform observance of the Factory and Workshop acts' which also allowed them to prosecute offenders who breached the Factory Acts and attend the prosecution hearing in the courtroom. In later years *The Times* described May as 'conspicuously successful at the conduct of prosecutions' where she showed 'a sense of fairness that won approval from the Bench and compliments from her professional opponents'.

During their first year as inspectors, the two women focused mainly on their initial concerns of illegal overtime and long hours of work, dangerous trades and poor sanitation. The average working day controlled by the Factory Acts was not to exceed twelve hours, especially in the textile industries; however, there were many other workers, particularly dressmakers, exceeding those hours, working up to fourteen a day. May often found during her inspections, women or young girls working forced overtime, hidden away in separate rooms, or sometimes they were in the display area covered in dustsheets. Inadequate sanitation was also a huge problem in the factories, with limited toilet facilities, often for the use of both sexes. Requests by any women for separate facilities were met with dismissal from their employer, who seemed to be uninterested in their necessities. Many workplaces were over-crowded, with poor ventilation and extreme unhealthy temperatures of both hot and cold. The employment of young children was a deep concern for May, many working long hours in conditions that were extremely dangerous and unhealthy, and being deprived of an education.

The inspectors encouraged the female workers to speak to them regarding any worries or grievances that they may have had in the workplace, but for many the fear of chastisement from their employers, often leading to dismissal, prevented them from offering any information on their employment. The solution to this problem came in communication from the women through the WTUL, where the inspectors investigated their complaints without the knowledge of their employer, a method which saw an increase in women coming forward with their complaints. Although May and Mary initially received a hostile reaction from many employers in their first year of inspections, there were also others that accepted their proposals for improvements and overall the ladies' work was concluded to be a success, not only by Sprague Oram, but by the public as well. This led to requests for the appointment of more female inspectors.

The home of Sir Charles and Lady Dilke had become the location for the meeting of the prospective female inspectors. Lady Dilke, helped by her husband's political status, and her leading position in the WTUL, had been influential in the recruitment of the pioneering lady inspectors, and she continued to have significant input in further employments. She had initially favoured appointing working women as factory inspectors, being aware of the likely willingness of the female workers to converse with them. But after meeting with them it became apparent that not only did they lack the diplomacy needed for this type of work, but also the office skills needed to write coherent reports. She was determined that female inspectors would maintain a level of competence equal to their male colleagues. So despite the campaigns for the recruitment of working women, approval went to the middle-class and educated, often to university level. The emphasis was placed on the occupation being middle class, when the woman was referred to as a 'Lady Factory Inspector'. Male applicants had been required to sit an exam when applying for the inspectorate, but May and Mary had been accepted through high recommendation. It was decided by the Home Office that further female recruits would be required to pass a Civil Service exam. Three more women were recruited, all after having gained the qualification and all of whom had social connections and experience with factory legislation and working conditions. Lucy Deane had trained as a nurse at Chelsea Hospital and was a sanitary inspector for the London Borough of Kensington and Chelsea, and also a member of the WTUL. Rose Squire had worked with Lucy as a sanitary inspector and the third lady was Adelaide Anderson, a graduate from Cambridge University and a clerk of the Royal Commission on Labour.

Although there were only the 'pioneering five' lady factory inspectors in the early years they covered an extensive amount of work, travelling across the whole of Great Britain. They visited countless factories, workshops and private homes, with each inspector travelling on average up to 10,000 miles each year. In 1895, May was appointed superintendent over the small group of inspectors and directed her team to cover all areas in the world of women's industrial work. A year later she published a book on factory legislation called *The Laws Relating to Factories and Workshops, Including Laundries and Docks*. Dangerous trades had been a major concern for May since starting her campaigning work alongside Lady Dilke. Lead poisoning was a huge threat to women, as was phossy jaw, a terrible affliction which affected women in the match-making industry through unguarded exposure to yellow phosphorous. During her investigations into the dangers of white lead, May was appointed to the Departmental Committee on Dangerous Trades in 1895, which had been set up by the Home Office to investigate hazardous working conditions in dangerous trades. It was there that May met her future husband, Harold John (Jack) Tennant, the Scottish Liberal MP for Berwickshire, chairman of the committee and brother-in-law to H.H. Asquith. He came from an affluent background and was the son of Sir Charles Tennant, 1st Baronet. He and May shared a deep mutual concern for the dangers of white lead and phosphorous to industrial workers. May's biographer and friend Violet Markham described her as 'beautiful and gracious, with dark hair, dark grey-blue eyes and an enchanting smile' which, along with her enchanting disposition attracted the attention of Harold, and in 1896 they married. Gertrude Tuckwell later recalled receiving the news of the wedding from May with mixed feelings, fearing the loss of such an important figure in public work, 'I was sorry and glad but not surprised. He adored her.'

May's marriage to Harold was effectively the end to her career as a Superintending Inspector of Factories. She had been determined to continue working, but was met with objections from her father-in-law, Sir Charles Tennant, who is said to have commented to his son, 'Have you married a lady or a factory inspector?' She also received little support from Matthew White Ridley, the Home Secretary, who wasn't as sympathetic to the female inspectors as his predecessor, H.H. Asquith, had been, but most importantly she had fallen pregnant, so she resigned the following year, before the birth of her first son, and devoted herself to family life. Adelaide Anderson expressed her regret at the loss, as she wrote in the Annual Report of the Factory Department:

> It is only by degrees that we can realize the extent of our loss, as we miss her knowledge and insight in the work for which we could not fail, while she was with us, to feel her rare gifts. It is for others in words to measure the extent of the loss in the public sense. I can but attempt here inadequately to record our official and personal recognition of what we had during the too short time in which she directed the work of this staff.

However, despite a growing family, and not giving up work completely, May still continued to campaign alongside her husband for the welfare of industrial workers, which she managed to combine with the commitments and responsibilities of her home life. Her continuing support and advice proved invaluable for her colleagues in the Factory Department, and she continued to attend meetings of the Dangerous Trades Committee up until 1899. In 1898 she became chairman of the Industrial Law Committee, which had been formed in 1897 to provide workers with information on their entitlement to legal protection and where to direct any complaints regarding violations of the law. The committee's indemnity fund provided compensation for workers who had been dismissed for giving evidence of breaches of the law to the inspectors, a procedure which the employer was completely permitted within the law to do. In 1909 Harold Tennant was appointed Parliamentary Secretary to the Board of Trade by H.H. Asquith, who had become Prime Minister in 1908 and was in the forefront of social welfare reforms. Winston Churchill had also been promoted from his seat in Manchester North West to a place in the Cabinet as president of the Board of Trade, in which he and Harold Tennant addressed the continuing problem of 'sweated labour', or long hours and low wages. Churchill argued that 'It is a national evil that any class of Her Majesty's subjects should receive less than a living wage in return for their utmost exertions.' The solution to this continuing problem came in the form of the Trade Boards Act, which was passed the same year, where a minimum hourly wage was set by Trade Boards in the lowest paid jobs. On the evening before the introduction of the Bill, Gertrude Tuckwell had dined at the Tennants' home with the Churchills and later recalled Winston Churchill speaking of the 'great revolutionary measure' he was going to introduce the next day. May had previously been involved in the first voluntary Trade Board, which had formed after its first meeting in her own home at Bruton Street, and had further played her part in the introduction of the Bill by pressurising her brother-in-law, H.H. Asquith, into passing the Bill through Parliament.

Also during 1909 May was appointed as member of the Royal Commission on Divorce and Matrimonial Causes, which looked into the present state of the administered English divorce and separation laws and recommended reforms, particularly for the poorer classes, as divorce was extremely expensive. The commission wanted equal grounds for divorce for both men and women, which would include drunkenness, desertion and cruelty. May was the only female member of the commission, but through her experience and high reputation gained as a factory inspector, she was seen to be an influential and beneficial advocate in women's social development. The outbreak of the First World War in 1914 saw May's involvement in women's welfare increase, as she worked as a welfare advisor in the War Office. The war had brought a serious increase in unemployment for women who had been employed in trades such as dressmaking, millinery, tailoring and pottery. The Central Committee on Women's Employment, which had been set up in 1914 by the Government to document the urgency of the problem and help the women find employment, opened workrooms for women across the country with the help of grants from Queen Mary's Work for Women's Fund. May became treasurer of the committee, a position which she held for the next twenty years.

In 1917, May became director of the Women's Section of the National Service Department. By now she'd had five children, but sadly tragedy struck when her eldest son, Henry, was killed in action in May of that year. May bravely continued her work as director, although her friend and deputy in the department, Violet Markham noted that 'she went about it as though half stunned' and those closest to her 'realized how mortal was the blow that she had received'. When the department closed she went on to act as chief advisor on women's welfare to the Ministry of Munitions.

After the war, in recognition of her services, the Government awarded May the Order of the Companions of Honour. Harold Tennant had lost his seat in the House of Commons in the 1918 general election and retired from political life. In 1910, the couple had bought Great Maytham Hall, a large country house in Rolvenden, Kent, which had been previously owned by the author Frances Hodgson Burnett, where the old walled garden had been the inspiration for her children's book, *The Secret Garden*. The beautiful grounds provided May with the peace and solace that she needed, and it was here she developed her hobby of gardening, becoming an expert and a member of the Royal Horticultural Society and director of the *Gardener's Chronicle*. Although her workload had decreased considerably, May still kept a hand in public affairs, becoming involved with the Nursing Association and the problems encountered in women's health, having particular concerns for maternal mortality. She became chairman of the Maternal Mortality Committee, which had been formed by the Government in 1928, to investigate the alarmingly high death rate of women during childbirth. After much publicity and recognition from Queen Mary, their campaign gained the support of many other women's organizations and with the introduction of effective medication to treat infections, there was a significant drop in maternal deaths during the following decade.

Harold Tennant had been in poor health and, after suffering a heart attack, sadly died in November 1935. The onset of the Second World War found May widowed and alone, as her remaining sons, John, Archie and Peter were away fighting for their country, and her only daughter, Alison, was in the Auxiliary Territorial Service, the women's branch of the British Army. During the first few months of the war May helped in the nurseries of The British Hospital for Mothers and Babies at Woolwich, a maternity hospital and training school for midwives, founded by midwife Alice Gregory in 1905. May had been involved with Alice's early efforts at lengthening and improving the training of midwives and was keen to offer her services at the hospital. Later, Maud Cashmore, successor to Alice after her death, expressed her warmth and gratitude to May when she wrote, 'My memory is of great thankfulness. Miss Gregory found in Mrs Tennant inspiration and encouragement through all the worst fighting time of her life. We of the staff at Woolwich fell under her charm and sympathy and shall never forget'.

May had moved into a smaller house called Cornhill, on the Maytham estate, and although her health was failing, she spent the duration of the war vigorously campaigning for the Royal Air Force Benevolent Fund, a service that was close to her heart, as her son Henry had served in the Flying Corps prior to his death. She worked tirelessly and raised a considerable amount of money for the fund by growing and selling plants and seedlings from her friends and her own grounds and from donations from churches of all denominations across the country. She continued her voluntary work right up until her death on 11 July 1946, after having been reunited with all her children after the war.

KATHLEEN LYNN
1874–1955

'Remember me in the nurseries of heaven.'

Obituary, Kathleen Lynn

Although she had a comfortable middle-class upbringing, Kathleen Lynn devoted most of her life to the health of the poor in Ireland. As well as having a political career, she was not only one of the first Irish women to qualify as a doctor, but one of the most prominent Irish female physicians of the twentieth century. A pioneering paediatrician, her love and passion for children and their welfare improved and saved numerous lives.

Kathleen Florence Lynn was born on 28 January 1874 into a middle-class Anglo-Irish Protestant family, in Mullafarry near Killala, County Mayo, and was the second of four children. Religion and medicine were prominent in her family background and both remained a constant guide and impetus throughout her life. Her maternal grandfather was Revd Richard Wynne of Drumcliffe in Sligo and her father, Revd Robert Lynn, was the son of a Sligo doctor who had graduated with a degree in divinity from Trinity College Dublin. Her mother, Katherine Wynne, was descended from aristocracy which included Mary Queen of Scots, and the Earl of Hazelwood, and also prestigious landowners of Sligo and Leitrim.

Mayo suffered considerable poverty in the 1870s, and was still struggling from the aftermath of the famine and the economic and social effects of the Land War. Like most Victorian clergymen's wives, Kathleen's mother was involved in charity work, and Kathleen would frequently accompany her whilst visiting the needy. She would have witnessed the poverty, disease and malnutrition suffered by the local people, seriously aggravated by the lack of medical services. Later, in 1882, when the family moved to Shrule, County Longford, Kathleen became greatly influenced by her cousin, Dr Smart, whose work

Kathleen Lynn. (Reproduced by kind permission of the Royal College of Physicians of Ireland. Ref: SU/9/4)

and assistance to the local people, she said, was, 'the fount of help and hope and so I decided to become a doctor.' The activities of the Ladies Land League in Mayo at the time, which gave women the opportunity to become politically active, were also an inspiration to Kathleen's later political views.

In 1886 Kathleen's father was appointed to a rectory through Lord Ardilaun of the Guinness family, who, with Lady Ardilaun, owned Ashford Castle in County Mayo. The grand and majestic castle, set in beautiful grounds on the shores of Lough Corrib, was the perfect setting for elite social gatherings and events for the affluent classes, including royalty. Kathleen and her family were invited to these high-class functions, and she would later recall the visit of the Prince of Wales to Cong. In stark contrast to Mullafarry, Cong may have been a haven for the rich, but there was discord amongst the tenant farmers and landlords and the political activity of the Ladies Land League would not have gone unnoticed with Kathleen. Although the family resided in Cong, Kathleen, after being tutored by a governess for several years, continued her education in Manchester, England and Dusseldorf, Germany and then eventually in 1891, in Alexandra College Dublin, the forerunner of university-type education for women.

Founded by Anne Jellicoe in 1866, Alexandra College initiated higher education for women, preparing the girls for degrees with the Royal University of Ireland and encouraging them to succeed academically in fields that were predominantly male at the time, such as law, journalism and medicine. Girls were inspired to be freethinking and liberal and female unity and philanthropy were fundamental to the college's ethos, with lectures on employment conditions for women, as well as poverty, housing and local government reform. Women's suffrage was also an important topic on the timetable, as Anna Haslam, founder of the Irish Women's Suffrage and Local Government Association or IWSLGA, frequently visited the college, which resulted in a number of pupils and staff becoming members.

As Trinity College Dublin did not accept women until 1904, Kathleen followed her ambition to become a doctor by attending lectures at both the Royal College of Surgeons in Ireland, which had permitted women in its classes since 1885, and the Catholic University School of Medicine, in preparation for her medical degree. Kathleen excelled as a medical student. In her first year of medical exams in 1896 she won £3 and a medal for coming first in practical anatomy, with Alexandra College showing their admiration in their magazine, describing it as, 'a distinction not hitherto achieved by a woman', and two years later she won the Barker Anatomical Prize from the Royal College of Surgeons. Students were required to reside at several different hospitals to complete their medical training and although Kathleen had been the first woman to be elected as a resident doctor at Adelaide Hospital, she was refused due to the lack of female accommodation and the objections from the other male doctors. Undeterred, she completed her training, gaining invaluable experience at Holles Street Hospital, the Rotunda Maternity Hospital, the Richmond Lunatic Asylum and the Royal Victoria Eye and Ear Hospital, where she was the first female resident. In 1899 she was awarded degrees in medicine, surgery and obstetrics from the Royal University of Ireland or RUI.

Once qualified, Kathleen had the difficult task of finding employment in her chosen field. Although a number of Irish women had qualified through the RUI and Ireland had gained prominence in medical training for women, there was still discrimination against female doctors.

She went on to finish her postgraduate degree in the United States and in 1909 became the third woman to become a fellow of the Royal College of Surgeons and eventually worked as a consultant and ophthalmologist at the Royal Victoria Eye and Ear Hospital from 1910 to 1916. She then went on to administer a general practice from her rented home at 9 Belgrave Road, Rathmines, in the middle-class area of south Dublin, also a hub for activism. Her neighbouring families included the Plunketts, who were involved in nationalist movements, the Haslams, the pioneering suffragists, the feminist, Margaret (Gretta) Cousins and later, in 1918, the militant suffragette, Hanna Sheehy Skeffington, came to live next door to her.

Already a member of the Irish Women's Suffrage and Local Government Association (IWSLGA) since 1903, Kathleen also joined the British Women's Social and Political Union in 1908, founded by the Pankhursts and in 1912, at a mass meeting in Dublin, she joined in the campaign to include votes for women in the Home Rule Bill. Many of the suffragettes were middle-class, educated women and, like Kathleen, had experienced discrimination in their profession, inspiring their interest in women's suffrage. In 1913 she replaced Dr Elizabeth Tennant as medical examiner to the suffragettes in prison and on hunger strikes.

It was through her involvement in the suffrage movement and the influence of Countess Constance Markievicz, a distant relative and president of Cumann na mBan, a support group for the Irish Volunteers, that Kathleen became interested in nationalism. Constance introduced her to Helena Maloney, who claimed to have converted Kathleen to republicanism and who was also a member of Cumann na mBan and Inghinidhe na hÉireann or 'daughters of Ireland', a radical nationalist women's organization founded by Maud Gonne in 1900. The Inghinidhe developed from the Patriotic Children's Treat Committee and ran classes in the Irish language, Irish literature, history, music and art, particularly amongst the young. They supported and promoted Irish-manufactured goods and sponsored entertainment for children and adults, performing tableaux vivants on Irish mythology and also protesting at recruitment to the British Army.

Kathleen also became good friends with James Connolly, who was the leader of the Irish Citizen Army (ICA). Connolly set up the Irish

Transport and General Workers' Union (ITGWU) to protect workers and picketers from the violence of the Dublin Metropolitan Police during the labour dispute of the 1913 Dublin Lock-out. Both Kathleen and Constance supported the relief efforts for the strikers and their families during the Lock-out and helped in the soup kitchens in Liberty Hall, where they saw first-hand the terrible plight of the unemployed, starving and diseased. This charitable work would determine Kathleen's and many other female activists' commitment to nationalism.

The ICA was the first Irish Army to allow female recruits and give them equality in its ranks. James Connolly wrote, 'Win the women to your cause and your cause is secure'. Kathleen admired James Connolly and his support for women's suffrage and agreed to teach first aid in the ICA, then she progressed to captain and chief medical officer, although she avoided taking part in the drilling, having little interest in militarism. It was in the ICA that she met Madeleine ffrench-Mullen, who wrote a children's column in the *Bean na hÉireann*, a newspaper of Inghinidhe na hÉireann, edited by Helena Maloney. The newspaper favoured women's suffrage and supported the introduction of school meals, a campaign in which Madeleine was active. The two women were opposite in appearance, Kathleen with her long plaited hair and feminine clothes and Madeleine, once mistaken for a man, with her short cropped hair. Although they came from different religious backgrounds, with Madeleine a devout Catholic, they shared many interests, most significantly their interest in children, women's suffrage and nationalism. She was to become Kathleen's intimate and lifelong confidante and companion, until Madeleine's death in 1944.

In preparation for the 1916 Rising, Kathleen, along with other members of the ICA, transported and collected weapons in her car and stored ammunition at her home in Belgrave Road. She was at this time still employed by the Royal Victoria Eye and Ear Hospital, where wounded British soldiers were being admitted. Kathleen had been assigned to deliver medical supplies to several stations and was appointed captain of the garrison at Dublin City Hall, situated next to Dublin Castle, the centre of British rule in Ireland. On Easter Monday, 24 April, the commandant, Sean Connolly, an actor and trade unionist, shot and killed a policeman, James O'Brien, who had blocked his way when he and his group had tried to enter Dublin Castle. Sean moved up to the dome of City Hall, attempting to raise the tricolour flag to the top, but was shot from the Castle clock tower by a British sniper. Kathleen bravely crawled along the rooftop under fire to help him, but he was already dead, leaving Kathleen in charge of the outpost. That same evening she told Sean Connolly's 15-year-old brother Matt to get some sleep and took over his post as sniper on the roof of City Hall, intending to avert another death in the same family. After surviving a horrendous night of gunfire and explosions, the next morning Kathleen and her comrades were over-powered by the British and she surrendered.

Kathleen's calm and assertive manner provided solace and reassurance to the other members of the ICA, especially during the traumatic events of Easter Monday in 1916, as it was later remembered; 'While on the roof of the City Hall with bullets smacking all round her, she straight-ened and covered the body of Sean Connolly'. James Connolly had great admiration for her, saying that of all the women in the ICA, she was the 'most amazing'. Following their capture, the women were detained for almost a week at Ship Street Barracks next to Dublin Castle, where, locked in a 'filthy store', they endured appalling conditions with flea- and lice-ridden blankets, very little food, poor sanitation and the dreadful stench of refuse bins. On 1 May Kathleen, along with many other repub-licans, was transferred to Kilmainham Gaol and imprisoned in the old west wing dating from the 1790s, where the conditions were just as dire as her previous confinement. The wing was damp and decaying, with no heat or light, and the executions of fellow republicans could be heard by the condemned. However, Kathleen's incarceration at Kilmainham was rendered bearable by sharing the cell with her close friends, Madeleine ffrench-Mullen and Helena Maloney.

After being moved and spending a week in Mountjoy Gaol, Madeleine was released. Kathleen was deported to England, where there was huge demand for doctors during the Great War. Jennie Wyse Power, founder of Inghinidhe na hÉireann and Kathleen's colleague in IWSLGA, managed to arrange for her to work as a locum with Dr Cusack, origi-nally from Galway, at Coleford House in Abingdon. In July that year, due to her sister Muriel's illness, Kathleen was allowed to return to Cong and, following a brief visit back to Bath, through representation from Lawrence Ginnell MP, she was released and allowed to return to Dublin in the autumn of 1916. However, after her involvement in the 1916 Rising, she was refused by the Royal Victoria Ear and Eye Hospital to return to her previous position and was unable to find employment with any other hospital, so she returned to her practice at her home in Rathmines.

At the 1917 Sinn Féin convention Kathleen was one of four women to be elected to the Sinn Féin executive of twenty-four people and was appointed Director of Public Health. She supported equality for men and women in the organization, which she stressed at the convention should be emphasised in all speeches and pamphlets. With her direct and no-nonsense approach, she appealed to her male counterparts and her comments were met with applause. Kathleen and her fellow feminists continued to promote suffrage within the organization and when Countess Plunkett proposed that women should be delegated to tackle health and welfare issues, topics which concerned Kathleen deeply, women were able to show their competence in these areas and prove their worth.

Kathleen spent several months 'on the run' in 1918 because of her membership and involvement with Sinn Féin. She was arrested in October under the Defence of the Realm regulations during an outbreak of the influenza epidemic, but avoided deportation and imprisonment after the Lord Mayor of Dublin persuaded the authorities that her medical expertise was needed amongst the sick and the poor during the pandemic. For her release she also signed an undertaking which stated that she would, 'take no part in politics, and not leave the area of Dublin Metropolitan Police'. After which she was continually watched and her home was frequently searched. The flu epidemic brought Kathleen into direct contact with the poor, as did her work in her own practice and the 1913 Lock-out, and she had witnessed first-hand the dreadful circumstances in which many children were born in Dublin. As there were no antibiotics or immunizations, the flu claimed millions of lives worldwide, with infant mortality rates in Ireland being amongst the highest, at 165 deaths per 1,000 children.

Dublin's hospitals were extremely overcrowded due to the flu epidemic
and the Irish soldiers returning home from the Great War. Many of them
were infected with syphilis and as a result many diseased babies were born.
Kathleen, along with Dr Richard Hayes, a Sinn Féin MP for east Limerick,
campaigned for every soldier to be detained until tested and cleared for
venereal disease and, with fellow activists, formed a VD committee, promoting awareness of sexually transmitted diseases, particularly among
female Irish doctors and nurses. This contributed to an increased outpatient
attendance at Lock Hospital, leading to a decline in numbers the following
year. Kathleen was also deeply concerned by the seriously high mortality rate in infants, especially those under one year old and in urban areas,
where the death rate was twice as high. Poor housing in the Dublin slums,
where families lived in one room, accelerated the spread of diseases.

Madeleine shared Kathleen's concern and in May 1919 in an old
rundown building at 37 Charlemont Street in Dublin, they opened
St Ultan's Hospital for Infants, the first in Ireland, with just two cots
and £70. It was named after the Bishop of Meath who, in the seventh
century, had cared for children during the yellow plague. At the time,
care for infants was not given precedence by the medical profession and
St Ultan's was the first Irish hospital dedicated to infant care for those
under one year of age. The hospital was also completely staffed by women,
making it the only one of its kind in Ireland and so providing professional medical opportunities for women denied elsewhere in favour of
their male contemporaries. The hospital's main aim was to provide much-
needed medical and educational facilities for infants and their mothers
and to reduce the alarmingly high mortality rate among Dublin's infants,
as the annual report of 1928 noted:

> The objects of St Ultan's were to provide treatment in an institution for
> babies under one year old, suffering from non-infectious diseases includ-
> ing summer diarrhoea, to train nurses for infants, and give opportunities
> for research into the disorders and the nutrition of infants.

Much needed funds for the hospital came from different sources such as
organised outings, fetes and musical concerts, and a book compiled by

Katherine MacCormack in 1920 entitled *Leabhar Ultáin, The Book of Saint Ultan*. A collection of pictures and poems by Irish artists and writers, it included contributions from artists Jack B. Yeats and George Russell and raised considerable funds for the hospital. Kathleen also used her republican connections to generate funds. Lady Carson, wife of Edward Carson, the unionist leader, donated two goats which provided tuberculosis-free milk for the infants, and the White Cross, created to support republican families, donated £2,000, which provided an outpatient clinic where mothers were given advice on hygiene, the importance of fresh air, and breastfeeding. A strong believer in breastfeeding and the connection between this and a reduction in infant mortality, Kathleen would stress in her talks, 'breast milk is the baby's birthright.' She provided the Abt's electric breast pump in her clinic to help mothers to produce milk.

Kathleen's upper-class connections, particularly Lady Ardilaun, visited the hospital and evidently provided funds, along with politicians and their wives and other patrons. She regularly visited hospitals in Britain and America, where she gained valuable knowledge from other physicians and paediatricians. She also received regular funding from America, where she had an office on Fifth Avenue, New York, for St Ultan's, to manage the funds. Farmers and grocers donated fresh food and many women gave second-hand baby clothes. Mindful of the connection between poverty, poor housing and illness, St Ultan's Hospital Utility Society built homes near the hospital to accommodate families from the slums.

Throughout the War of Independence Kathleen remained politically active, though not as prominent. Her main concerns were for housing, public health, education, working conditions and holiday schemes for workers. She was elected to Dáil Éireann for Dublin county as a Sinn Féin candidate, but like many anti-treaty republicans, she declined her seat and in the 1927 election was unsuccessful. However, she did remain active in local government and continued as a councillor with Rathmines Urban District Council, where she had been elected onto the Public Health Committee in 1920 and later, in 1923, the Child Welfare Committee. She was a huge influence in ensuring that doctors included 'infant consultations' in their health visits and in 1926 proposed the provision of school meals in the child welfare centre. Gradually her involvement in politics lessened as her work with children and St Ultan's became the main priority in her life.

Kathleen devoted almost all her time to the hospital and, being quite a radical for that time in her method of childcare, she believed that not just medicine, but love, consoling and soothing a child, was extremely important in aiding their recovery. Her love for children was evident as she would often be seen in the hospital holding a child in her arms. She was also interested in education for children and greatly admired Dr Maria Montessori, the Italian physician known for her method of child-centred education. At St Ultan's Kathleen opened the first hospital Montessori ward in the world, which Dr Montessori came to see in 1934. The hospital continued to grow and through the Hospital's Commission receiving funds from the new national lottery, it received a financial boost, which in 1930 enabled them to increase their number of cots to thirty-five and build an out-patients department, a laboratory and an x-ray department. Extensive research was carried out at St Ultan's, especially regarding the spreading of infection through microbes on babies' comforters. This was very important in fighting the infectious disease gastroenteritis, which was the biggest killer in the hospital.

Tuberculosis was a huge problem in Ireland at the time, and had been the cause of many deaths in the early part of the twentieth century. Although the numbers had declined by the 1930s, Ireland's mortality rate was extremely high compared to the rest of Europe and America. The increasing threat of the disease and its connection to poor housing and poverty was regularly reported by Kathleen and Madeleine. Many prominent Irish female doctors of the time worked at the hospital, including Dr Dorothy Stopford-Price, who had carried out research and clinical trials there, and pioneered the arrival of the BCG vaccine into Ireland at St Ultan's in 1937, making it the first hospital in Britain and Ireland to use it, leading to a mortality drop from 77% to 28%. However, as both Britain and Ireland doubted its efficiency, even though it had been used in Europe since the 1920s, it was to be ten years before the vaccine was used widely across Ireland, and eventually in 1949 the National BCG Committee's headquarters was opened at St Ultan's.

The immediate post-war years saw an influx of German refugees entering Ireland. Kathleen's colleague at St Ultan's, Dr Kathleen Murphy, had introduced a plan to support the welfare of the German children known as 'Operation Shamrock' within the Save the German Children Society. Kathleen became vice-president of the society in 1948 and as it became apparent that preference was given to Catholics rather than those of other religions, she went on to help establish the German-Irish Society in 1951. Later, in 1956, four months after Kathleen's death, a sculpture commissioned by the German government showing their appreciation for Ireland's help was unveiled by Dr Kathleen Murphy, remembering Kathleen's support to the society.

Kathleen remained active in her work at St Ultan's right up until six months before she died at the age of 81, on 14 September 1955, at St Mary's Nursing Home, Ballsbridge, Dublin. She was buried at the family plot in Deansgrange cemetery with full military honours and nurses in uniform lined the streets outside St Ultan's as the coffin passed. An avid believer all her life that plenty of fresh air for good health, Kathleen's summer cottage at Glenmalure, County Wicklow was donated to the youth organisation An Óige after her death, a group she had been actively involved in, and was opened as a youth hostel in her memory. At the time of her death, St Ultan's had progressed to having ninety cots and 15,000 outpatients. Sadly, due to insufficient funds, the hospital closed in 1984 and became Charlemont Clinic, a private medical clinic.

LILIAN BLAND

1878–1971

'It is quite a new sensation being charged by an aeroplane.'

Lilian Bland

Lilian Bland's career as an aviator may have been short, but she made a distinctive mark in aviation history. She was largely overshadowed by other aviation pioneers of her time, particularly Amelia Earhart, her American counterpart, who was only just twelve years old when Lilian made history as a pioneering aviatrix.

Although Lilian Emily Bland was born in Kent in England, she came from a long line of Irish descendants, dating back as far as 1670. Her family background was fairly privileged and middle class. Her grandfather, the Revd Robert Wintringham Bland, was the Dean of Belfast and also a Justice of the Peace. His eldest son, John Humphrey Bland, born in 1828, received a BA at Trinity College Dublin, and travelled to Paris to study art at the École des Beaux-Arts, then went on to exhibit his work at the Royal Academy in London. He married Emily Charlotte Madden of Burgh Apton in Norfolk in 1867 and they had three children. Lilian was the youngest and was born on 28 September 1878 at Willington House near Maidstone, in Kent. John moved his family back to his native Carnmoney in County Antrim, Ireland in 1900, when Lilian's mother, Emily, became ill. They lived at Tobarcooran House, with her father's widowed sister, Sarah Smythe, but, due to her

Lilian Bland, 1907. (Courtesy of Guy Warner)

illness, Lilian's mother moved to the warmer climate of the Mediterranean with Lilian's sister, Eva, and later died in 1906.

In Carnmoney Lilian became interested in photography. She would often wander over Carnmoney Hill, her favourite place, where she would watch and photograph the birds soaring overhead and dream of joining them up in the sky. She wasn't the conventional granddaughter of a Dean of Belfast, and as a young woman certainly wasn't bland. Much to the dismay of her aunt, she dressed in breeches, smoked cigarettes, tampered with motor car engines, rode astride horses, and was one of the first women in Ireland to apply for a jockey's licence. She also engaged in hunting, fishing and shooting activities, at which she showed great skill; activities which were not appropriate for a young lady in the Edwardian period, especially in County Antrim.

Lilian established herself as a renowned sports journalist and photographer for London newspapers, winning prizes for her photographs. While staying with friends on the west coast of Scotland, in the summer of 1908, she would spend all day watching and photographing the seagulls manoeuvring in the skies above her, increasing her longing to be up there with them and hence sowing the early seeds for her interest in flying. She exhibited a collection of her coloured photographs from Scotland at the Royal Photographic Society in London that year, which are believed to be the first colour plates taken of live birds. On 25 July 1909 the Frenchman, Louis Blériot, became the first aviator to fly across the English Channel and Lilian received a postcard from her Uncle Robert from France of Louis Blériot's monoplane with its dimensions written on the card, which further fuelled her aspirations of aviation.

Interest in aviation was beginning to grow in Britain in the early part of the twentieth century, with competitions and prizes offered by the *Daily Mail* for new advances in flying. Aviation meetings and air displays were also taking place. The first one held in Britain was instigated by Lord Northcliffe after he attended the world's first public air display at Rheims in France, in August 1909. Later that year, in October, the first official aviation meeting was held in Blackpool, attended by 200,000 spectators. Lilian was amongst the crowds, taking careful note of the construction of the aircrafts on display and recording details of the measurements and dimensions in her notebooks. In a letter to her father she wrote, 'The few English machines are, I imagine, no good – much too small and fitted with motor-bike engines … most of them are covered with tyre fabric, lashed on like lace boots sewn or tacked … the wheels are on castors with small springs'. On observing the aviators in flight she noted that, 'in flying they keep their heads to the wind and turn a corner by drifting round tail-first'.

The success of the American aviators, the Wright brothers, a few years earlier, impelled Lilian further in pursuing her dream of building and flying an aeroplane. She had read all the information she could in books and magazines, especially *Flight* magazine, which was first issued in January 1909, and was determined to build and fly her own plane. She set to work at Tobarcooran, in her late uncle, General Smythe's, well-equipped workshop, situated at the back of the house. First she built a model biplane glider with a wingspan of six feet, which she flew successfully as a kite. Encouraged, she drew the plans and in the winter of 1909 she started work on her full-size glider, intending to add an engine if it worked. Lilian regularly wrote letters and articles to *Flight* magazine, giving updates on the progress of the construction of her biplane and in the December 17 issue, following 'considerable interest' and at the 'request of the editor', the full process was published.

In January's *Flight* she recorded using materials such as bamboo, spruce, elm and ash. Ash was used for the main spars and, remembering the seagulls she had spent hours observing in Scotland, Lilian steamed the ash to bend it into shape to emulate the slight curvature at the tip of their wings. Spruce was used for the ribs and stanchions and, to make it waterproof, she soaked unbleached calico in a mixture of gelatine and formalin. The skids were also made of ash and the outriggers were bamboo. The engine bed, made from American elm, was fastened by wires attached to the upper and lower wings, to keep it secure and in position, the wires also adding strength to the wings. The fuel tank was housed in the chassis with the pilot's seat which was made from canvas and was enclosed and secured by four straps, to prevent the pilot from falling out. The elevator control bar was in front of the seat. The entire chassis was held in place by four bolts, but could be detached in one piece, with or without the engine.

The controls were a bicycle handle bar, which when turned to the right lifted the right-hand elevator and lowered the left. The elevators were connected to the horizontal tail planes, which worked in the opposite direction to the elevators. She specified that 'all controls are double, wire and strong waterproofed whipcord'. The back seat controlled the balancing planes, which were hinged to the rear stanchions. Leaning to the right pulled down the right-hand balancer and to the left the left-hand balancer. The engine controls consisted of a butterfly valve which regulated the fuel supply, the air throttle, and a lever to the magneto, which cut out when one cylinder was started. The vertical rudder was worked by pedals. Although, as Lilian stated, the 'controls may sound complicated', she realised that 'in practice they are quite simple to work'.

The biplane was made in sections in the workshop and then moved to the larger coach house also at Tobarcooran, to be assembled. The finished glider had a wingspan of twenty feet and seven inches and weighed two hundred pounds. Due to some doubt about its flying capability, Lilian, with deliberate irony, named it the *Mayfly*. The glider was taken to the slopes of Carnmoney Hill, where Lilian had the help of three men on its trial flight. As the wind swiftly took the glider up, two of the men let the tethered rope slide through their hands. Luckily, Lilian and the third man grabbed hold of the rope, limiting the damage to the biplane. In a letter published in *Flight* magazine in February 1910, Lilian wrote, 'I enclose two photos of my biplane, the "*Mayfly*". I made her entirely myself, with the exception of the metal clips, and, of course the sockets, strainers, etc., were bought from English firms. I think she is the first biplane made in Ireland'. She continued to give an account of its first trial flight at Carnmoney Hill:

I had her out again today, wind of 18m.p.h. My only difficulty is at present to prevent her flying when I do not want her to … we got the machine soaring beautifully for some time until a down-ward gust caught the elevators, which I had fastened, when she dived down and broke both skids, but did no other damage.

Adjustments were made to the steering arrangement, so that the elevators could be controlled from the ground, and with the glider flying with vertical ropes 'she rises straight off the ground when faced to the wind. If we bring her gliding down in a steady wind, she lands as soft as a feather.' The skids were reinforced as 'they both broke where the wood was cross-grained, but I have the greatest difficulty here to get good wood. The skids are American elm, which is very springy, and I must say they were severely tried.' To determine if the aircraft could carry an engine, Lilian enlisted the help of four six-foot tall, burly members of the Royal Irish Constabulary, along with Joe Blain, her aunt's gardener. All five hung on to the *Mayfly* as it rose into the air. The four constables promptly let go, leaving Joe to hang on and bring the glider back down to the ground. Lillian concluded that if the *Mayfly* could carry the weight of five men it could quite easily manage an engine.

Lilian Bland and the *Mayfly* on Carnmoney Hill. (Courtesy of J.M. Bruce/G.S. Leslie Collection)

The pioneer aviator Alliot V. Roe, along with his brother Humphrey, founded the A.V. Roe Aircraft Company in Manchester in January 1910, which went on to be the very successful British aircraft manufacturer, Avro. At Lilian's request they agreed to make her a two-stroke air-cooled engine for the sum of £100. However, the order was delayed and in the summer of 1910, Lilian, unable to wait any longer, travelled by ferry to England. As she eagerly watched the initial test of the Avro engine, which produced twenty horse-power at 1,000rpm, the propeller spun off and shattered into pieces. Fortunately, no one was hurt and with a new adjustable-pitch propeller, measuring six feet six inches in diameter, and the engine supplied by Avro, Lilian took it back to Ireland on the boat train, much to the astonishment of the other passengers. In her letter to *Flight* magazine in July she wrote, 'I have at last got my engine. To hasten matters, I went over to England and brought it back not quite under my arm, but on two spars; it fitted very neatly into a railway carriage and also onto an outside car'.

Back in Ireland, Lilian wasted no time in testing the engine, which she did late one night and in the heavy rain. While she was waiting for the fuel tank to arrive, for the first test she devised her own alternative method by using a whiskey bottle and her aunt's ear trumpet to feed the engine with petrol. Lilian's letter to *Flight* continued:

> Under the circumstances the engine behaved better than I expected, it was like a cat-fight on a very enlarged scale. The natives, I hear, thought one of the mills had blown up, but as the noise continued they put it down to a thunderstorm; in the meantime I found the mechanic while deeply interested in the engine, was literally pouring the petrol over the main plane instead of down the ear-trumpet, and the engine subsided with a sigh.

Accompanying the letter were two photos of Lilian's plane and engine, one showing her standing next to it dressed in mechanics overalls, which she advised were, 'the best things to wear; skirts are out of the question with all the wires ... not to speak of oil.'

The new fuel tank arrived and was fitted, but the engine was slow to start and when it did the vibration loosened the bolts and snapped the wires between the struts. Further alterations were made to strengthen the biplane, so a T-bar control yoke was fitted, and a tricycle undercarriage. As the steamed ribs did not keep the correct shape, they were removed and replaced with ribs that were cut in a solid curve and bored out for lightness. The fabric was doubled and laced on, enabling it to be tightened when it had stretched and any alterations to be made without spoiling the fabric. Heavier wheels and tyres were also fitted, as Lilian stated in *Flight*:

> I have wasted much time in trying to run the machine on ball-bearing wheels and spindles, fitted with various springs, rubber bands etc, none of which were satisfactory. The spindles were always bending or breaking, and the wheels are now rebuilt onto 7in hubs, which run on the axle. The axle is clipped to the skids, and the only spring is that afforded by the Palmer tyres.

As the field at Carnmoney was considered too small, Lord O'Neill's 800 acre park at Randalstown was loaned to Lilian to use for the flight trials of the *Mayfly*. The front and rear booms were removed and small wheels were attached to the skids so that the *Mayfly* could be moved to Randalstown and be re-assembled. The park was perfect, but it had one disadvantage in that Lilian had to share it with a bull, as she wrote in *Flight* magazine, 'If it gets annoyed and charges I shall have every inducement to fly!' When the weather was appropriate for flying, she would cycle twelve miles with Joe Blain to Randalstown.

As the engine was housed behind the pilot, the *Mayfly* was started by Joe Blain standing between the tailbooms and swinging the propeller. In August 1910 Lilian made her first powered flight, although the flight wasn't particularly smooth, with the plane making faltering hops at short distance. The test flights had to be postponed for several weeks due to a very wet, stormy August, but after several more attempts in September, it did fly to an altitude of thirty feet and stayed in the air for a quarter of a mile. Despite Lilian remarking that the Avro engine was a 'beast to start and it got too hot', she was delighted and in disbelief kept checking the wheel tracks on the wet grass to confirm that she had taken off. 'I have flown!' she wrote in a letter to *Flight* magazine, 'The quaintest thing was that I did not know that I was off the ground! I was only a few feet up, and was intent on the engine and levers, and I could not believe it till I went back to trace the wheels'. Additional adjustments were made to the vertical tail and the skids, and protective canvas screens were placed on either side of the seat. Lillian discovered that black enamel paint prevented the wires rusting in the damp weather of Northern Ireland, and she also varnished the woodwork with copal for protection. Even though the biplane had been kept outside for four months, the fabric had endured the wet weather and remained water-resistant. She also stated in her letter that she always started the *Mayfly* on one cylinder and 'let her pick up slowly as it is less strain on the engine'. She went on to say that 'The "*Mayfly*" is evidently going to behave as she did as a glider, when she always rose at once and was difficult to keep on the ground, however, I think all credit is due to the engine, which pulls like a Trojan, or rather pushes' and regarding the achievement, she modestly added, 'I am naturally awfully pleased, having made and designed her myself. It is a very small, but promising start anyway.'

In the November 1969 issue of *Flying*, Lilian's *Mayfly* was described as apparently 'not a pretty sight' and one biographer is thought to have noted that, 'No great effort was expanded to rig it square or true, and it sagged and bulged in all directions'. However, in September 1910, Lilian not only flew Ireland's first powered biplane, but was also the first woman in the world to design, build and fly an aeroplane, which also gave her distinct approval and recognition in the expanding aviation circle.

Apart from the description of the biplane, Lilian's three-page article in the 17 December issue of *Flight* in 1910 also included scale drawings and photographs of the *Mayfly,* and gave good practical advice for other enthusiastic amateur aviators, though she proclaimed that she was 'not a good enough pilot yet to give much advice'. She suggested that they could learn a considerable amount from watching competent pilots, as she had been lucky in observing the flying of the 'masters of the art' in Farman, Louis Palhan and Latham. She advised the reader that plenty of spare time and money were essential, allowing for extra costs for any repairs, which Lilian had encountered with the *Mayfly*. Despite all her hard work and effort, Lilian had not lost her enthusiasm and passion for aviation, concluding that 'it is the finest sport in the world, and well worth all the hard work', though there was still 'room for improvement, both in the aeroplanes, engines and propellers'. Lilian had plans to improve the design of the *Mayfly* and in the same article she offered to take orders for gliders or full-size machines, on condition that she would use her own designs. She guaranteed that the machines would glide and fly and be of the best quality. However, she specified that the engine and propeller must be 'reasonably efficient, otherwise it is only a waste of time'. She started her business in the early months of 1911 and advertised her biplanes for £250 (without an engine) and her gliders for £80.

In March 1911 Lilian had built a scale model of the improved thirty foot span *Mayfly 2*, which she had intended to build and fly, but her enterprise was short-lived, as in the same year her father, who had been worried and anxious about her precarious exploits, enticed her to leave aviation by buying her a 20hp Model T Ford motor car instead. She taught herself to drive and became Ford's first agent in Northern Ireland, but after further disapproval from her family, particularly her aunt, regarding her 'unladylike' pursuits, she married her cousin, Lieutenant Charles Loftus Bland, in October 1911. According to an article in *Flight* magazine in December, Charles, who was living in Vancouver in Canada, read of 'her perseverance and pluck and came to the conclusion that they must surely be indicative of just those qualities so essential to the pioneer settler in a place like Vancouver'. Lilian was lauded for 'her plucky pioneer work with her gliders and her aeroplane in Ireland, and particularly the frank, instructive, and often amusing letters that so enlivened our correspondence pages'. *Flight* also stated that Lilian was 'disposing of her aeroplane' and was 'willing to pass on, for the cost of carriage and packing, to some club which is putting in practical work amongst its members'. In response to the many letters received by Lilian regarding the *Mayfly* she asked *Flight* to publish a reply, which they did in their issue of 6 January 1912, confirming that she had presented her biplane to the newly founded Dublin Flying Club.

Simultaneous to Lilian, although separately, a motor car mechanic named Harry Ferguson, from Dromore, near Hillsborough in County Down, also had strong aspirations in aviation. Harry was also fascinated and inspired by the Wright brothers and after visiting various aviation events in Britain and Europe, he built his own engine-powered monoplane. On 31 December 1909 he was the first man to successfully fly an aeroplane in Ireland and is also said to have carried the first aviation passenger in Ireland. Like Lilian, Harry's aviation career was short lived, which may have in part been due to a serious accident at Magilligan Strand in October 1910. Affectionately nicknamed the 'mad mechanic' due to his love of racing and the stunts that he attempted, he is better known for his innovations in developing farming machinery, later becoming world-famous for the Ferguson tractor. Although both had made a huge achievement, becoming aviation pioneers, in later years Lilian became less well known as Harry Ferguson gained prominence in Irish history. Hugh Conway, the managing director of Short Brothers & Harland Ltd, the pioneering aircraft production company, stated in a letter to Lilian in 1964:

> I can at last send you photocopies of the local paper dealing with Harry Ferguson's first flight and then yours. You will see that you were the first biplane, but that he was the first aeroplane. At any rate you must have been the first woman in the world to build and fly an aeroplane, which isn't so bad.

Lilian joined Charles in Canada in April 1912, and helped him run a 160-acre farm in British Columbia. They had one daughter, who after an accident contracted tetanus and sadly died at the age of sixteen. In 1935 Lilian travelled back to England and lived at Penshurst in Kent, with her brother, Captain Robert Bland, where she became a gardener. She spent the remainder of her life in Cornwall and as she told the *New York Times* in 1965, 'I gambled my wages on the stock market and was very lucky. I made enough to come here (Sennen in Cornwall) ten years ago. I now spend my time painting, gardening and gambling a little'. Lilian died at the age of 92 on 11 May 1971 and is buried in the churchyard in Sennen, near Land's End in Cornwall. Shortly before she died, the *Belfast Telegraph* quoted her as saying 'that the only excitement left to her was gambling'.

EILEEN GRAY

1878–1976

'The future projects light, the past only shadows.'

Eileen Gray

For most of her career Eileen Gray was overlooked, eclipsed by her male contemporaries, but today she is celebrated as one of the most influential designers and architects of the twentieth century, an inspiration to both the Modernist and the Art Deco movement. Her innovative furniture pieces are among the most valuable and sought-after in the world and her pioneering, iconic villa is considered a landmark in modern architectural history.

Kathleen Eileen Moray Smith was born into an aristocratic family and grew up in Brownswood, a grand manor house set high above the banks of the river Slaney, near Enniscorthy, County Wexford. Her mother, Eveleen Pounden, was the granddaughter of the 10th Earl of Moray, and she, at twenty-one, had run off to Italy with James Maclaren Smith, a keen amateur painter and nine years her senior. Much to the disapproval of her parents, they married in 1863 and soon after they started a family. Eileen, born on 9 August 1878, was the youngest of five children, with two brothers and two sisters. Her birth date would often be inaccurately stated as 1879, but that didn't appear to bother Eileen, as, according to her biographer, Peter Adam, when she was questioned in her later years about whether she was ninety-six or seven, she simply replied, 'Is there a difference?'

Eileen Grey. (By kind permission of
Enniscorthy Castle, Wexford)

Eileen's childhood was mostly spent divided between Brownswood House and the family's other home in South Kensington, London, where, apart from short periods in a private school abroad, she was mainly educated at home by governesses. Her father, James Maclaren, whom she adored, would often be absent on painting trips abroad in Europe, particularly Italy and Switzerland, so Eileen was brought up predominantly by her mother. However, she did accompany her father to Europe on occasions, where he encouraged her artistic abilities and instilled in her a sense of adventure. Despite having older brothers and sisters, Eileen's childhood at Brownswood was quite lonely and from an early age she developed a sense of being unloved. She was also an extremely frightened child and often fearing the creaking of the big old house at night, would get up from her bed and creep down the dark corridor to her mother's bedroom where she would quietly put two chairs in front of her mother's door and fall asleep there until dawn when the servants found her. Many years later she wrote, 'I have instinctive fears, fears of ghosts, of people. This fright never left me and I have often tried in vain to conquer it'.

Though both of Eileen's parents initially kept up the pretence of their marriage, her father seldom came home and he finally settled permanently abroad. Upon the death of her great-uncle in 1893 Eileen's mother inherited the title Baroness Gray and, being separated from her husband, subsequently changed her children's surname to Gray. As Eileen grew into a young woman she resented the pomposity of her class, not caring much for 'titles' and yearned to gain her independence away from Brownswood, where she felt stifled and restrained. In 1895 the house was restored beyond recognition and Eileen watched as her beautiful childhood home turned into an ostentatious mock Tudor-style brick building which she hated. She felt that the family house was no longer home. At twenty years of age she managed to persuade her mother to allow her to enrol at the highly prestigious Slade School of Fine Art in London. Founded in 1871 with funds bequeathed from lawyer and philanthropist Felix Slade, the school offered female students education on equal terms as men. It was renowned for the curriculum based on the French system of art education. Although initially Eileen entered Slade full of enthusiasm, she soon found both the atmosphere and academic training in the school uninspiring and too traditional, and gradually lost interest in drawing and painting. However, she did enjoy her freedom in London and thought the city fascinating. She spent much of her time exploring the little back streets and the museums, in particular the Victoria and Albert Museum, where she first discovered the art of Asian lacquer work. It was in Dean Street in Soho that Eileen came across a lacquer repair workshop run by Mr D. Charles who specialised in restoring antique furniture and screens. She later recalled, 'I remembered old lacquer screens, and had been fascinated by that matière. Charles was very nice and said I might come and work there, which I did. They used mostly coloured European varnishes to repair the old screens but also real lacquer from China.' Eileen would remain in contact with him throughout her career, receiving tips and advice and exchanging new methods of lacquer work.

In 1900 Eileen's father died in Switzerland and in the same year she made her first trip to Paris with her mother to see the World's Fair, or Exposition Universelle. This grand exhibition was held in Paris between 15 April and 12 November, to celebrate the achievements of the past century and to accelerate development into the next. It was visited by around fifty million people and was a mammoth showcase for progress, science and the arts, displaying many new inventions, including diesel engines, escalators, talking film, the telegraphone (the forerunner to modern-day sound recording), and Matryoska dolls (Russian nesting dolls). More significantly, the World's Fair publicised Art Nouveau, a new style in architecture and design, showing furniture, ceramics, jewellery, glass, textiles and metalwork. Eileen was excited and captivated by the futuristic exhibits on show, the daring architecture and the mechanical walkways, known as *platforme mobile electrique* which carried pedestrians throughout the city.

The cosmopolitan city of Paris was also the centre of the art world, where artists would congregate to learn of new developments in modern art. Eileen loved Paris and was drawn to the city's vibrant streets, occupied by chic and sophisticated shops and department stores, concert halls, theatres and variety palaces. In England she had admired the work of Charles Rennie Mackintosh, the Scottish architect and Art Nouveau designer, but in Paris the popular Art Nouveau designs were far more prominent. She would have seen work by France's foremost designers, such as buildings designed by the architect Hector Guimard, jewellery by René Lalique and glassware by Émile Gallé. Eileen made up her mind to move to Paris with the intention of studying there. She persuaded two of her friends, Jessie Gavin and Kathleen Bruce, to go with her and in 1902 the three friends arrived in Paris, where they found lodgings at 7 rue Barras, near Montparnasse, a popular area for resident artists. They enrolled at the Académie Colarossi and then the Académie Julian. In her memoirs, *Self-Portrait of an Artist*, published later in 1949, Kathleen Bruce wrote, 'Off and away to Paris! I had two friends who thought that to go to Paris and to be an artist was a fine idea'. She described Eileen as 'more lovable' than Jessie:

> … though rather remote. She was fair, with wide-set, pale blue eyes, tall and of grand proportion, well-born and quaintly and beautifully dressed. But for a rather vague look and absent-minded manner, she would have been wonderful. I thought she was wonderful and when, one night she told me that she lived her whole life in terror because there was madness in her family, I thought her not only wonderful to look at, but also the most romantic figure I had ever seen.

It is most likely that the 'madness' Eileen was referring to was her family's eccentricity.

The Académie Colarossi in the rue de la Grande-Chaumière in Montparnasse was a private, international art school that had been founded in the nineteenth century by the Italian sculptor, Filippo

Colarossi, as an alternative to the State academies, some of which in the opinion of many talented young artists had become too conservative. The school was one of the few that accepted female students and allowed them to draw from nude male models. Unlike Kathleen, who was uncomfortable at the sight of nudity and would look away, embarrassed, Eileen appeared totally indifferent. Kathleen later recalled passing one of the studios and seeing Eileen 'standing composedly with her head critically on one side, whilst at the end of the studio passed one by one, a string of nudes, male models'. The three women soon moved on to the Académie Julian, in the rue du Dragon, a very popular private art studio school founded by painter and art administrator Rodolphe Julian in 1868. Like its counterpart the Académie Colarossi, it was an international school, attracting students from all over the world, particularly Americans, as only fees, not qualifications, were required for entrance.

In the early twentieth century, the left bank of Paris was a popular place of residence for American and European expatriate artists and writers, and the centre for Bohemian lesbian culture. Eileen was bisexual and was acquainted with the avante-garde intellects of that period such as Gertrude Stein, Djuna Barnes, Natalie Barney and Romaine Brooks, but while she enjoyed an active social life she preferred to remain slightly aloof, maintaining that 'Freedom, as I imagine it, can only be bought with an existence lived in solitude'. However, Eileen's friendship with Jessie Gavin developed further into a relationship and the two women would often be seen visiting the bars and clubs of Paris. Jessie would dress in disguise as a male, donning a wig and moustache and tell Eileen, 'I can take you to places where you can't go without a man.' Eileen recalled on one occasion when she and Jessie, who was dressed convincingly as a male Spaniard with a wig and beard, entered a club and the Spanish national anthem was played for them.

In 1905 Eileen returned to London to be with her ailing mother. While she was in Kensington she went back to Mr Charles's studio to complete her apprenticeship. She returned to Paris in 1906 with a little more experience, a supply of Chinese lacquer and a list of some contacts that would prove to be beneficial in her career. Shortly after Eileen moved out of her shared lodgings into a rented apartment in the rue Bonaparte, near the church of Saint-German-des-Prés, which she bought a few years later, and it remained her permanent home for the rest of her life. She came into contact with Seizo Sugawara, a lacquerer from Jahoji, a small village north of Japan famous for its lacquer work. Sugawara had settled in Paris after arriving there in 1900 as part of the Japanese national delegation to the Exposition Universelle, to oversee the lacquerware sent from Japan. He became prominent as a master of the art of lacquer, teaching western-ers Oriental lacquer techniques.

Lacquer is a hard, waterproof substance made from the resin of the *Rhus Verniciflua*, a deciduous shrub or tree native to Eastern Asia, particularly China and Japan. The process of lacquering was extremely time-con-suming, requiring a considerable amount of patience. Eileen worked in her apartment under the guidance of her mentor, Sugawara. She meticu-lously recorded in a notepad the successes and failures of the procedures used in her experiments with lacquer, such as attaining the right colour and texture, and how to avoid imperfections in the finish such as rippling. She spent many hours painstakingly working towards perfection, some-times having to apply many coats of lacquer to get the desired effect, or if it went wrong, she would patiently start the whole process all over again. 'Lacquer takes so long, twenty coats, sometimes forty coats, and the other side of the wood has to be lacquered too, otherwise it will warp,' she said. A local craftsman supplied Eileen with wooden pieces, such as panels and screens, to work on. At first, the colours were limited, but after adding a natural dye she achieved other colours such as reds, deep greens and blue, a colour that Mr Charles had told her was virtually impossible to achieve in lacquer. She then went on to add inlays of mother of pearl and gold or silver leaf. Her lacquer screens reflected a distinctive French and Far Eastern influence, and were unique in her application of both abstract and figura-tive themes. Being a nonconformist, Eileen was developing her own style, preferring simpler lines and later said that her screens were 'an attempt to simplify the figurative with almost geometrical designs and to replace those ghastly drapes and curves of Tiffany and Art Nouveau.'

Around 1908 Eileen travelled to Algeria, in northern Africa with Evelyn Wyld, a family friend who had arrived in Paris a year earlier. Evelyn had an interest in rug making and so the two friends spent some time in the Atlas

Mountains learning the techniques of weaving and dyeing from the local artisans. Following their trip Evelyn went to England to learn more about weaving and rug making, and Eileen returned to Paris, where she acquired a small workshop on the top floor of 17 rue Visconti in Saint-Germain for their carpet business. They obtained wool and looms from England and hired a teacher from the National School of Weavers. Eileen designed the rugs in abstract, geometric patterns, while Evelyn oversaw their production of the carpets. The rugs took less time to produce and were less expensive than Eileen's lacquered furniture and so proved to be very successful. In the meantime Eileen had transferred her lacquer workshop to a larger space in a building on the rue Guénégaud, near the river Seine, where she opened a studio with Sugawara.

Although she was based in Paris, Eileen would make regular trips home to London and Ireland. She loved anything modern and mechanical and it was in England that she developed an enduring passion for aviation and motor cars, making regular visits to the annual Motor Show. In 1909, after acquiring her driver's license, she bought her first motor car, a Chenard-Walcker. It was through a friend of her mother's, C.S. Rolls of the Rolls Royce family, that Eileen became acquainted with several prominent aviators of the time, including the French aviation pioneer, Hubert Latham and flew with Chéron in his bi-plane near Marseilles. She was also one of the first passengers to fly on the airmail plane from Mexico City to Acapulco, later in the 1920s. Her love of flying and motor cars would later be echoed in some of her designs.

In 1913 Eileen exhibited for the first time at the eighth Salon de la Société des Artistes Décorateurs in the Pavillon de Marsan in Paris. Her work comprised of a decorative lacquer panel of figures, entitled *Le Magicien de la Nuit* (The Magician of the Night), a frieze, a yellow and silver library panel, and a mantelpiece entitled *Om Mani Padme Hum*. The *Art et Décoration* magazine stated, 'Miss Gray uses that admirable material lacquer and creates with it interesting and unusual mantelpieces, friezes, and library panels. Seeing her entries, one regrets that this beautiful technique is not more favoured by our decorators'. Her exhibits attracted the attention of several influential people and future patrons, including the French writer Élisabeth de Gramont, the Duchesse de Clermont-Tonnerre and foremost couturier and fashion designer Jacques Doucet, who became Eileen's first major client. He purchased a red-lacquered, four-panel screen from her studio, decorated with three figures on one side and an abstract image on the other. The screen, entitled *Le Destin* (Destiny), had been inspired by a drawing of a madman she had seen at the La Salpêtrière hospital in Paris. Jacques' purchase not only gave her professional recognition, but also recommendation to new clients. Eileen was very reluctant to sign her work, but through Jacques' insistence, *Le Destin* was one of her few signed and dated pieces.

Jacques Doucet was an avid collector of modern artefacts and was so impressed with Eileen's work that he commissioned her to design several other pieces of furniture for his new apartment at 46 Avenue du Bois. The Lotus table, the smaller Bilboquet table and a small red lacquer table designed for Jacques are some of her most important early pieces. She also designed and made decorated lacquer frames for his Van Gogh paintings. However, the outbreak of the First World War in 1914 disrupted Eileen's work for Jacques Doucet. Despite her mother's pleas to return to London, she initially remained in Paris, working with Evelyn Wyld as a volunteer ambulance driver under the supervision of the Duchesse de Clermont-Tonnerre. By 1915 Eileen felt that her services were no longer needed in Paris and, accompanied by Sugawara, she returned to London where she intended to pursue her career. She rented a workshop in Cheyne Walk in Chelsea, but like Paris, London was also affected by the austerity of the war and the demand for luxuries such as expensive furniture had fallen dramatically. Her venture in London was unsuccessful, despite being favourably received by the critics. An article published in *Vogue* magazine in 1917 on Eileen's work, entitled 'An Artist in Lacquer,' read, 'She stands alone, unique, the champion of a singularly free method of expression'. Later that year, Eileen and Sugawara returned to Paris, where she reopened her workshops.

The Armistice was signed on 11 November 1918, and after the dreadful hardships of the war years the people of Paris were feeling more positive about the future. Post-war Paris saw a trend for change, particularly in the homes of the affluent, initiating a demand for designers and architects. 'Modern luxury is insatiable', wrote the Duchesse de Clermont-Tonnerre. Eileen's clientele rapidly increased to include some of the elite

of Paris. In 1919 Suzanne Talbot (Madame Mathieu-Lévy), the successful milliner and owner of the boutique Salon de Modiste, commissioned
Eileen to refurbish her apartment on the rue de Lota, requesting that she
create 'something extravagant'. It was a highly ambitious project which
allowed Eileen the means and freedom to create the entire interior of a
domestic space, designing wall and floor coverings, rugs, lighting and furniture, as she liked. It took her four years to produce a result that was an
extremely opulent yet simplistic design, and ten years ahead of her time.
The whole apartment was predominantly finished in lacquer, for which
she had to employ additional assistants to help Sugawara. She lined the
walls of the entrance hall with hundreds of small lacquered black panels
texturised in eggshell, which gave the effect of bricks in a wall, and from
which she would develop the design of her highly acclaimed Block Screen.
The existing mouldings on the walls and ceilings, which Eileen regarded as
'disgraceful', were covered with panels of dark lacquer inlaid with silver and
mother of pearl arabesques, providing a dramatic backdrop for the stylish
lacquered furniture. Among Eileen's stunning designs were the Pirogue
sofa, a canoe-shaped daybed in lacquer with tortoise shell effect, complete
with large matt gold cushions and her iconic futuristic Bibendum chair
composed of three large curved leather tubes, stacked upon one another
on a leather seat, supported by a chrome plated tubular steel base. It was a
design that had been inspired by the Michelin man, reflecting her love of
motor cars. Her thick, luxurious hand-woven wool rugs of abstract geometric motifs and blankets made of fur and silk completed an apartment
that was an innovative mix of art deco and high modernism.

The apartment enabled Eileen to extend her creativity significantly as an
interior architect. It was highly praised by the critics – *Harper's Bazaar* declared:

> Paris and London are quite mad on the subject of lacquer rooms. The last
> word in interior decoration demands walls of lacquer with furnishings to
> match. Paris is still however ahead of the English capital for it possesses
> Miss Gray, admittedly the master of her difficult art. Her style is thor-
> oughly modern although there is much feeling for the antique ... Miss
> Gray's work stands out because of its beauty ... She was the first in the
> field to show an unusual perfection of workmanship.

In an exclusive article on her work in a French art journal, *Feuillets d'Art*, the Duchesse de Clermont-Tonnerre wrote, 'She aims to create interiors adapted to our lives, to the proportions of our rooms and the aspirations of our sensibility'.

In 1922, whilst Eileen was working on the rue de Lota apartment, she opened a shop to display and sell her avante-garde, functional yet luxurious designs, on the fashionable rue du Faubourg Saint-Honoré, which she named Jean Désert. She changed the shop's old-fashioned façade to a stylish black and white, framed the widened windows in white curtains and painted the interior white. Eileen was quite shy and modest, especially regarding her work, so she preferred to stay in the background and hired a sales woman to sell her pieces. Business was slow at first, but soon Jean Désert attracted several prominent clients such as the French politician Maurice Thorez, film director René Clair, Prime Minister Raymond Poincaré, Sylvia Beach, James Joyce and the French singer Damia, who became Eileen's lover. Both women loved the vibrancy and eccentricity of Paris, where they would ride in Damia's car, accompanied by her pet black panther. Eileen had also gained a clientele abroad and her work was praised in newspapers as far as America. An article in the *Chicago Tribune* admired Eileen's 'unusual decorative perception and her rare grasp of detail and art' and described a visit to

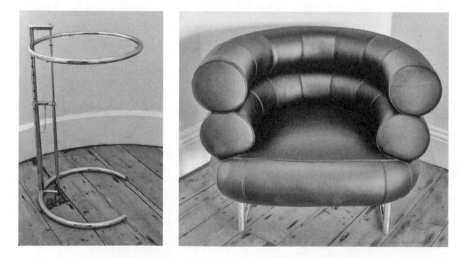

Reproductions of Eileen Grey's designs for an adjustable table and Bibendum Chair. (By kind permission of Enniscorthy Castle, Wexford)

her shop, Jean Désert, as, 'a sojourn into the never before seen, never before heard'.

At the annual Salon des Artistes Décorateurs in 1923 Eileen exhibited the multi-functional 'Bedroom-boudoir for Monte Carlo', an entire room designed for luxury and dual-purpose living. The room was a bold combination of stark white walls with dark lacquered furniture, dark carpeting and geometric rugs. Two block screens were placed next to a black lacquered daybed covered in fur and mounted on white sculptured block feet, which was placed in front of dark red and white lacquer panels. The innovative lighting was in parchment of 'African' style with appliqué motifs in red, white and ivory, and also a futuristic floor lamp, resembling a rocket, in copper and black lacquered wood. The room was a far cry from the popular Art Deco interiors favoured in Paris at the time and Eileen received some negative reviews from the critics, with descriptions such as 'strange' and 'frightening' and 'the room of the daughter of Doctor Caligari in all its horror'. *Art et Décoration* invited its readers to 'take a look at the strange bedroom of Madame Eileen Gray. It is comical and it is abnormal'. However, her room was admired by several designers, including the prominent French architect and designer Robert Mallet-Stevens, but it was the Dutch designers and architects who really appreciated and understood her work. She received a postcard from Jacobus J.P. Oud, the leading Dutch architect of the De Stijl movement, requesting to see more of her work, and her lamps that had been criticised by *Art et Décoration*, as being of 'unsettling appearance' were commended by the writer and architect Albert Boeken when he wrote:

What variety in these lamps! What fantasy in the use of white parchment together with a black design, white or coloured glass, cassowary egg shells combined with a geometric lacquered base ... These lamps are complete in themselves; they penetrate and wholly constitute the interior with their astonishing light.

By the mid-1920s Eileen had exhibited her furniture alongside some of the most prominent French designers of that period, and her name had become synonymous with Pierre Chareau, Francis Jourdain and Pierre Legrain.

She also had a growing interest in architecture, which was progressively apparent in her furniture and was moving away from her previous lacquer designs. Her designs were increasingly geometric, using different woods and materials such as chrome and tubular steel. She said of her previous work, 'I never really felt like doing these things. I did them because everybody wanted them.' She saw her wall screens as 'a revolt against Art Nouveau'. Eileen's career move towards architecture was greatly encouraged by Jean Badovici, a Romanian architect and architecture critic who she had met and befriended after the First World War, whilst he was studying architecture in Paris. He had become editor of *L'Architecture Vivante*, a leading French magazine for avant-garde architecture, and also contributed to several other artistic journals. Jean showcased Eileen's work in an article for a Dutch art magazine *Wendingen* in 1924 and wrote:

> Eileen Gray occupies the centre of the modern movement. In all her tendencies, visions, and expressions she is modern … She knows that our time, with its new possibilities of living, necessitates new ways of feeling … her creations testify to a rare audacity and reveal a singularly original vision. She is not interested in presenting mere natural form, she wants to find the geometric equivalent. The beauty of her work does not stem from scientific laws, it is derived from an original and lyrical élan which gives her objects their profound unity … a systematic unity gives all her designs a unique, architectonic significance.

Eileen shared Jean Badovici's enthusiasm for the Modern Movement and he introduced her to some of the most prominent European architects and their work, most notably Le Corbusier, one of the pioneers of modern architecture, whom she admired. She and Jean travelled together, observing the buildings of prolific modernist Dutch and German architects such as Gerrit Rietveld, Bruno Taut and Ludwig Mies van der Rohe. Eileen often assisted Jean with the production of *L'Architecture Vivante*, contributing to its layout and article content. She included it in the growing collection of textbooks and magazines on architecture, which provided the primary source of her training. She had always loved architecture but had lacked the confidence to design and build her own home. Her chance to put theory into practice came when Jean Badovici persuaded her to build them a 'little refuge' in the South of France. By this time they had become lovers and Eileen was captivated with the handsome architect, who was fifteen years her junior. Following several trips to the south of France Eileen bought a perfect plot overlooking the Mediterranean, tucked away in a secluded, remote area in Roquebrune-Cap-Martin, which could only be accessed by a small footpath. As Eileen had no knowledge of drawing architectural plans she produced a model of the house to show Jean, which he liked.

Work began on the construction of the house in 1926, which would take three years to finish. The progress of the build was hampered by the restricted access to the site meaning the workmen had to transport the building materials by wheelbarrow. Eileen moved to Roquebrune and remained on or near the site to oversee its construction, while Jean occasionally visited, offering advice and ideas. During that time she led a solitary life and saw only the workers, later recalling, 'I had very little encouragement. I was strong and keen but often it was difficult and very hard to get one's enthusiasm going.' Although the project was difficult, to Eileen it was a labour of love which she completely funded herself, listing Jean as the owner. She said, 'As in music, the value of a thing is based only on how much love goes into it.' She called the house E.1027, a numeric code for both Eileen and Jean's initials, E for Eileen, 10 for J, the tenth letter of the alphabet, 2 for B in Badovici and 7 for the G in Gray.

The white flat roofed villa stood on *piloti* (concrete piers) and faced south with covered terraces, taking full advantage of the Mediterranean views, with the bedroom to the east in order to see the sunrise. Eileen maximised the light which flooded through large floor-to-ceiling, folding screen windows, designed using the same principal as her lacquered screens. It was her intention to design a home that was both compact and open, allowing the occupants complete freedom and independence, 'There must still be the impression of being alone, and if desired entirely alone.' Screens and sliding doors were incorporated throughout, to allow flexible changes and privacy to the rooms according to the occupant's lifestyle. It was designed for a 'minimum of space and maximum of comfort' – simple and efficient, incorporating built-in cupboards and multi-functional furniture, which Eileen designed specifically for the house. A spiral stairway led to a glass and metal exit on the rooftop, where the Bay of Monaco could be seen on the horizon. She said, 'Avante-garde architecture doesn't have a soul, things must not only look right, they must also feel right. It is about creating homes for people.'

E.1027 was completed in 1929 and for the next few years Eileen and Jean would mainly occupy the villa in the summer months. Eileen had also employed a maid, Louise Dany, who would prove to be a life-long, trustworthy companion. In the same year she closed her shop in Paris, as she wanted to concentrate more on architecture. She often entertained guests at E.1027 such as the French writer and playwright, Claude Roger-Marx, the artist Fernand Léger, and Le Corbusier who greatly admired the house, to the extent that it became an obsession. However, Jean was a heavy drinker and womaniser, and by 1932 Eileen had moved out of E.1027, taking only one item of furniture, her adjustable side table made in pioneering tubular steel and glass, designed for her sister Thora, who liked to have breakfast in bed. Le Corbusier had wanted to buy the villa but Eileen had refused. Nonetheless, his fixation grew and after her departure, whilst staying there with Jean, he painted eight large sexual murals on the walls, one of which depicted Jean on the right and Eileen on the left, with a figure sitting in the middle which he said was 'the desired child which was never born.' Eileen had not been consulted and was furious, seeing the defacement of her architecture as 'an act of vandalism'. Although Le Corbusier had made his mark on E.1027, he failed to ever purchase it and later, after the Second World War, he acquired a small site behind the house, on which at first he built a small wooden cabin, followed later by a two-storey house on *pilotis*.

Le Corbusier had a perfect viewpoint from which to observe the villa. He would be seen taking a daily swim in the sea in front of the house and his presence at the villa, along with the publication of his photographs of the murals, overshadowed the fact that Eileen had been the designer of E.1027. For many years he was falsely attributed in numerous architectural and design magazines as the architect of the house.

While E.1027 was being built Eileen had purchased a small plot of land nearby at Castellar. After parting from Jean she started the construction of a smaller new house which she called Tempe à Pailla, taken from an old, Provencal proverb, 'With time and straw, the figs ripen'. As with E.1027, she meticulously designed the house down to every last detail, with innovative built-in storage spaces and multi-functional furniture. Again, the rooms were designed to maximise the natural light which, in the living room, could be controlled by adjusting the vertical metal slats at the windows and a skylight added 'other lighting effects'. Although Eileen was sociable she also enjoyed seclusion at times and so the house was built for both socializing and privacy, with partially roofed terraces, adding extra living and entertainment space and private rooms for Eileen to withdraw to when she wanted. It was designed purely for Eileen's own needs and lifestyle, 'E.1027 was for a man who likes to entertain; Temp à Pailla is for a woman whose main pleasure is to work,' she said.

Eileen spent the years leading up to the Second World War designing projects on a larger commercial scale rather than individual homes, but unfortunately they did not progress further than her sketches and models. She lived in Tempe à Pailla until 1940, when for her own safety she was forced to move further inland in Provence, where she lived with Louise in a rented house in Lourmarin. Towards the end of the war Eileen returned to Castellar where she found that her home had been entirely looted and the flat she had purchased before the war in nearby St Tropez had been bombed by the Germans. She was devastated and returned to the rue Bonaparte, her apartment in Paris, which thereafter became her main residence. However, she yearned for St Tropez and the following years were spent between Paris and the south of France, where she repaired and refurbished Tempe à Pailla, a task which took seven years. But by then she felt that the house had lost its magic and she sold it in 1954.

In 1956 Eileen received the news that Jean Badovici had died. She had remained good friends with Jean and was deeply upset. Despite his promises to Eileen, he had not made a will and E.1027 went to his sister, who was living in Romania. Le Corbusier was still very much obsessed with the house and persuaded his close friend, Madame Schelbert, to buy it. On the understanding that Le Corbusier had designed E.1027, Madame Schelbert bought the house and its entire contents at auction in 1960 and Le Corbusier received a payment for the wall murals. Eileen was not aware of the auction until after the sale and received nothing. Her response was, 'I like to put things in motion, but I despise owner-ship.' Five years later, in August 1965, Le Corbusier died of a heart attack whilst taking his daily swim in the cove directly in front of E.1027.

Back in Paris, Eileen worked on further architectural projects, includ-ing a large cultural centre, but sadly these did not materialise. She did undertake one last project back in St Tropez, converting a small dwelling for herself in a vineyard that she had previously purchased before the war. She called it Lou Pérou and although it was small, it was a big renova-tion, which she undertook at the grand age of eighty. Despite her age, poor eyesight and trembling hands, Eileen continued designing, working with new materials such as plastics and plexiglass and in her nineties she supervised some small pieces of furniture. She had been leading a quieter, more reclusive life for a number of years and was almost forgotten. But in 1972 she was rediscovered when the sale of her early screen, *Le Destin*, at a major auction of Jacques Doucet's furniture, set a new world record for any furniture from that period. Philippe Garner, a director of Christies, described Eileen as receiving the news with 'bemused detach-ment'. Renewed interest in Eileen's work grew, and in February 2009 her 'Dragon' armchair or *Fauteuil aux Dragons* which had been originally owned by her early patron Suzanne Talbot, then later part of the Yves Saint Laurent collection, sold at a Christies auction in Paris for a stag-gering €21.9 million ($28.3 million), setting another auction record for twentieth-century decorative art.

In 1973 Eileen, now in her nineties, met interior designer and furniture dealer, Zeev Aram and worked with him on the reproduction of some of her most famous pieces. In an interview in 2013 Zeev recalled Eileen as being puzzled at the revived interest shown in her work. He described her as 'Very frail and very elegant, but not in an ostentatious kind of way. She was very shy, but at the same time she knew exactly what's what.' He also remembers her as being 'so precise, so accurate and so confident', discussing her designs down to the last centimetre. Eileen gave Zeev Aram the exclusive license to produce her designs worldwide, which are still sold today from Aram Designs in Drury Lane, London.

On 25 October 1976, Eileen sent Louise out to buy some wood for a table design which she had been working on. When Louise returned she found Eileen unconscious, after having fallen near her workroom in the apartment. She never recovered and died in hospital six days later on 31 October. Her ashes were placed in a grave numbered 17616, in the world-famous cemetery of Père Lachaise, in Paris. It was her loyal house-keeper Louise Dany who placed a small black marble plaque, inscribed with Eileen's name and date of death on her grave. She did not put her date of birth, 'because Mademoiselle did not like to speak of her age'.

LADY MARY HEATH

1897–1939

'To fly is an adventure and at the same moment a
time of spirit renewal and refreshment.'

Lady Mary Heath

During the mid to late 1920s, Lady Heath was one of the most famous women in the world, making headline news worldwide as the first pilot ever to fly solo in a small open-cockpit plane from Capetown to London. By the time she had accomplished this tremendous feat, she had already established herself as a professional athlete, leading the way for women into the Olympics in Britain.

Sophie Theresa Catherine Mary Pierce Evans was born on 10 November 1896, in the village of Knockaderry, near the town of Newcastle West in County Limerick and was baptised in the local Church of Ireland church. Her father, John Pierce Evans, came from a respectable, comfortable, professional background. He was the only boy of eight children and was quite a problematic child. As he progressed into adulthood it became evident that he also had a violent temper. His mother's death and subsequently his father's second marriage to an older woman, who had difficulty in coping with a large family, may have added to his unruly behaviour.

After his uncle's death, John inherited the substantial Knockaderry House. With no idea how to manage such a property he adopted the unorthodox system of challenging tenants who could not pay the rent to a fight, in which if the tenant won, the rent would be overlooked. This encouraged rogues and villains from nearby Newcastle West and soon the house became a regular bolthole for the local lowlifes.

John employed Catherine Teresa Dooling from Castlemaine, County Kerry, as his housekeeper. Unlike John, Catherine came from a less fortunate background of peasant farmers and was also illegitimate, as was her mother before her. He had been in a sexual relationship with his previous housekeeper Catherine Keane, but she had repeatedly fled from her employer through fear of his temper. He would come after her and when he found her, he would assault both her and her husband, which led to him spending a month in prison on one occasion. This behaviour was repeated with Catherine Dooling, but unlike her predecessor, she stayed put and, after a stormy relationship, they married on 29 May 1895.

Their marriage continued to be turbulent and didn't improve after Sophie was born. Her father was increasingly unpredictable and his

Knockaderry House, Lady Mary Heath's birthplace. (Courtesy of Byron Smith)

temper was worse than ever. Poor Sophie was stuck in the middle of their battles, with either parent periodically leaving the house and marriage, with Sophie in their arms. Once, her father, in a fit of rage, set off with Sophie in a holdall under his arm, with the intention of taking her to America. However, while he was in Cork looking for lodgings his odd behaviour caught the attention of a local woman, who, out of concern for the child, informed the police, which led to his arrest. Sophie's mother came to collect her and all three returned home to Knockaderry.

The couple were often heard quarrelling in public and were frequently summoned to court for various reasons. John was mainly called for attacking his wife and feuding with his neighbour, William Power, whom he accused of raping Catherine, which the authorities thought may have been a fabricated story to try and gain money from William. After the jury could not agree on the case, the pair were described as 'half mad' and thrown out of the court. Catherine's drunken, antisocial behaviour at one time led to a two-month prison sentence, where the court heard that she 'did not appear to be right in the head'.

Mrs Eliot-Lynn with a display of her medals she won during her athletics career. (Courtesy of the Langford family)

The fighting and quarrelling between Sophie's parents escalated to a climax on 8 December 1897, when she was just one year old. Her father murdered her mother at their home. At first, the newspapers reported that Sophie's mother had been shot, but then it became apparent that she had been repeatedly kicked and beaten to death by her husband. The *Limerick Chronicle* reported that 'it is evident that the poor creature had a most agonising end, and that the fiendish attack made upon her must have been the result of a fit of temporary insanity'. All through the trial, John appeared very weary and vacant and 'seemed to take a listless interest in the whole proceedings', except when a garment belonging to his deceased wife was presented, only then did he 'bury his face in his hands and weep'. The verdict was guilty of murder, but with insanity, and John was detained for life at the Central Mental Hospital in Dublin.

Following her mother's death, Sophie was taken to live with her grandfather, Dr George Pierce, and her aunts at their house in Newcastle West. The murder trial hung over the family and the aunts endeavoured to protect Sophie from any slander by restricting her to playing within the privacy of their garden, and she was always accompanied when out in town. She later said, 'My childhood has made me love freedom of every kind today.' After attending several schools she eventually boarded at St Margaret's Hall in Dublin, where she became a keen hockey and tennis player, activities which had been restricted by her aunts at home. In Newcastle West, Sophie's vibrant personality had been suppressed and she had been at times unruly, showing traits similar to those of her father, but at St Margaret's Hall her wilfulness and determination contributed to her high academic achievements, which secured her a place at the Royal College of Science in 1914. Whilst studying for her degree, she became involved in the writing and publishing of the student magazine *The Torch*, showing a natural talent for writing in her contributions of articles and poems.

During the First World War, in the summer of 1916, Sophie's father died and in the same year she met and married Captain William Davies Eliott-Lynn, a forty-one-year-old bachelor and officer with the Royal Engineers. Shortly after her marriage she decided to take a temporary break from her studies and enlisted with the War Office as a dispatch rider in the Women's Auxiliary Army Corps, where she was billeted in England. After spending two years as an ambulance driver on the front line in France, she returned to Dublin to her husband, and to continue her studies.

After a short, troubled period together, William returned to Africa, to work as an engineer, as he had done during the latter part of the war, and Sophie stayed in Dublin to complete her studies, where she gained an honours degree in agricultural science. William financially supported

Sophie through university, but she was very reckless with money and her carefree attitude towards spending meant that she was constantly asking her husband for financial assistance, which caused disagreements in their marriage. When Sophie finished university William stipulated that she was to seek employment, which she did at Aberdeen University in Scotland, as a lecturer in zoology. It was at Aberdeen that Sophie discovered athletics as a diversion from her strained marriage. She excelled in sports at Aberdeen, and pursued athletics to competition level back home in Dublin in the summer of 1921. She competed locally and at the Clonliffe Harriers Athletics Club in Landsdowne Road, and she came second in Britain and Ireland in the high jump that year. Her height of nearly six feet proved to be a great asset in athletics, especially with the high jump and javelin, where she would later achieve the most success.

In the autumn of 1921 Sophie arrived back in Aberdeen and started campaigning for greater recognition of women athletes, and a year later, in 1922, with the help of Major Marchant and Florence Birchenough, a competitor in the Monte Carlo games, the Women's Amateur Athletic Association or WAAA was formed. Although women's athletics at that time was considered by the men to be 'unladylike', the WAAA rapidly gained support, and by 1925 there were 500 clubs with over 25,000 members, varying from factory workers to university students. The first Women's Modern Olympic Games were held at Pershing Stadium in Paris, where in front of 20,000 spectators, the British team triumphed over the French and American teams. It was much publicised by the local and international press and was a leap forward in women's sports, gaining them respect for the first time. The games were subsequently held every four years, like the traditional Olympic Games, an event where women were still forbidden to compete.

In October 1923 Sophie joined her husband in Africa, to work on their coffee farm of 1,000 acres that had been given to William in place of some of his army pay, but their relationship continued to be tense and Sophie found the colonial life style constrained her outgoing, adventurous nature. Her eagerness to join William on safari triggered arguments between them, as it was not orthodox at that time for a woman to take part in hunting pursuits in Africa. Alone in the farmhouse, with only servants for company, Sophie consoled herself by writing poetry and training daily, practising her javelin skills. She adopted the Masai technique holding the javelin low with both hands, one on the grip, the other balancing the spear at the end: 'I noticed that they always held their spears well behind the centre of gravity and so ensured that they came down point first.'

Mrs Eliot-Lynn throwing the javelin. (Courtesy of the Langford family)

Sophie returned to England in the following spring, where she took part in numerous competitions and in August 1923, at the first English Women's Athletics Championships in Bromley, she became Britain's first women's javelin champion and then went on to set the world record for the high jump of four foot ten inches. She had also become a well-known public figure, through her athletic success and her vivacious personality, regularly featuring in articles in the newspapers. At the end of the athletic season Sophie made her last visit to Africa in an attempt to save her marriage, but unable to settle into the expected tradition of a married woman and with the failure of their coffee crop adding to their marital problems, Sophie returned to London. With her marriage virtually finished, she immersed herself in athletics, competing internationally and winning countless medals. She also became involved with the National Playing Fields Association, campaigning for more adequate open spaces for sporting activities. Her book of poetry, *East African Nights and Other Verses*, was published in 1925 and later in the same year *Athletics for Women and Girls – How to be an Athlete and Why*, was also published, the first book of its kind. The profits from the sales of both books went to the WAAA and the Playing Fields Association.

Sophie continued her campaigning and in 1925, she travelled by aeroplane for the first time, to the 8th Olympic Congress in Prague, where she proposed the inclusion of 'track and field' events for women on the Olympic programme. Subsequently three women's events were included in the Amsterdam Games in 1928, where Sophie was a judge. Although it was to take some years before women would be included in all Olympic Games, the foundations had been set by Sophie. It was after a conversation with the pilot, Captain Reid, on her flight home from Prague, that Sophie's passion for flying began. He encouraged her to join the new London Light Aeroplane Club. Full of enthusiasm Sophie became a member and after David Kettel generously gave her his place on the club's first half-hour flight, she took to the air in the club's small bi-plane, the dual-control de Havilland Moth and became the club's first passenger and first woman member.

As part of the Air Minstry's 'Policy of Encouragement and Assistance' towards the 'Formation of Light Aeroplane Clubs' in Britain in the early

1920s, light aeroplane clubs were emerging all over Britain, providing not just flying schools but prestigious social clubs which attracted the wealthy and elite. Sophie enjoyed the glamour and attention that came with the club membership and apart from enjoying the thrill of flying, saw it as an opportunity to gain further publicity and a regular income to ease her financial problems. After 1919 the Air Navigation Act stipulated that a PPL – Private Pilot's Licence or 'A' licence was compulsory in order to fly for pleasure and carry passengers and goods, but not commercially. A pilot could qualify for the PPL after three hours of solo flying, a test of technical knowledge and a medical examination. This gave the new pilot use of the club's planes for a fee and enabled them to take part in displays, stunts and races.

Sophie took her first solo flight in October 1925, after which she took her test for her 'A' licence. Despite poor visibility due to the mist, she calmly and proficiently completed her manoeuvres and reached a height of 6,000 feet, before landing the plane safely, proving she had a natural ability with flying. Later she stated, 'After a very short time, flying became second nature to me. I fly nearly every day and can remain a long time in the air without feeling fatigued'. She received her 'A' licence on 4 November, just before her twenty-ninth birthday and during the summer air shows, she entertained thousands of people displaying her skills as a pilot, which included stunt flying and racing and provided her with a good income.

Sophie's main aim was to become a commercial pilot, but the International Commission for Air Navigation excluded women from 'any employment in the operating crew of aircraft engaged in public transport', and stated that the commercial pilot 'must be of the male sex'. They suggested that women would be less competent than men in commercial flying and that their 'menstruating bodies' would be a hindrance. Undeterred and as determined as ever, Sophie started her campaign for equality for female commercial pilots and approached the international commission and, at their request, demonstrated her flying skills and proved that her abilities as a pilot were unaffected by her being a woman.

During her campaign, Sophie continued to encourage other women to fly, stating, 'Flying really is absurdly easy – and it is only those who fly themselves who realise this.' She proclaimed that flying was safer and cleaner than travelling by road, as 'you can arrive at your destination much cleaner and fresher than if you came on a dusty or muddy road.' She also claimed that there was no need for any special clothing, such as a helmet or goggles, as a loose skirt and a warm fur coat was sufficient in cold weather. Always immaculately dressed herself, even when flying she would always wear a smart suit or evening dress under her flying coat and silk undergarments that would roll up without creasing and despite carrying the minimal amount of personal luggage, an evening dress and shoes would always be included for social occasions.

Having passed her theory exams for the 'B' licence, but unable to carry passengers due to the existing ban, she continued to earn her living by delivering newspapers between London and Paris and by taking part in exhibitions and various daring stunts, where her pluckiness along with her 'courage, beauty and charm' attracted further publicity. She was the first female pilot to fly a loop-the-loop and in April 1926, she became the first woman to parachute jump from a plane in Hereford. Her first attempt the day before had almost ended in disaster. When she had climbed on to the wing of the aeroplane at 1,500 feet, intending to jump off, the engine had sputtered, making the plane dive rapidly. She clung on desperately as the plane just missed a hedge and landed in a football field. Luckily no one was hurt and after the successful second attempt the following day, Sophie told the reporters, 'The sensation of landing by parachute was about the same as a jump from a six-foot wall. I could have wished, however, that the ploughed field could have been a little bit softer.'

Lady Mary Heath on arrival at Le Bourget airport, Paris, on her homeward flight from Cape Town. (Courtesy of the Langford family)

Eventually the ban was lifted in May and after completing her practical flying tests, Sophie at last received her 'B' licence and became Britain's first female commercial pilot. Still keen to promote women and flying, in May 1927, with her friend and fellow Irish aviator, Lady Mary Bailey as passenger, Sophie set an altitude record of 16,000 feet. An article published in *Flight Magazine* read, 'It is still a common practice for women, as aviators, to be rather disdained. Mrs Eliott-Lynn has perhaps done more for her sex than any other woman'. She went on to give lectures on aviation in Britain and Ireland and toured Central Europe. After *Flight Magazine* stated that an aeroplane 'can fly where it will but it cannot land where it will', Sophie flew 1,300 miles around Britain, landing at seventy-nine aerodromes, and proved the magazine wrong.

Also in 1927, her estranged husband William, having returned to London, was found drowned in the River Thames. Later that year in October, Sophie married Sir James Heath, 45 years her senior and a very wealthy colliery owner. She had been using her middle name of Mary, so she now became known as 'Lady Mary'. Being an aviation enthusiast himself, her new husband bought her the latest Avro Avian biplane, to add to the other three she already owned and shortly after the wedding, on 18 November, they travelled to Cape Town by ship with her new biplane in a crate in the ship's hold. It had been Lady Mary's dream to fly across Africa and later in her book, *Woman and Flying*, published in 1929 and written with her friend and supporter, Stella Wolfe Murray, she wrote, 'It had always been in my mind that I would some day fly over the length of Africa, to me the most fascinating Continent of the whole world'.

Although Africa had been assessed for flying potential by the Air Ministry after the First World War, much of the continent was still unexplored. Aware of the challenges she may encounter on her flight, Lady Mary had visited Africa previously on several occasions and had studied the ground and climate conditions of the various regions of her planned route and gathered information on flying conditions and petrol supplies. As she was unable to find any information of the flying route to Cairo in Cape Town, she flew up to Johannesburg. En route she visited several flying clubs, giving joyrides to passengers at £1 a time, earning over £1,200, which she gave back to the flying clubs and with the remainder she later established flying clubs back in England, to inspire other women to learn to fly.

During her journey to Cairo, Lady Mary also toured and gave lectures, all the time raising money for the Light Aeroplane Clubs of South Africa. At Port Elizabeth, she attended a presentation ceremony in which a Westland Widgen monoplane was presented to the flying club and was duly named *The Lady Heath*. Her tours boosted her popularity in Africa and she quickly became well known, so that the natives of the small towns greeted her with much interest and delight. In the town of Tsolo, near the Drakensburg Mountain, a witch doctor presented Lady Mary with a bead head-dress in token of her 'greater magic.' She was also proving to be of great interest to the journalists who followed her every move and her photograph would often appear in the local newspapers, alongside an article covering her latest exploits.

Always in pursuit of new challenges, Lady Mary planned to carry on her journey from Cairo to London. As her book states, 'When I conceived the idea of flying northward from the Cape to Cairo, and then on to Croydon, I realised I would have many more difficulties to face than the ordinary male pilot, especially in the event of a forced landing in jungle or swamp, or among hostile natives'. And at 7.30 a.m on 25 February 1928, after the South African Air Force gave the Avian a complete overhaul, Lady Mary set off from Pretoria on her solo flight back to London. She travelled well equipped, with a kit which included basic medical supplies such as morphine, iodine and bandages, clothing, a Bible, some novels and a tennis racket and tennis shoes.

Six hours into her flight and flying 8,000 feet above the great quartz hills of Matobo in Zimbabwe, Lady Mary began to feel a pain in the back of her head, neck and shoulders. She knew it was sunstroke, having suffered from it before. She tried desperately to reach her flying topee or pith hat but was unsuccessful and despite pulling off part of her underclothing and wrapping it around her head and shoulders, it was too late. With her sight fading and slowly slipping into unconsciousness, she somehow managed to safely and skilfully land the plane. She woke up four hours later, laying on her fur coat under some thorn bushes, with 'three native girls in various stages of scanty undress, sitting back on their haunches and laughing at me!' The girls helped Lady Mary to the harem hut and after staying there for the night, the Lord Mayor of the nearest town of Bulawayo, sent Captain Mail, who flew her out to the hospital, where she slept for eighteen hours. After a few days recovery her temperature returned to normal and she continued with her journey.

After an eight hour nonstop flight from Rome, Lady Mary landed in Marseilles, where she met Stella Wolfe Murray, who mentioned in their book, 'she looked as if she had stepped out of a bandbox, having changed her flying helmet for a little black cloche hat'. After tea and sandwiches she changed into her overalls to work on her engine, 'while an admiring group of mechanics stood round open-mouthed'. Stella continued, 'I have never seen anyone unpack or pack so quickly, or undress and dress so quickly, as she did, contriving to look like a fashion plate all the same'.

During her epic journey, Lady Heath had endured not just sunstroke, but also rheumatic fever, blistering heat of 120 degrees Fahrenheit and heavy torrential rain, all in an open cockpit. She had persevered with a hazardous flight, been shot at over the North African coast and had her lifejacket of two inflated tyres burst at 7,000 feet over the sea, when water was her biggest fear. She landed in Croydon on 17 May to the cheering crowd including her husband, journalists and various support- ers. She later wrote in her book of the last lap of the journey, 'The last lap was, as the papers say, without incident, except for a storm in the Channel that blew me up to Deal. I was so annoyed by this, and so cold, that I landed at Lympne, to have a cup of tea before going on to Croydon. I had not expected anybody to come out to Croydon to meet me, and I was so surprised and pleased to find two aeroplanes circling round me as I approached the aerodrome'.

The *Daily Express* reported that 'Lady Heath stepped out of the machine wearing a silk dress, fur coat and a black straw hat proclaiming that, "it is so safe that a woman can fly across Africa wearing a Parisian frock and keeping her nose powdered all the way".' She told the *Irish Independent*, 'My Avian is as comfortable as a motor car, you really do not need special flying kit in these light planes. Why, I have flown practically from Capetown in this outfit.' Of her 'delightful experience' of flying along the River Nile, she added indifferently, 'As Cairo is an important place, I thought I must appear respectable, so I poked out a pair of silk stockings from the back locker and managed to put them on in mid-air.' She also claimed to have read a novel and eaten chocolates as she flew along the river Nile.

Her 10,000-mile flight was not only the first solo flight from any British overseas colony to London, but she was the first woman to fly solo from South Africa to London, her achievement making headline news across the globe. She later said of her success, 'My ambition was not to be the first woman flying over any area, but to bring my machine safely back to England, and prove that the organization of such a flight could be made as well in the Colonies as in England.'

Back in England, Lady Mary became involved in various aviation committees and societies and after much persuasion secured a job as a commercial pilot with KLM, the Royal Dutch Airline, flying passengers from London to Amsterdam. She travelled to America where she had made quite an impression, appearing on the front pages of the newspapers and she continued to give lectures and demonstrations. It was during the National Air Races in Cleveland that a near-fatal accident effectively ended Lady Mary's flying career, when the plane she was flying plummeted from the sky and crashed through the roof of the Mill Company factory next to the flying field.

Sadly, the accident left her with not just physical but mental scars, and although she did eventually recover, her head injuries required a metal plate to be fitted in her skull. After the accident her personality seemed to change. She became erratic and eccentric, developed a drinking problem and was unable to fly for some time. Her marriage to Sir James Heath had broken down and after their divorce she married Reginald Williams, or 'Jack' as he was known, in 1931, who came from a wealthy background on the Caribbean Island of St Lucia and was also an aviator. He was nearer her age than her two previous husbands, with her being three years older than him; as she said after the wedding service, 'This is the first time I've married a younger man.'

In the summer of 1932 she decided to leave America with her new husband and returned to Dublin, where she established the National

Junior Aviation Club, which was the first such club for teenagers in Europe and a lasting success, leading on to the present-day Irish Aviation Authority. After briefly running their own aviation company, Dublin Air Ferries in 1936, the corresponding opening of Aer Lingus in the same year proved to be too much competition and DAF closed in 1938. By this time Lady Mary's drinking was spiralling out of control and Jack went back to Trinidad while she went to London, where she was often found drunk in public places. Lady Mary was just a shadow of her former self. Gone was the vibrant, courageous, powerful role model, who had made headlines across the world; instead a poor, ragged, unstable alcoholic would be seen staggering about the streets of London. After making several appearances in court, she eventually spent two days in Holloway Prison. She vowed to make a fresh start and proposed to study medicine, but tragically on 7 May 1939, after boarding a tram car at Highgate Hill, she fell down the stairs from the top deck and died in hospital the next day.

She had requested, in the event of her death, that her ashes be scattered from an aeroplane over her home town of Newcastle West in Ireland, to shower over Captain Richbel Curling, a man she had despised since childhood, at the precise time he would be standing by the church, as he had done for many years watching the world go by. In typical Lady Heath style, eccentric to the last, her final wish was carried out, much to the bemusement of Captain Richbel Curling!

14

Dame Ninette de Valois

1898-2001

'You cannot have innovation without a firm bedrock of tradition.'

Dame Ninette de Valois

Highly regarded as one of the most influential women of the twentieth century, Ninette de Valois devoted her life to her passion for theatre and dance. Through her tenacity and dedication she fulfilled her dream of establishing one of the most prestigious and leading repertory ballet companies in the world today, The Royal Ballet.

Dame Ninette de Valois at the Abbey Theatre, 1929. (T13/B/355, Shields Family Archive, James Hardiman Library, National University of Ireland, Galway)

Dame Ninette de Valois was born as Edris Stannus on 6 June 1898 to Anglo-Irish Protestant parents, Lieutenant Colonel Thomas Stannus, a British Army officer, and Elizabeth Graydon-Smith, a glassmaker. She was the second of four children and spent the early years of her childhood with her elder sister Rose and her younger brothers, Trevor and James, in a large Irish country house near Blessington, County Wicklow. In her memoirs, *Come Dance with Me*, Ninette wrote of happy memories playing with Rose in the beautiful grounds of Baltiboys, where their lives were 'very sheltered' and 'cut off from all communal interests'. She described herself as 'a delicate, undersized child ... intensely reserved and as obstinate as a mule'. The children were educated at home in the nursery and schoolroom located above the stables, by a succession of English nursery governesses – 'strange starched ladies, with elegant mutton-sleeves, pork-pie hats or boaters, and haughty English accents – one of their main tasks was to rectify our brogues'. Edris and her sister thought them almost foreign. She was an extremely shy child and dreaded going to children's parties in other nearby country houses, where she was promptly 'sick, cried and came home again' unlike her sister who 'was in a constant frenzy of delight'.

The governess would often take Edris and Rose to visit the herdsman and his wife Kate at the home farm near Baltiboys. It was Kate who taught Edris how to perform an Irish jig on the stone floor of the farmhouse, which was her 'first experience of any self-expression' and infused her with a love of dance. At a much dreaded children's party at a later date, Edris was standing on a chair, watching what her mother had told her was a skirt dance, accompanied by a lady playing the piano. She disapproved of rather than admired the dance, and suddenly yearned to perform her own much-loved Irish jig, which she thought was 'by far the better dance'. She became so absorbed with the dancer that she completely forgot her shyness and with her mother's permission, she danced in front of all the people at the party. Her only concern was that the pianist would understand what she wanted and 'get things right' to play the exact tune that she had requested. This early sign of professionalism would be consistent throughout her later career. When she had finished her dance, she evidently ran back to hide behind her nurse's skirts. She later wrote that this experience and a previous trip to the Gaiety Theatre in Dublin to see the pantomime of *The Sleeping Beauty* were 'two small symbolic moments', glimpses of her future life.

Unable to afford the upkeep of their country estate, the family moved to England to live with Edris's grandmother at her house in the small coastal town of Walmer, adjacent to Deal. Seven-year-old Edris quickly adjusted to her new life in Kent and soon came out of her shell, enjoying the parties as much as her sister. Not forgetting her trip to the theatre in Ireland, she would entertain her siblings in the nursery with plays that she had written, using the deep windowsill as the stage. She attended weekly dance classes with her sister, taught by an assistant teacher of the famous Mrs Wordsworth in London, who enlightened Edris's mother with regards to her daughter's talent. In between her classes a space would be cleared in the drawing room where Edris would dance with intense passion in front of her grandmother. She later said, 'as I danced I wove strange stories around my improvisations' and afterwards felt 'a strange sense of happy achievement'.

By the time Edris was eleven years old the family had moved to Earls Court Square in London. She continued her dance classes with Mrs Wordsworth which had increased to four times a week, and was taught 'fancy dancing', a combination of rudimentary and fancy steps, which Edris thought was, 'harmless and good fun'. Mrs Wordsworth abhorred any form of theatrical dance and wholly discouraged her pupils in that direction, but that was the path Edris wanted to take. She had been enthralled when her mother had taken her to see the prima ballerina Adeline Genée in the production of *The Belle of the Ball* at the Empire Theatre, the Diaghilev Ballet at Covent Garden and the Coliseum and Anna Pavlova at the Palace Theatre. Her combined enthusiasm and ability prompted her mother to cancel her classes with Mrs Wordsworth and send her thirteen-year-old daughter to train professionally at the Lila Field Academy, a theatre school for children. Mrs Wordsworth didn't receive the news very well as Edris later recalled, 'She informed my mother that she would scrub floors before a daughter of hers went near the stage; but my mother grimly assured her that she would have me trained so as to avoid my having to scrub floors for myself.'

German sisters, Bertha and Lila Field came to England and formed their popular stage school, which taught its pupils 'something of everything'. Edris was 'almost immediately set aside to specialise in the classical ballet section'. Her first stage appearance was in *The Goldfish*, a children's fairy play in three acts, which opened at the Little Theatre. Edris played the queen alongside Alfred Willmore, better known as Micheál MacLiammóir, as the king and Noël Coward as Prince Mussel, also making their debut. In 1913, fourteen-year-old Edris went on tour with The Wonder Children, a group of pupils from the Academy, who performed short ballets and plays under the strict charge of Bertha Field. Following her mother's advice, she took the stage name Ninette de Valois, decided by the historic family connections with the French royal house of Valois. The group was very successful, performing in seaside pier theatres around the country. She later wrote, 'It is not difficult for me to recall that springboard sensation one experienced when hurrying along the gas-lit pier deck'. There were no wardrobe mistresses and no dressers and Ninette's mother had to buy her costumes. 'Obliging' relatives assisted the children, and they were responsible for 'packing and unpacking, mending, ironing, and all necessary laundry work of the costumes and the care of shoes and tights'. Ninette later recalled, 'of having danced on every old pier theatre in England! We worked very hard; I made ten solo appearances every night and received a salary of £4 per week. Out of this I kept myself, paid my term's tuition fees and saved.'

The performances included short character dances, an abridged version of *The Goldfish*, the *Russian Ballet*, and a set of classical and *demi-caractère* dances, in which Ninette danced solo. At the end of the programme came *A Children's Revue: Impressions of Famous Artists*, where Ninette gave an enthusiastic performance as Anna Pavlova in *The Dying Swan*, which she later remembered as 'dying twice nightly on all the coastal piers, for my "death" was always ferociously encored'. Although a critic for *The Dancing Times* was less enthused, 'I would suggest that when she takes an encore she does not repeat "The Swan" – there is something incongruous in a swan dying twice in five minutes'. Whilst the group were touring during the summer of 1914, war was declared and The Wonder Children were disbanded at Lemington Spa. Ninette spent 'the rest of that terrible

summer at Walmer within sound of the heavy gunfire in France and
with the news growing evermore grave'. Her mother had not entirely
been in favour of the tours and hoping to find her a placement in London,
had sent Ninette to various auditions, but they had been unsuccessful.
However, in the autumn of 1914, when she was sixteen, she auditioned at
the Lyceum Theatre and was cast as a principal dancer for the Christmas
pantomime, making her debut in the West End.

As ballet was not recognised as an art form in the British Theatre,
professional training was scarce and in order to find work dancers had
to extend their abilities to perform in various productions such as opera,
musical comedy, pantomime and music hall. Ninette said:

> In those days England had no Sadler's Wells, no Arts Council, no big
> private schools, and no institution such as the Royal Academy of Dancing
> devoting its work to raising the standard of teaching and giving advice …
> dancers were accepted as individuals on their individual merits and they
> had to search for their own teachers, how they arrived at their eventual
> state of execution was no-one's concern.

Nonetheless, this diverse training would give Ninette a broader understanding of the performing arts that would later be imperative to her career.

Ninette performed at the Lyceum Theatre annually throughout the
First World War, dancing in *Robinson Crusoe, Mother Goose, Jack and the
Beanstalk* and *Cinderella*. Unlike The Wonder Children tours, the cast
were provided with costumes and wigs by 'Little Willy Clarkson' who,
Ninette remembered, 'with his tiny pinched-in waist, his rouged cheeks,
top-hat and frock coat – resembling a French barber in a comic opera –
would trip round gesticulating and offering everyone costumes from his
vast theatrical stores … He lived and breathed wigs, and complimented
me on mine and asked me where I had got it; I had to explain, to his
disappointment, that it had grown on my head'. During her time at the
Lyceum Ninette received a considerable amount of fan mail and would
find in her dressing room 'anonymous gifts of jewellery, flowers, and even
crates of fruit'. But, despite her growing popularity, she knew that she
needed classical training to improve her technique and took two private

lessons and one class three times a week with the renowned producer and ballet master of the Empire Theatre, Edouard Espinosa. To fund her expensive tuition she travelled weekly by train to Eastbourne to teach private lessons to children. At the weekends she worked in the kitchen of a military hospital in Park Lane, and later as a shift supervisor at the Victoria Station soldiers' canteen. Edouard was an expert in teaching ballet techniques from the French school and his lessons specialised in proficient footwork, focusing on *terre à terre* work, such as *petit batterie* and *pirouettes*, with precise musicality and rhythm. When Ninette suggested showing him *The Swan Dance*, Edouard is reputed to have said, 'If anyone else comes here and does that I'll murder them!' At the start of her training he took her pointe shoes away and instructed her to work in soft shoes for four months to correct her feet. She wrote, 'His care of feet, ankles and knees were superlative. We were never allowed to go home in ordinary walking shoes; we had to wear laced or buttoned boots as to support the ankles and keep them from swelling'. Her footwork would become her greatest strength, which she later attributed to Edouard's training.

In 1918 the English conductor and impresario, Sir Thomas Beecham, was staging excerpts from operas and ballets at the Palladium. Ninette appeared in *Faust*, *Carmen* and *Phoebus and Pan*, which was Sir Thomas's version of Bach's cantata; this not only gave her the opportunity to work with conductors and opera singers, but also to choreograph her own solos. In the winter of that year she performed her last pantomime at the Lyceum and as Edouard had left Britain for Australia, she continued her studies with Hilda Bewicke, a former dancer with the Diaghilev Russian Ballet. In the spring of 1919, Hilda rejoined the Diaghilev and introduced Ninette to the ballet master, Enrico Cecchetti, who had opened a school in London the previous year. He was instructing the dancers of the Diaghilev Ballet, who were performing at the Coliseum. Ninette joined his classes, which were usually of about ten pupils and were held at the Chandos Hall, a 'miserable place' with no mirrors and a dressing-room that was often visited by rats. But despite the grim and dreary environment, Ninette was thrilled to be taking lessons from the 'maestro' who had taught Anna Pavlova and to be able to meet members of the Russian

Ballet. She would arrive early for her class, so that she could watch the end of Lydia Lopokova's private lesson, where she was preparing for her solo in the forthcoming production of *Boutique Fantasque*.

Enrico devised the Cecchetti method, which is a strict classical ballet training programme of planned daily exercise routines, with specific emphasis on body line. 'From Cecchetti I learnt the meaning of symmetry, the hidden beauty of the studied detail, the harmony that can be achieved in movement and the meaning of *ports de bras*.' In the absence of the Ballet Russes during the summer, Ninette received 'a series of gruelling but wonderful private lessons' where she learnt the perception and skill of mime and her aspirations in choreography were encouraged, 'He was an ideal professor for young choreographers to study with ... To really understand space as he taught it ... you had to be aware of drawing your body in space ... to see the balance of the legs, the arms, the head and the body when they are inventing movements is one of the most *important* things they can *possibly* study.'

In conjunction with her studies, Ninette continued to work in the commercial theatre, appearing as principal dancer in the topical revue *Laughing Eyes*, which was an instant success. In one of the scenes entitled 'The Dope Fiend', she played an ingenuous character lured into an opium den and given a cigarette that produced amazing balletic dreams. In the summer of 1919, she was engaged as *première danseuse* at the Royal Opera House, Covent Garden, for the first post-war international season of Grand Opera, appearing in five operas: *Le Traviata*, *Thais*, *Aida*, *Louise*, and *Nail*. One critic described her as 'an extremely lithe and graceful dancer' and *The Dancing Times* wrote of her 'magnificent display' in *Aida*. The following year Ninette branched out into musical comedies, where she was cast in *Oh! Julie!* at the Shaftesbury Theatre, which gave her the experience of yet another form of theatrical work. A review in *The Stage* read, 'It is difficult to describe her dance. It is partly operatic and partly eccentric. Nevertheless she is too good for this kind of work'. At the young age of twenty-one she had gained significant experience in opera-ballets, pantomimes and musicals. She was in demand, receiving a good salary and becoming increasingly famous, often appearing in magazines such as *The Tatler* and *The Sketch*.

Ninette had a love of folk dancing, particularly morris dancing, and had been studying with the Hungarian dancer and choreographer Friderica

Derra de Moroda, who was a folk dance recitalist and had also taken ballet lessons with Enrico Cecchetti. Ninette was keen to choreograph her own troupe of dancers and in 1921 she formed the Gulliver Hall group and toured the theatres of suburban London, performing a combination of ballet and folk dance, with her group of eight girls and a male partner, Russian trained Serge Moroscoff, who was later replaced by a New Zealand dancer, Jan Caryll. Jan later wrote, 'Ninette's presentation was ahead of its time and the numbers sat rather uncomfortably within a typical music hall bill'. The following year Ninette was presented with the ideal opportunity to work with Léonide Massine, principal dancer and choreographer with Diaghilev's Ballet Russes, who had formed a small company with Lydia Lopokova. She joined their tour of Britain, which included performances in a show at the Royal Opera House that combined ballet and film. The Russian dancers had worked with the most prominent *demi-caractère* choreographers of that time and were adept at both acting and dancing. Ninette later wrote, 'The choreography was of an order undreamt of in any of my previous experiences, and the disciplined routine of class and lengthy rehearsals in preparation for the opening filled me with a sudden feeling of dedication that was an entirely new sensation'.

By 1923, Enrico Cecchetti had returned to Italy and Ninette was attending 'classes of perfection' with Russian ballet master Nicholas Legat. In September of that year, through Enrico Cecchetti's recommendation, Ninette joined the Diaghilev Ballet in Paris. Created by Sergei Diaghilev in 1909, the Ballet Russes were an avant-garde dance troupe, famous for their innovative artistic collaboration between young talented choreographers, composers, artists and dancers. Their unique productions were an amalgam of creativeness, performed by dancers of an exceptionally high standard. Ninette said that the Ballet Russes were, 'a repertory company running classical and modern ballet side by side – and what is more important – in many cases blended'. Diaghilev was a tough and even fearsome taskmaster, to which Ninette later admitted that she had been too scared of him to look him in the face. However, Diaghilev admired her dancing but apparently considered her stage name to be, 'Half tart, half royal family of France'. During her time with the Ballet Russes Ninette gained invaluable experience working with the most prominent choreographers of that time, including Bronislava Nijinska, who shared her interest in folk dancing and was to be a huge influence on her future outlook. Ninette appeared in various roles of some of the company's most famous productions, including several of Nijinska's new ballets such as *Le Train Bleu*, *Les Noces* and *Les Biches*. After touring for two years, Ninette was 'anxious to take up production work' and left the Ballet Russes to return to London. She later wrote that all she had learned of value to do with 'the presentation of ballet, the study of choreography and the development of the artist … came from this apprenticeship in the most famous of companies'.

Ninette had been suffering since her early teens from a previously undiagnosed illness, which she now knew to be polio. Knowing that eventually she would have to give up dancing altogether, she started to concentrate on teaching. The ballet companies that visited Britain at the time were usually Russian and Ninette's vision was that Britain should have its own National Ballet School. She was determined to start a repertory ballet company and school and to establish a national style of dance. In the summer of 1926, she founded The Academy of Choreographic Art, on the ground floor of 6A Roland Gardens, Gloucester Road, Kensington, where, in addition to ballet, the prospectus included courses in folk dance, production and costume design, and mime. She wanted her company to have a theatre for her pupils to gain professional experience in productions on the stage and so she approached Lilian Baylis, the formidable owner of the Old Vic Theatre. Known as 'The Lady' to her associates, Lilian had inherited the Old Vic from her aunt, the Victorian philanthropist, Emma Cons and had transformed the disorderly music hall into a venue providing drama and opera that was affordable to all classes. Her Cockney accent was treated with disdain by some of the middle class, but nevertheless she presented successful productions of a high standard on a minimal budget, coaxing the actors to work for very little money, which they saw as 'doing our bit for the Vic'. She was a deeply pious woman, whose faith greatly influenced the running of the theatre and would often be found next to her desk, 'down on her knees, praying for a tenor'. Any actors who asked for a raise would be told in earnest, 'Sorry, dear, God says No'.

Although Lilian thought Ninette 'a slightly fanatical young woman' she 'liked her face' and her proposed plans, even though Ninette had stressed that 'the running of such a ballet company would never be a money-making concern' but at that time she was unable to accommodate her due to lack of money and space. However, she had purchased and started a campaign for the renovation work on the old derelict Sadler's Wells Theatre in Islington, which would have the prospect of housing a British ballet company in the future. In the meantime, she was looking for 'someone to teach the drama students how to move' as they 'all had dreadful hands ... someone to arrange any little dance required in the Shakespearean productions ... someone to give a look to her office workers' who performed (unpaid) in the opera ballets, and a 'short (expenses only) ballet performance put on at Christmas, before *Hansel and Gretel* by some good ballet school and a lot more angels from the same source for the opera itself'. Ninette accepted Lilian's offer of '£1 per week for teaching, £2 for choreography' and engaged her students in the theatre's productions, giving them professional stage experience. She wrote, 'Thus, briefly, did Lilian Baylis contract me to the services of the Old Vic for four years, ever dangling in front of my eyes the rebuilding of Sadler's Wells in the dim future'.

During the years leading up to the opening of Sadler's Wells Ninette was kept busy with her school and her work at the Old Vic. She was also teaching once a week at Heathfield School at Ascot and had accepted the position of choreographic director at the new Festival Theatre in Cambridge, founded by her cousin Terence Gray. She choreographed the festival's debut production, *The Orestia*, where her students made up the chorus line, after which their time was divided between dancing at the Old Vic and in the chorus of Greek plays and short ballet performances at Cambridge. In 1927, William Butler Yeats, who had seen and admired Ninette's work, invited her to produce and perform every three months in his *Plays for Dancers* at the Abbey Theatre in Dublin and supply a teacher for his new ballet school. So Ninette took a former student Vivienne Bennett (the actress) to Dublin and the Abbey Theatre School of Ballet was opened in a small studio behind the theatre. To draw the public's attention to the school Ninette choreographed the opening performance of a new production called *Venetian Suite*, which included her own dancers from London as well as local students. The *Irish Independent* wrote that it was 'an experience far and away beyond what many people anticipated … What amazed one most was the extraordinary intelligence and supreme grace with which every movement was apparently spontaneously developed'.

The following years were spent mostly travelling between Cambridge and London, where after the first night of a production in Cambridge, Ninette would often be 'stretched out in a third-class carriage' of the milk train to get to her school on time the following morning. Aside from her teaching and choreography work she also continued dancing, performing on several occasions with Anton Dolin and with the Diaghilev Ballet in London, which brought in extra money for her repertory theatre, where she was sure that 'therein lay the future of an English Ballet Company'. Shortly after the death of Sergei Diaghilev in 1929 and the end of the Ballet Russes, an important group was formed to enhance the development of British ballet by staging productions and promoting British dancers and choreographers. Named after Marie Camargo, the famous eighteenth-century ballerina, the Camargo Society was established by Arnold Haskell, a dance critic, and Philip Richardson, editor and founder of *The Dancing Times* magazine. There were a number of artistic supporters involved, which included the conductor and composer Constant Lambert, Edwin Evans and Lydia Keynes (formerly Lopokova) on the general committee. Ninette joined Anton Dolin on the advisory committee.

A yearly subscription of two or three guineas provided the funds for the Camargo Society. Productions of original and classical ballets were performed four times a year at a West End theatre. Their first production was held at the Cambridge Theatre on 19 October 1930, where Ninette and Anton Dolin danced a *pas de deux*. The Camargo was an instant success, with productions attracting large audiences and positive reviews from the newspapers. The *Daily Mail* said, 'The whole representation had a beauty both strange and dignified – more, one would say that at times sublimity was attained'. Ninette choreographed a number of productions for the Camargo that were equally successful, including *Cephalus and Procris*, *Rout*, *La Création du Monde* and *Danse Sacrée et Danse Profane*, danced by pupils from the Academy. The Camargo Society had shown that there were sufficient talented dancers, composers, designers and choreographers in Britain to form an English ballet and that it need not be just a tradition for the continent.

The Sadler's Wells Theatre was finally reopened in January 1931; Ninette's dream of nearly five years could start to materialise. There had been very little money for the rebuilding of the theatre and the majority of the funds had come from private benefactors. Ninette had managed to source a wooden floor from a generous mother of one of her students, after Lilian had informed her that a concrete floor would have to suffice. The new Vic-Sadler's Wells Opera Ballet Company was to receive no financial assistance and to be totally self-supporting. Ninette offered her flourishing Academy as goodwill, in exchange for operating her ballet company and school at the theatre. She presented the accounts from the Academy to Sir Reginald Rowe, the Old Vic's Governor, to show that there was a sufficient turnover to finance the salary of six dancers for the next six months, who would perform in both the Old Vic and Sadler's Wells theatres. Profits from the school would be put back into the ballet company and Ninette would work unpaid as principal dancer, director and choreographer, living on the income from her teaching position at Heathfield. She sold the remainder of the lease on her dance studio and bought a small flat in Bloomsbury. She later said, 'I was virtually self-sold to the one institution for which, during nearly five years, I had worked with this one end in view.'

To attract audiences early productions had guest appearances by leading dancers, who agreed to work for minimal or no fees, such as Anton Dolin and Lydia Lopokova, which proved to be invaluable to the initial success of the company. The small ballets performed at the Old Vic were so popular that Lilian Baylis decided to present a whole evening, which sold out, with people being turned away. She repeated the programme at the Sadler's Wells, which was just as successful. The management stated in the Annual Report that it had been 'astonishingly satisfactory to discover so large and enthusiastic a public waiting for the presentation of this difficult and eclectic form of art, which has not hitherto been treated seriously in London unless it hailed from a foreign country'. The company's first full season, opened by a performance of *Job*, a ballet based on the *Book of Job* from the Bible, was a huge success, showing Ninette's expertise as a choreographer. It was the first ballet produced entirely by a British creative team and was fundamental in the development of British ballet.

The company struggled financially until around 1935, when they received a monetary boost from a sympathetic and wealthy sponsor, whose generous contribution subsidised them until they were sufficiently established. Traditional ballets were included in the repertory, with new productions added through the years. Two of Ninette's most notable works were produced in this period, *The Rake's Progress*, based on the paintings of William Hogarth, and two years later, *Checkmate*. A number of prominent artists had joined the company; Frederick Ashton had been employed as resident choreographer, Constant Lambert as musical director, and Alicia Markova, who had been under Ninette's charge in the Ballet Russes, was appointed the Company's first Prima Ballerina and was a huge attraction. When she left to start her own touring company in 1935, Ninette knew instantly who her successor would be, a sixteen year old student from the Vic-Wells Ballet School. 'Little Hookham' otherwise known as Peggy, who at their first meeting had listened to Ninette declare that 'something wonderful and beautiful had come had come into our midst' would go on to achieve international fame as Margot Fonteyn. Robert Helpmann, the young Australian dancer, had also impressed Ninette at their first meeting, with his distinctive theatrical qualities, as she remembered, 'This unknown young man impressed me with a strange sense of power; here, possibly, was an artist of infinite range …' Lilian Baylis also spotted his potential and charisma, but with just one reservation, 'I like the boy, dear, who puts too much brilliantine on his hair; do stop him, his head's rather large anyway, and it makes one keep looking at him.' To which Ninette politely pointed out that perhaps that was his intention. He would become the Company's leading male dancer, partnering Margot Fonteyn in many successful productions. On 6 July that year, Ninette married Dr Arthur Blackall Connell, a general practitioner in Barnes, south-west London, which also became their marital home. They had no children.

In November 1937, Lilian Baylis died of a heart attack. Ninette wrote, 'My gratitude towards her is something that I can never fully express … We owe her our greatest debt, for regular employment, artistic achievement and recognition could only be made possible once this selfless point of view was taken by someone who was engaged in the management of a theatre'. War was declared in September 1939 and in the same year the company was renamed the Sadler's Wells Ballet. In the spring of 1940, the British Council and the Foreign Office, sent Ninette and her Company on a cultural propaganda tour of Holland, in order to reinforce Britain's associations with neutral and allied countries. They received a warm welcome from audiences at The Hague's Royal Theatre, Hengelo, Eindhoven and Arnhem, with their performances closing under a shower of tulip petals from the roof of the theatre. But they were not long into the tour when they had to make a hasty retreat back to Britain, running from the imminent invasion of German forces, leaving behind costumes, musical scores and orchestral parts for several major ballets. Back in London, amidst the bombings and air raids, Ninette's new ballet of the summer season, *The Prospect Before Us*, performed to a full Sadler's Wells Theatre. But by September 1940, her male dancers were gradually being called up and the Sadler's Wells Theatre was taken over as a shelter for bombed-out families, although she was able to continue her school in the rehearsal room of the theatre. The Sadler's Wells Ballet had no option but to go on tour around Britain, with a limited repertoire, reduced scenery and lights, two pianos replacing the orchestra and the artists on very low salaries. Nonetheless, the tour would prove to be extremely beneficial to the company, building an audience and gaining them popularity right across the country. Ninette later said, 'It was the war that turned us from a struggling repertory theatre company into a prosperous commercial venture.'

From 1941 Ninette and her dancers were able to use the National Theatre as a base for performances, which provided a much appreciated break from touring. During this time the theatre experienced a 'boom', with escalating ticket sales, which in turn demanded more performances. Although the company was faced with food and clothing rationing, travel, accommodation and heating difficulties, the threat of overhead bombs (particularly the dreaded drone of the Vi or 'doodle-bug') and the stress of imminent air raids whilst performing, their work load increased as people of wartime Britain wanted entertainment. They toured throughout the war, playing to packed theatres and boosting the nation's morale. In a working environment, Ninette was a perfectionist, a strict disciplinarian and at times unpredictable, flying into short bursts of rage, earning her the nickname 'madam', which she accepted with good spirits, even signing it in correspondence. She also had a side that was warm, kind and selfless, and she was very concerned for the well-being of her dancers during the war years, working extremely hard on very little sleep and insufficient nourishment. She gave them glucose, which seemed to help them with their strenuous routines. 'It was taking toll of everyone's reserves and even the reserves of the youth were fully taxed.'

Shortly after the end of the Second World War in 1945 a decision was made to re-open the Royal Opera House in Covent Garden, which had served as a dance hall during the war. The Sadler's Wells Ballet, which by now was becoming something of a national institution, was invited to become the resident ballet company and to expand the school, with a second company at Sadler's Wells. Initially the governors of the company were hesitant, but Ninette knew that the move would be beneficial, 'We were the fruits of ten years pioneer work, and this decision meant that it would become possible for us to develop along lines that would not be possible, on account of its dimensions, in the Sadler's Wells Theatre.' She relocated her 'bedraggled, war-weary Company' and despite some reservations, started preparing for the opening in less than six months. 'It could be likened to a crazy nightmare, wherein I might be given Buckingham Palace, a few dusters, and told to get on with the spring cleaning.' The new revived full-length production of *The Sleeping Beauty*, with Margot Fonteyn as the princess Aurora and Robert Helpmann as Prince Florimund, was shown on 19 February 1946, in the presence of the Royal Family and the full Cabinet. Ninette recalled the hectic preparations before the rise of the stage curtain, '… the last stitches were being put into the new costumes, the final flower sewn on the fairies costumes … fifteen year old Princess Margaret's concern because someone had hinted that Margot Fonteyn's third-act costume was not yet finished!' Within three days any uncertainties were diminished when it was confirmed that every seat for every performance (seven in the week) was sold for the full month's run and when the following month's programmes of triple bills were publicised, 'the queues at the box office appeared, to my reeling senses, to be longer than ever'.

The Royal Ballet School, White Lodge, Richmond Park. (Courtesy Noriko Honda)

In the subsequent years the Sadler's Wells Ballet toured across Europe and in 1948, by invitation of the Turkish Government, Ninette founded the first Turkish National School of Ballet. This was followed by the first of many tours of America, where their opening performance in New York in 1949 was met with huge acclaim. By the mid-1950s the company had travelled to South Africa, Canada and Russia and was now an international success. In 1955 the Sadler's Wells Ballet School relocated permanently to the grand historic White Lodge in Richmond Park, Surrey and a year later the company, its sister company, and school were granted a Royal Charter and subsequently renamed The Royal Ballet, Sadler's Wells Royal Ballet and The Royal Ballet School. Later, in 1990, the Sadler's Wells Royal Ballet relocated and became the resident ballet company at the Birmingham Hippodrome Theatre, where it was changed to the Birmingham Royal Ballet and although it maintains strong connections with the Royal Ballet in London, it is now an independent company.

In 1963, Ninette retired, handing over the directorship with confidence to her 'associate director' Sir Frederick Ashton. 'Women are good for the pioneer work,' she said, 'but when it has developed to a certain point the

men must take it over.' However, she remained devoted to the school
for the next decade and worked with the Royal Ballet Benevolent Fund,
providing support and financial assistance to dancers in times of need.
She continued to attend performances by her students, watching the con-
tinuation of the work that she had started with just six dancers all those
years before and spent her hundredth birthday at White Lodge watching
a celebratory programme by the younger pupils. She was given a CBE in
1947, a DBE as Dame Ninette in 1951, was designated a Companion of
Honour in 1981 and received the definitive honour of the Order of Merit
in 1992. She also received numerous awards and honorary degrees from
several British universities and wrote three books about dance: *Invitation
to the Ballet* (1937), *Come Dance with Me* (1957) and *Step by Step* (1977).

Ninette died at the grand age of 102, at her home in Barnes, London,
on 8 March 2001, outliving her husband, Arthur Connell, by fifteen
years. Arts Minister Alan Howarth said after her passing, 'Her influence on the development of ballet in this country cannot be overstated,
and her life's work has provided a legacy that will continue to flourish
and inspire dancers and audiences alike for decades to come.'

DAME KATHLEEN LONSDALE
1903–1971

'There is a sense in which she appeared to own
the whole of crystallography in her time.'

Dorothy Crowfoot Hodgkin

Dame Kathleen Lonsdale was an early pioneer of X-ray crystallography. She achieved many firsts, including being the first woman to gain worldwide recognition in a field which, at the time, was traditionally preserved for men. In addition to her ground-breaking scientific research, she also campaigned tirelessly for prison reform and world peace, both of which were as equally important as her scientific achievements.

Kathleen Yardley was born into an impoverished family in Newbridge, County Kildare on 28 January 1903. She was the youngest of ten children, four girls and six boys, four of whom died in infancy. She once wrote, 'Perhaps for my sake, it was as well that there was no testimony against a high birth rate in those days'. Her father, Harry Frederick Yardley, had been a regimental sergeant major in the British Army and had fought in the Boer War. On his return to Ireland he became a postmaster at Newbridge post office, managing a staff of six, sorting mail for the Black and Tans, the former British soldiers recruited to assist the Royal Irish Constabulary (RIC) during the Irish War of Independence. He had an inquisitive mind and was a keen reader of encyclopaedias, having a widespread interest in

Kathleen Lonsdale. (Courtesy of Smithsonian Institution Archives - image #SIA 2008 – 5424)

virtually any subject. His collection of books, which he had mostly picked up from junk stalls, covered topics ranging from the antiquities of Peru to the birds of Western Australia. Kathleen later wrote, 'I think that it was from him that I inherited my passion for facts'.

Harry's drinking problem added to the family's poverty and eventually, in 1908, Kathleen's Scottish mother, Jessie Cameron left Ireland and took her children to Seven Kings, Essex in England. Jessie was of a strict Baptist faith and later Kathleen recalled her 'very faint' memories of her early childhood in Ireland, attending the Sunday morning service in the Church of Ireland in Newbridge and the Methodist Sunday school in the afternoon. Her father's visits to Essex were infrequent and she later said after his death, 'I think he was fond of us and did not know how to show it. I wish that I could have been fonder of him.'

From 1908 to 1914 Kathleen attended Downshall Elementary School and, after winning a scholarship, went on to the County High School for Girls in Ilford, where she proved to be a very conscientious and intelligent student, excelling in all her subjects, especially mathematics and science. She was the only girl at the time to attend classes in physics, chemistry and higher mathematics at the High School for Boys, as her school did not offer these subjects. After achieving distinctions in six subjects in the Cambridge Senior Examination she was awarded a County Major Scholarship and, at only 16, she was allowed to enter Bedford College for Women, part of the University of London. The local education authority wanted her to stay on at school to try for Cambridge University and offered to increase her county scholarship, but Kathleen was keen to start university as soon as possible.

Kathleen's eldest brother, Fred, had also won a scholarship from school, but due to the family's financial difficulties, he had to forgo any further education and, along with his other four older siblings, had to work to help support the family. However, he did manage to achieve a successful career as one of the first wireless operators in 1910, and receiving the last distress signals from the *Titanic* in 1912. He also founded one of the first schools of wireless telegraphy in the north of England.

Not wanting to pursue a career in teaching, which Kathleen felt was her only option as a mathematician, she decided to switch to physics at the end of her first year, ignoring the advice of her old headmistress, who believed that she would not be able to compete in a 'man's field' such as physics. However, her decision was vindicated, when in 1922, she came top in the University of London honours BSc examination, achieving the highest marks in ten years. Her success was noted by one of her examiners, Professor William Henry Bragg, the eminent physicist and pioneer of X-ray diffraction. W.H. Bragg and his son, Sir William Lawrence Bragg, derived Bragg's Law, the fundamental law of X-ray crystallography, to explain the connection between an X-ray light shooting into and its reflection off of a crystal surface. Together they were awarded the Nobel Prize for physics in 1915. Kathleen readily accepted an invitation from W.H. Bragg to join his research team at University College London, with a grant of £180 a year, which helped enormously with the family's financial outgoings.

Kathleen was greatly encouraged by W.H. Bragg, her mentor, who would be a continual support in her career for many years. She later wrote, 'He inspired me with his own love of pure science and with his enthusiastic spirit of enquiry and at the same time left me entirely free to follow my own line of research'. Following the professor's advice, she chose to work on solving the structure of simple organic crystals and, further inspired after reading Professor Hilton's 1903 book on mathematical crystallography, Kathleen worked with fellow student W.T. Astbury, calculating tables of x-ray patterns in common crystals. They presented their momentous paper, 'Tabulated data for the examination of the 230 space-groups by homogenous X-rays' to the Royal Society, which was published in 1924, and was the first table of space-groups.

In 1923, Kathleen moved with W.H. Bragg to the prestigious Royal Institution in London, where she joined his newly appointed international team of twelve young researchers. Female scientists were scarce as they were not widely accepted at the time and initially Kathleen was one of three women in the group, but due to W.H. Bragg's encouragement, in the following years the numbers increased significantly. Both he and his son, W.L. Bragg, created a peaceful, friendly, non-competitive environment which, combined with their congenial nature, was fundamental in attracting women to the field of crystallography. Many years later, Anne Sayre, journalist and wife of the pioneer crystallographer, David Sayre, wrote:

> I have often wondered how much the Braggs were responsible for the unaggressive low-key friendly atmosphere that long prevailed in the field (and no longer seems to very much). Somehow the first and second and a few of the third generation crystallographers consistently conveyed an impression of working for pleasure, for the sheer joy of it – the idea of competition didn't seem to emerge very strongly until the 1960s or so. Uncompetitive societies tend to be good for women.

Kathleen completed her master's degree in 1924, during which time she assembled a set of 230 space-group tables, mathematical descriptions of the crystal symmetries that became essential tools for crystallographers. Whilst working for her PhD she met fellow engineering research student, Thomas Lonsdale, and they married in 1927. He was the son of James Jackson Lonsdale, senior science master at the Sloane School in Chelsea, who had also worked on researching gaseous ions. Chemistry Nobel Laureate, Dorothy M.C. Hodgkin, her friend and colleague, recalled Thomas' proposal to Kathleen in the *Biographical Memoirs of Fellows of the Royal Society*, 'He proposed to her by letter and when he received her reply accepting him, he was so very happy he dried his face on a clean shirt hanging up instead of a towel'. The couple moved to Leeds, where Thomas found employment as an assistant with the Silk Research Association, centred in the Textile Department of the University of Leeds. Kathleen was prepared to forgo her scientific research and settle into the conventional domestic life that was expected of a married woman, but Thomas encouraged and supported her, insisting that 'he had not married to get a free housekeeper'. Unlike most husbands of that time, Thomas willingly shared the domestic chores with Kathleen, which gave them both more time to continue their scientific studies at home. Thomas performed experiments for his PhD on an apparatus he had set up in the kitchen, while Kathleen did her mathematical calculations, which she would have done by hand, using logarithm tables.

Women who pursued a scientific career usually remained single, but if they chose to marry they were expected to leave the laboratory and settle into a domestic life. Although she received full support from her husband, Kathleen's decision to combine marriage with her scientific career would be met with criticism, particularly from her colleagues. Sir Alfred Yarrow, founder of the Yarrow shipbuilding dynasty, believed that high intellect was inherited from the mother's side, but agreed with many others that women should not become scientists, as invariably they would leave the laboratory upon marriage. Allegedly Kathleen retorted, 'Where are your intelligent mothers to come from, if only those with no profession are allowed to marry?' She was more than aware of the difficulties that married women faced in pursuing a scientific career and in later years she wrote in one of her works entitled, 'Women in Science – Why so Few?,' her own recommendations:

> For a woman, and especially a married woman with children, to become a first class scientist she must first of all choose, or have chosen, the right husband. He must recognise her problems and be willing to share them. If he is really domesticated, so much the better. Then, she must be a good organiser and be pretty ruthless in keeping to her schedule, no matter if the heavens fall. She must be able to do with very little sleep, because her working day will be at least twice as long as the average trade unionist … She must be willing to accept additional responsibility, even if she feels she has more than enough. But above all she must learn to concentrate in any available moment and not require ideal conditions in which to do so.

Through the arrangement of Professor Whiddington, who had previously worked on X-rays with W.H. Bragg, Kathleen gained a part-time demonstratorship in Leeds University, where she would begin her most important and successful pioneering research and become one of Britain's most prominent crystallographers, gaining international recognition. She received a grant from the Royal Society for £150, with which she was able to buy a new ionisation spectrometer and electroscope, and studied the crystals of hexamethylbenzene, given to her by the British chemist, Sir C.K. Ingold from the Chemistry Department. Since Auguste Kekulé, the prominent German chemist, had suggested in 1865 that benzene had a six-member ring structure, chemists had argued as to whether the ring was planar or puckered. As benzene was a liquid at room temperature, Kathleen used hexamethylbenzene, a solid that could be obtained in large single crystals, and with her spectrometer and some X-ray photographs from the Royal Institution, she proved that the benzene ring was both flat and hexagonal in shape. It was the first experimental proof and an enormous breakthrough in organic chemistry. She was also the first scientist to use Fourier analysis, a type of mathematical analysis, to demonstrate the structure of hexachlorobenzene, equally a difficult structure to analyse. She published her account in the *Proceedings of the Royal Society of London* in 1929, which finally resolved the long-standing debate between crystallographers and organic chemists about the structure of the benzene ring. Sir Ingold said of her publication, 'One paper like this brings more certainty into organic chemistry than generations of activity by us professionals.'

Shortly after the birth of their first child Jane in 1929 the family returned to London, where Thomas obtained work at the Testing Station of the Ministry of Transport. Their second child Nancy was born in 1931, followed by Stephen in 1934. It is clearly apparent that Kathleen's passion and enthusiasm for her work never wavered, as she later wrote, 'My work was fun. I often ran the last few yards to the laboratory. Later on I took my mathematical calculations with me to the nursing homes where my babies were born; it was exciting to find out new facts'. Whilst she was at home with her children she compiled crystallographic tables to assist scientists in obtaining chemical structures

from X-ray photographs more easily. As she had no access to a laboratory she used reference books and old X-ray photographs, and used her
mathematical skills to work the calculations by hand, progressing on to
a second-hand typewriter to type the long formulas. These tables were
to be a major and invaluable contribution to her field of work. She later
said of this period of her life, 'I was not idle while I had my three children, far from it. It gave me the opportunity of standing back, as it were,
and looking at my work. And I came back with new ideas.' Through
recommendation from the influential W.H. Bragg, she received a grant
of £50 from the managers of the Royal Institution to employ daily help.
In 1931 Kathleen received a letter from W.H. Bragg in which he eagerly
wrote: 'A piece of good news! Sir Robert Mond is giving me £200 with
which you are to get assistance at home to enable you to come and work
here. Can you come and see me soon?' She was able to return to her
research work with W.H. Bragg at the Royal Institution, where she
stayed for a further fifteen years, continuing after his death in 1942 with
his successor Sir Henry Hallett Dale. She was awarded the DSc by
University College, London in 1936.

By the onset of the Second World War, Kathleen and Thomas, who
were both committed pacifists, had become increasingly convinced by
the Quakers Peace Testimony, which opposed war and violence in any
form, and in 1935 they joined the Religious Society of Friends. Kathleen
had started questioning the validation of war during her childhood
in the First World War, when she and her siblings watched the bombs
being dropped from the 'suicidal gas-filled Zeppelins' near their home
in London. She later recalled, 'We sometimes watched them being shot
down in flames and my mother cried, because she had read that some of
the German crews were boys of sixteen. Somehow this seemed to have
very little connection with the science I was learning, but it may have had
something to do with my own growing feeling that war was utterly wrong.'
This experience, followed by her later charitable work with the Society of
Friends during the Depression and providing shelter for German refugees
in the Lonsdale's home, deepened her belief that war was unjustified.

During the Second World War it was mandatory for women to register for fire-watching duties against incendiary bombs from the enemy

planes. As Kathleen's children were under the age of fourteen she was technically exempt from all war duties, but was required to register for civil defence duties. As a conscientious objector, she refused to register and was consequently summoned, but refused to pay the £2 fine for non-registration and so spent a month in Holloway Prison in 1943.

According to Dorothy Hodgkin, one of Kathleen's minor concerns prior to her entering prison was, 'Do the police come for one or do I just have to go to prison myself?' Although she did find prison horrendous, Kathleen later wrote that she was so frightened beforehand that prison itself came as something of an anti-climax. In her prison memoirs, written after her release, she described the dreadful conditions and deprivations of prison life, particularly those affecting the personal hygiene of the prisoners. She wrote of the inadequate and filthy toilet facilities, where healthy and diseased prisoners were forced to share toilets which were often out of order. 'The stench from the W.C.s in the mornings, when everyone was emptying 14½ hours' slops, and many women were discarding soiled sanitary towels into and over an uncovered pail, was often almost unbearable', she wrote. Wartime shortages meant that necessities needed for daily hygiene, such as soap and hot water for baths were a scarce commodity. The prisoners' monthly allowance of one small piece of soap for their personal use and cleaning their cell rarely lasted and the clothes had to be boiled without using the soap. Kathleen wrote, 'It was quite obvious that the underwear and nightgown with which I was supplied had never seen the soap: they were stained from the previous wearer's menstruation and streaked with the dirt of ages'.

Initially Kathleen's work included carrying heavy containers of cocoa and coal scuttles up three flights of stairs, but after collapsing one day she was given lighter work in the prison officer's quarters, cleaning the baths, sinks and toilets. Following a request from Sir Henry Dale, she was permitted to have scientific papers and instruments sent in from the head laboratory technician at the Royal Institution, to work with in her cell in the evenings. She became friendly with some of the other inmates and listened intently during their conversations about their criminal lives. On leaving Holloway her experience and observations of prison life led her to become involved in penal reform, starting with a letter to the Governor, Dr Matheson. After thanking him for allowing her to have her papers in her cell, with which she accomplished 'about seven hours each day of really concentrated scientific work', she proposed ways in which the hygiene and prisoners' lives could be improved. She continued to support these proposals after the war, when in 1949 she became a member of the Board of Visitors, Aylesbury Prison for Women and Borstal Institution for Girls, and also vice-chairman of the Board of Visitors of a borstal in Essex. She attended regular meetings to discuss the welfare and the misfortunes of the prisoners, as she conveyed in a letter to a fellow prison visitor, Lady Pitman, 'The usual problems of broken homes, husbands or boyfriends in prison, babies in care, drugs or neurotic troubles.' Her husband Thomas later said, 'Going to prison was the single most formative experience in her career.'

In the same year, Kathleen was invited to lecture at the Dublin Institute for Advanced Studies Summer School, chaired by Austrian Nobel physicist, Erwin Schrödinger and attended by the Taoiseach, Eamon de Valera. This was the start of many future trips abroad, where Kathleen attended numerous scientific conferences in different countries around the world, lecturing mainly on crystallography and the ethics of science, often combining it with her work for the Society of Friends. She was extremely popular in Japan, where she was greeted with a mass of flowers which filled the rooms in the small hotel where she stayed. In Russia she visited a prison near Moscow which housed 885 men and 15 women in temporary huts. Kathleen asked the prison governor specific questions concerning the prison's organization, which led to her interpreter being asked, 'How is it that such a nice lady knows so much about prisons?' Although the interpreter knew how, he chose to tell them that Kathleen was an 'important British prison official'. She recorded in a notebook her observations during her visits to different laboratories. During one particular visit to China, she was asked, 'How far behind the West are we in our technology?' to which Kathleen tactfully replied, 'About twenty years.' After much laughter they said, 'Splendid, we have caught up ten years in one year. Professor Bernal was here last year and he told us we were thirty years behind.' After having difficulty obtaining

a visa to visit the United States, she was told by one Embassy official,
'You've been to the three most difficult places: Russia, China and gaol.'

On 17 May 1945 Kathleen and microbiologist Marjory Stevenson
were the first two women to be elected as Fellows of the Royal Society
in London. Established by a group of twelve scientists, including
Christopher Wren, in 1660 at Gresham College, this prestigious institution is the oldest in the world still in existence and election to fellowship
is considered the highest accolade a scientist can achieve. In 1946, at the
age of forty-three and after many years of living on grants and fellow-
ships, Kathleen finally gained her first permanent academic position as
Reader (associate professor) in Crystallography at University College,
London and in 1949 she was the first woman to be appointed as Professor
of Chemistry and Head of the Crystallography Department. By now she
was editor-in-chief of the *International X-ray Tables* and she published
her popular textbook *Crystals and X-rays*. She established her own international research school in the College, introducing two new courses in
crystallography for undergraduates and graduates, where the research
was varied and included methonium compounds, urinary calculi and
synthetic diamonds. According to Dorothy Hodgkin, many of Kathleen's
students found her lectures difficult to understand:

> She was a little impatient with those who could not follow her line of
> thought, forgetting perhaps that, though she might feel herself inad-
> equately trained, her mathematical background was much more solid than
> that of most chemistry students. At the same time she would often spend
> a great deal of her own time guiding beginners through the critical stages
> of research; and her general lectures, on many occasions, were a joy to
> listen to, easy to follow and brightened by stories and illustrations.

It was during this time that Kathleen began working with science
student Judith Grenville-Wells (later Milledge). She had arrived from
South Africa to study diamonds with Kathleen for her PhD. Initially
she assisted in some of the secretarial work on the *International X-ray
Tables* in exchange for lodgings at the Lonsdale's, but gradually she
became a permanent loyal companion and scientific colleague on almost

all of Kathleen's scientific work. Their studies included natural and arti-
ficial diamonds, minerals at high temperatures and high pressures and
the process of solid state reactions. Judith collaborated with Kathleen
on her publications and carried on much of her work after her retirement, eventually becoming her literary executor after her death. In 1966,
a rare hexagonal form of diamond was named Lonsdaleite in honour of
Kathleen's exploratory work on the structure of diamonds. In response
Kathleen wrote, 'It makes me feel both proud and rather humble that it
shall be called lonsdaleite. Certainly the name seems appropriate since
the mineral only occurs in very small quantities (perhaps rare would be
too flattering) and it is generally rather mixed up!'

Following the atomic bombings in the final stages of the Second
World War Kathleen and Thomas worked together in a relentless campaign to promote world peace, which she would uphold throughout
her life. She wrote numerous articles and at the annual meeting of the
British Quakers in 1953 she delivered the Swarthmore Lecture under
the title, *Removing the Causes of War*. She also attended several Pugwash
Conferences on World Affairs and became vice-president of the newly
formed British Atomic Scientists Association and President of the
Women's International League for Peace and Freedom. At a conference
on 'The biological hazards of atomic energy' in 1950 her paper, entitled
'The Scientist's Responsibility as a Citizen', raised the issue of safety and
protection measures for the uranium miners suffering from the biological effects of radiation. In her investigations she had found that there
were extremely high numbers of deaths, particularly from lung cancer,
and very few safety procedures. Although it would be several more years
before official action was taken in controlling the exposure of workers
to radiation, Kathleen's talk had set the wheels in motion. She strongly
opposed nuclear weapons, and in 1956, in response to the extensive
nuclear testing in Russia, America and Great Britain, she wrote her book,
Is Peace Possible?, in just six weeks. The book examined the connection
between world peace and world population needs, as seen through her
personal experience of being the youngest of ten children. In the fore-
word she stated:

When the news of the dropping of the first atomic bomb on Hiroshima appeared in the British newspapers, an actress friend of mine, not a pacifist, came to me in a fury and said, 'Do you see what you scientists have done now?' This is an attempt to answer that question. It is written in a personal way because I feel a sense of corporate guilt and responsibility that scientific knowledge should have been so misused. It includes an even more limited attempt to suggest what we, the scientists, and all those who desire a world in which our grandchildren can grow up happily, ought to be doing.

In the same year, just a day after the first of her ten grandchildren was born, she was given the title Dame Commander of the Order of the British Empire. Dorothy Hodgkin described Kathleen as 'short, with very fuzzy hair usually cut for her at home by Thomas. She had rather little time or money to spend on clothes, but she was fond of lovely things and liked to be nicely dressed for occasions; she made herself a small hat of a piece of lace, some coloured cardboard and nine-pence worth of ribbons from a little wool shop near her home, for her investiture at Buckingham Palace'. Dorothy also recalled on one occasion, following one of her television appearances, Kathleen's secretary playfully saying to her, 'You look such a sweet, gentle, elderly grandmother, but you are a fraud; you are really a very tough character.' Kathleen replied, 'Yes, I know it is a gimmick, but it is one I like.'

In the early 1960s Kathleen began an extensive study of kidney, bladder and gallstones. Dr D.A. Andersen, an urologist and chief medical officer with the Salvation Army, consulted Kathleen on the analysis of a collection of human stones which he had brought back from his travels abroad. Through his observations he had found that they were common among children from underdeveloped countries and were the cause of many deaths. Kathleen received a grant from the Medical Research Council and the help of a crystallographer, Dr June Sutor. By the late 1960s they had studied over a thousand stones, including those preserved in museums. Kathleen also enjoyed showing an x-ray diffraction photograph of Napoleon III's bladder stone.

In 1965 Thomas retired and they moved to Bexhill-on-Sea, where Kathleen travelled five hours a day to work until her own retirement three years later, upon which she was given the honorary title of Professor Emeritus, which enabled her to continue her scientific and educational work. She also remained politically active and Thomas, who had always been extremely supportive of his wife's career and causes, helped her with the huge amount of correspondence regarding peace and prison reforms which had been sent to her from all over the world. In 1966 she was elected as the first female president of the International Union of Crystallography, and a year later, the first female president of the British Association for the Advancement of Science, promoting science education for young people. 'Never refuse an opportunity to speak at schools,' she noted to herself. The physicist, microbiologist and crystallographer, Michael Rossmann, claims that his interest in crystallography stemmed from hearing Kathleen speak at his school. She received honorary degrees from several universities including Oxford, Bath, Leeds, Manchester, Leicester and Wales.

Kathleen had been feeling ill for a while, and at first it was thought that she had contracted an illness from her travels abroad, but sadly she was diagnosed with cancer of the bone marrow. Despite being extremely ill she was determined to complete her book on *Human Stones* and during the last weeks of her life, which were spent in hospital, the nurses would find her working in bed for up to thirteen hours a day. She was allowed home briefly to celebrate Thomas' seventieth birthday, but died in hospital shortly after on 1 April 1971.

Ten years after her death the chemistry building at University College, London was renamed the Kathleen Lonsdale building in her honour, and also, in 1998, another building at the University of Limerick in Ireland. She is remembered in her native County Kildare at the National University of Ireland in Maynooth, where the annual Lonsdale Prize in Chemistry is awarded to the student who achieves the highest results in the final exams for the science single honours (chemistry) degree.

In his tribute to Kathleen following her death, Sir William L. Bragg wrote:

Others have written about Dame Kathleen Lonsdale's scientific achievements; I wish to add a tribute to her as a person. She was one of the most thorough, high-principled, and courageous people I have known. We who work in the field of X-ray analysis, cannot be too grateful for all she did to help us. Her early collaboration with Astbury in preparing an exhaustive survey of space groups was typical. The set of formulae for structure analysts, and the work on International Tables for the union, were models of accuracy and ordered arrangement. No trouble was too great for her, and it was all done disinterestedly for the general good, much of it behind the scenes and in helping others.

With reference to her book he wrote:

The last letter I had from her was on 24th March, only a week before her death. She wrote cheerfully and competently about the plans for it; one could never had guessed from her letters how seriously ill she was. Talking of her good progress she said, 'So the postal strike was not wasted on me, nor the enforced "leisure" in hospital!'

PICTURE CREDITS

My thanks goes to Guy Warner, Donna and Mary at Enniscorthy Castle, Barry Houlihan, the Langford family, Vivienne Keely, Harriet Wheelock, Aileen Ivory, Clare Boulton and Byron Smith.

BIBLIOGRAPHY

All quotations within the chapters are from the following material:

Dr James Miranda Barry

Cook, Bernard A. (ed.), *Women and War: A Historical Encyclopedia from Antiquity to the Present, Volume One* (ABC-CLIO Inc.; California, 2006) ISBN-1-85109-770-8

Depuis, Nicola, *Mná Na hÉireann*: Women who shaped Ireland (Mercier Press; Cork, 2009) ISBN-978-1-85635-645-9

Haines, Catherine M.C., *International Women in Science: A Biographical Dictionary to 1950* (ABC-CLIO Inc.; California, 2001) ISBN-1-57607-090-5

Holmes, Rachel, *Scanty Particulars: The Life of Dr James Barry* (Penguin Books Ltd; London, 2002) ISBN-0-670-89099-5

Laver, James, *Costume and Fashion: A Concise History* (Thames and Hudson Ltd; London, 1995) ISBN-0-500-20266-4

Robson, Pamela, *Wild Women: History's Female Rebels, Radicals and Revolutionaries* (Murdoch Books Pty Ltd; Australia, 2011) ISBN-9781741966329

Rose, June, *The Perfect Gentleman: The Remarkable Life of Dr James Miranda Barry, the Woman Who Served as an Officer in the British Army from 1813 to 1859* (Hutchinson & Co. Ltd; London, 1977) ISBN-0-09-126840-0

Margaret Louisa Aylward

Bourke, Angela (ed.), *The Field Day Anthology of Irish Writing Vol V: Irish Women's Writing and Traditions* (Cork University Press; Ireland, 2002) ISBN-0-8147-9907-8

Cullen, Mary and Luddy, Maria (eds), *Women, Power and Consciousness in 19th Century Ireland* (Attic Press; Dublin, 1995) ISBN-1-85594-0-787

Gibbons, Margaret, *The Life of Margaret Aylward, Foundress of the Sisters of the Holy Faith* (Sands & Co.; London, 1928)

Luddy, Maria, *Women and Philanthropy in Nineteenth-Century Ireland* (Cambridge University Press; Cambridge, 1995) ISBN-978-0-521-47433-7

Preston, Margaret H., *Charitable Words: Women, Philanthropy, and the Language of Charity in Nineteenth-Century Dublin* (Praeger Publishers; Westport, 2004) ISBN-0-275-97930-X

Prunty, Jacinta, *Margaret Aylward, 1810-1889, Lady of Charity, Sister of Faith* (Four Courts Press; Dublin, 1999) ISBN-978-1-85182-438-0

PAPERS

Brady, Donald, *Margaret Louisa Aylward 1810-1889* (Waterford County Council; Waterford, 28 September 2009)

Curran, Eugene C.M., 'Margaret Aylward and the Sisters of the Holy Faith – Part II', *Colloque: Journal of the Irish Province of the Congregation of the Mission*, No.39 (Spring 1999)

WEBSITES

www.holyfaithsisters.org/heritage

JOANNA BRIDGEMAN

Bolster, Evelyn, *The Sisters of Mercy in the Crimean War* (Mercier Press; Cork, 1964)

Callista, Roy, Sister, Jones, Dorothy A. (eds), *Nursing Knowledge Development and Clinical Practice: Opportunities and Directions* (Springer Publishing Co.; New York, 2007) ISBN-0-8261-0299-9

Dolan, Josephine A., Fitzpatrick Louise M., Herrmann, Eleanor K., *Nursing in Society: A Historical Perspective* (Philadelphia; W.B. Saunders Co., 1983) ISBN-0-7216-3135-5

Fealy, Gerard M. (ed.), *Care to Remember: Nursing and Midwifery in Ireland* (Mercier Press; Cork, 2005) ISBN-185635-456-3

Fealy, Gerard M., *A History of Apprenticeship Nursing Training in Ireland* (Taylor & Francis e-Library, 2006) ISBN-0-203-00795-6

Hayes, Alan, Urquhart, Diane (eds), *Irish Women's History Reader* (Irish Academic Press; Dublin, 2004) ISBN-0-7165-2702-2

Luddy, Maria (ed.), *The Crimean Journals of the Sisters of Mercy, 1854-56* (Four Courts Press; Dublin, 2004) ISBN-1851827560

Murphy, Denis G., *They Did Not Pass By; The Story of the Early Pioneers of Nursing* (Longman's Green and Co. Ltd; London, 1956)

Nelson, Sioban and Rafferty, Anne Marie (eds), *Notes on Nightingale: The Influence and Legacy of a Nursing Icon* (Cornell University Press; United States, 2010) ISBN-978-0-8014-4906-2

Nightingale, Florence, *Letters from the Crimea* (Mandolin; Manchester, 1997) ISBN-1-901341-02-X

Ó Cléirigh, Nellie, *Hardship & Hard Living: Irish Women's Lives 1808-1923*
   (Portobello Press; Dublin, 2003) ISBN-0-9519249-1-5

Russell, William Howard, *The Crimean War: As Seen By Those Who Reported It*
   (Louisiana State University Press, 2009) ISBN-0807134457

Sullivan, Mary C. (ed.), *The Friendship of Florence Nightingale and Mary
   Clare Moore* (University of Pennsylvania Press; Philadelphia, 1999)
   ISBN-0-8122-3489-8

Taylor, Fanny, *Eastern Hospitals and English Nurses: The Narrative of Twelve
   Months' Experience in the Hospitals of Koulali and Scutari* (Hurst and Blackett;
   London, 1856)

Wintle, J.W., *The Story of Florence Nightingale: The Heroine of the Crimea*
   (The Sunday School Union; London, 1913)

Woodham Smith, Cecil, *Florence Nightingale* (Constable and Co. Ltd; London,
   1950)

WEBSITES

www.victorianweb.org/history/crimea/florrie.html
www.spartacus.schoolnet.co.uk/REnightingale.htn

FRANCES POWER COBBE

Cain, Barbara, *Victorian Feminists* (Oxford University Press; Oxford, 1992)
   ISBN-0-19-820170-2

Cullen, Mary and Luddy, Maria, *Women, Power and Consciousness in 19th Century
   Ireland* (Attic Press; Dublin, 1995) ISBN-1-85594-0-787

Driver, Felix, *Power and Pauperism: The Workhouse System 1834-1884*
   (Cambridge University Press; Cambridge, 1993) ISBN-0-521-38151-7

Hamilton, Susan (ed.), *Animal Welfare and Anti-Vivisection 1870-1910: Nineteenth
   Century Woman's Mission* (Routledge; London, 2004) ISBN-0-415-32142-5

Jeffreys, Sheila (ed.), *The Sexuality Debate* (Routledge; Oxon, 2001)
   ISBN-978-0-415-25691-9

Mcdonald, Lynn (ed.), *Women Theorists on Society and Politics* (Wilfrid Laurier
   University Press; Canada, 1998) ISBN-0-88920-290-7

Mitchell, Sally, *Frances Power Cobbe: Victorian Feminist, Journalist, Reformer*
   (University of Virginia Press, 2004) ISBN-0-8139-2271-2

Power Cobbe, Frances, *Criminals, Idiots, Women and Minors* (A. Ireland and Co.;
   Manchester, 1869)

Power Cobbe, Frances, *Essays on the Pursuits of Women* (Emily Faithfull; London, 1963)

Power Cobbe, Frances, *Life of Frances Power Cobbe: As Told by Herself* (Swan
   Sonnenschein; London, 1904)

Williamson, Lori, *Power and Protest: Frances Power Cobbe and Victorian Society*
   (River Oram Press; London, 2005) ISBN-1-85489-100-6

NEWSPAPERS

Guardian, 9 March 2001
Spectator, 11 May 1878

ANNE JELLICOE

Atkinson, Norman, *Irish Education; A History of Educational Institutions* (Allen Figgis; Dublin, 1969)

Cullen, Mary and Luddy, Maria (eds), *Women, Power and Consciousness in 19th Century Ireland* (Attic Press; Dublin, 1995) ISBN-1-85594-0-797

FAS Training Unit and Mountmellick Development Association, *The Quakers of Mountmellick: A Short History of the Religious Society of Friends in the Town of Mountmellick, 1630–1900* (1994) ISBN-0-86335-008-9

Harford, Judith and Rush, Claire (eds), *Have Women Made a Difference? Women in Irish Universities, 1850–2010* (Peter Lang AG; Switzerland, 2010) ISBN-978-3-0343-0116-9

Harrison, Richard S., *A Biographical Dictionary of Irish Quakers* (Four Courts Press; Dublin, 1997) ISBN-1-85182-304-2

Hastings, George Woodyatt (ed.), *Transactions of the National Association for the Promotion of Social Science* (Longmans, Green, Reader and Dyer; London, 1868)

Luddy, Maria, *Women in Ireland 1800–1918, A Documentary History* (Cork University Press; Cork, 1995) ISBN-1-85918-037-X

Mulvihill, Mary (eds), *Lab Coats and Lace* (WITS (Women in Technology and Science); Dublin, 2009) ISBN-978-0-9531953-1-2

O' Hógartaigh, Margaret, *Quiet Revolutionaries; Irish Women in Education, Medicine and Sport, 1861–1964* (The History Press Ireland; Dublin, 2011) ISBN-978-1-84588-696-7

Raftery, Deirdre and Parkes, Susan M., *Female Education in Ireland 1700–1900, Minerva or Madonna* (Irish Academic Press; Dublin, 2007) ISBN-978-0-7165-2650-6

Wigham, Maurice J., *The Irish Quakers: A Short History of the Religious Society of Friends in Ireland* (Historical Committee of the Religious Society of Friends; Dublin, 1992) ISBN-0-9519870-0-3

WEBSITES

www.iol.ie/~rjtechne/tyndall/tyndall_books/prometheus/ch19/ch19v.htm

ANNA MARIA HASLAM

Crawford, Elizabeth, *The Women's Suffrage Movement in Britain and Ireland: A Regional Survey* (Routledge; Oxon, 2006) ISBN-0-415-38332-3

Cullen, Mary and Luddy, Maria, *Women, Power and Consciousness in 19th Century Ireland* (Attic Press; Dublin, 1995) ISBN-1-85594-0-787

Ó Céirin, Kit & Cyril, *Women of Ireland, A Biographic Dictionary* (Tír Eolas; County Galway, 1996) ISBN-1-873821-06-9

Harrison, Richard S., A *Biographical Dictionary of Irish Quakers* (Four Courts Press; Dublin, 1997) ISBN-1-85182-304-2

Hayes, Alan and Urquhart, Diane (eds), *The Irish Woman's History Reader* (Routledge; London, 2001) ISBN-0-415-19913-1

Luddy, Maria, *Women in Ireland 1800-1918: A Documentary History* (Cork University Press; Cork, 1995) ISBN-1-85918-037-X

Quinlan, Carmel, *Genteel Revolutionaries* (Cork University Press; County Cork, 2002) ISBN-1-85918-328-X

Rappaport, Helen, *Encyclopaedia of Women Social Reformers, Volume 1* (ABC-CLIO Inc.; California, 2001) ISBN-1-57607-101-4

ELLEN (NELLIE) CASHMAN

Chaput, Don, *Nellie Cashman and the North American Mining Frontier* (Westernlore Press; Arizona, 1995) ISBN-0-87026-093-6

Clum, John P., *Nellie Cashman, The Angel of Tombstone* (The Arizona Historical Review; United States, 1931)

Kales, David, *The Boston Harbor Islands: A History of an Urban Wilderness* (The History Press; Charleston, 2007) ISBN-978-1-59629-290-1

Ledbetter, Suzann, *Nellie Cashman – Prospector and Trailblazer* (Texas Western Press; United States, 1993) ISBN-0-87404 194-5

Mayer, Melanie J., *Klondike Women: True Tales of the 1897-1898 Gold Rush* (Swallow Press/Ohio University Press; United States, 1989) ISBN-0-8040-0927-9

Murphy, Claire Rudolf and Haigh, Jane G., *Gold Rush Women* (Alaska Northwest Books; Portland, 1997) ISBN-0-88240-484-9

NEWSPAPERS

Tombstone Epitaph, 25 October 1891

Tombstone Prospector, 16 September 1897

Mohave County Miner, 1 January 1898

The Western Liberal, 22 February 1899

Bisbee Daily Review, 25 September 1908

Daily Colonist, 15 February 1898, 11 January 1925

Arizona State Miner (Wickenburg), 24 January 1925

ALEEN CUST

Ford, Connie M., *Aleen Cust Veterinary Surgeon: Britain's First Woman Vet* (Biopress Ltd, Bristol, 1990) ISBN-0-948737-11-5

Haines, Catharine M. C., *International Women in Science: A Biographical Dictionary to 1950* (ABC-CLIO Inc.; California, 2001) ISBN-1-57607-090-5

Hunter, Pamela, *Veterinary Medicine: A Guide to Historical Sources* (Ashgate
    Publishing Ltd; Hampshire, 2004) ISBN-0-7546-4053-1
McEldowney, John, Grant, Wyn and Medley, Graham, *The Regulation of Animal Health
    and Welfare: Science, Law and Policy* (Routledge; Oxon, 2013) ISBN-978-0-415-50474-4

PAPERS

Anon, 'The First Woman Veterinary Surgeon', *British Medical Journal*, Vol.2.
    No.3234 (23 December 1922), p.1236

WEBSITES

www.fortunatusfamilia.com.au
www.ymca.net/history/founding.html
www.worldwar1.com/dbc/ymca.htm

MARGARET MARY EDITH (MAY) TENNANT

Blackburn, Sheila, *A Fair Day's Wage for a Fair Day's Work? Sweated Labour and
    the Origins of Minimum Wage Legislation in Britain* (Ashgate Publishing Ltd;
    Hampshire, 2007) ISBN 978-0-7546-3264-1
Drake, Barbara, *Women in Trade Unions: A Classic Account of Women and Trade
    Unionism* (Virago Press Ltd; London, 1984) ISBN-0-86068-405-9
Drake McFeely, Mary, *Lady Inspectors, The Campaign for a Better Workplace,
    1893-1921* (University of Georgia Press; Georgia, 1991) ISBN-0-8203-1391-2
Harrison, Barbara, *Not Only the Dangerous Trades: Women's Work and Health in
    Britain, 1880-1914* (Taylor & Francis e-Library, 2005) ISBN-0-203-99307-1
Hart, Vivien, *Bound by Our Constitution: Women, Workers and the Minimum Wage*
    (Princeton University Press; New Jersey, 1994) ISBN 1-4008-0351-9
Israel, Kali, *Name and Stories: Emilia Dilke and Victorian Culture* (Oxford
    University Press Inc.; New York, 1999) ISBN-0-19-512275-5
Jones, Helen, *Women in British Public Life, 1914-50, Gender, Power and Social Policy*
    (Pearson Education Ltd, 2000) ISBN-0-582-27731
Markham, Violet, *May Tennant, A Portrait* (The Falcon Press; London, 1949)
Soames, Mary (ed.), *Winston and Clementine: The Personal Letters of the Churchills*
    (Houghton Mifflin Company; New York, 1998) ISBN-0-395-96319-2
Soldon, Norbert C., *Women in British Trade Unions 1874-1976* (Gill and
    Macmillan Ltd; Dublin, 1978) ISBN-0-8476-6056-7

NEWSPAPERS

London Gazette, 2 December 1892
Evening Post, 1 July 1893

WEBSITES

www.hse.gov.uk/aboutus/timeline/index.htm

KATHLEEN LYNN

Bourke, Angela, *The Field Day Anthology of Irish Writing Vol 5: Irish Women's Writing and Traditions* (Cork University Press; Ireland, 2002) ISBN-0-8147-9907-8

Cullen, Mary and Luddy, Maria, *Female Activists, Irish Women and Change 1900–1960* (The Woodfield Press; Dublin, 2001) ISBN-0-9534293-0-X

Hopkins, Frank, *Rare Old Dublin: Heroes, Hawkers and Hoors* (Marino Books; Dublin, 2002) ISBN-1-86023-150-0

Matthews, Ann, *Renegades Irish Republican Women 1900–1922* (Mercier Press; Cork, 2010) ISBN 978-1-85635-648-8

Mulholland, Marie, *The Politics and Relationships of Kathleen Lynn* (The Woodfield Press; Dublin, 2002) ISBN-0-9534293-2-6

Ó Hogartaigh, Margaret, *Kathleen Lynn: Irishwoman, Patriot, Doctor* (Irish Academic Press Ltd; Dublin, 2006) ISBN-978-0-7165-2843-2

LILIAN BLAND

Byrne, Liam, *History of Aviation in Ireland* (The Blackwater Press; Dublin, 1980) ISBN-0-905471-10-5

Lebow, Eileen F., *Before Amelia* (Brassey's Inc.; Virginia, 2002) ISBN-1-57488-532-4

MacCarron, Donal, *A View from Above: 200 years of Aviation in Ireland* (The O'Brien Press; Dublin, 2000) ISBN-0-86278-662-2

Mulvihill, Mary (ed.), *Lab Coats and Lace* (WITS (Women in Technology and Science); Dublin, 2009) ISBN-978-0-9531953-1

Warner, Guy, *Lilian Bland: The First Woman in the World to Design, Build and Fly an Aeroplane* (Ulster Aviation Society, 2010) ISBN-978-1-90598-951-5

MAGAZINES

Flight magazine, 1 January, 19 February, 5 March, 11 June, 16 July, 10 September, 17 December, 1910

Flight magazine, 23 December 1911

Flight magazine, 6 January 1912

Flight magazine, 23 January 1964

EILEEN GRAY

Adam, Peter, *Eileen Gray, Architect Designer: A Biography* (Thomas & Hudson Ltd; London, 1987) ISBN-0-500-28218-8

Baudot, Francois, *Eileen Gray* (Thames and Hudson Ltd; London, 1998) ISBN-0-500-01853-7

Campbell, Gordon (ed.), *The Grove Encyclopedia of Decorative Arts Volume 1* (Oxford University Press Inc.; New York, 2006) ISBN-978-0-19-518948-3

Constant, Caroline, *Eileen Gray* (Phaidon Press Ltd; London, 2000)
    ISBN-978-0-7148-4844-0

Garner, Philippe, *Eileen Gray, Design and Architecture, 1878-1976* (Taschen;
    Germany, 2006) ISBN-978-3-8228-4417-5

Rault, Jasmine, *Eileen Gray and the Design of Sapphic Modernity: Staying in*
    (Ashgate Publishing Ltd; Surrey, 2011) ISBN-978-0-7546-6961-6

Scott, Kathleen Lady, *Self-Portrait of an Artist, from the Diaries and Memoirs of
    Lady Kennet* (J. Murray; London, 1949)

WEBSITES

www.christies.com

FILMS

Invitation to a Voyage, Eileen Gray: Designer and Architect, Kick Film for RTÉ, 2006.
    Produced and directed by Jord Bundschuh

MAGAZINES

Dezeen Magazine, 9 September 2013

Lady Mary Heath

Boase, Wendy, *The Sky's the Limit: Women Pioneers in Aviation* (Osprey Publishing
    Ltd; London, 1979) ISBN-0-85045-318-6

Haines, Catherine M.C., *International Women in Science: A Biographical Dictionary
    to 1950* (ABC-CLIO Inc.; California, 2001) ISBN-1-57607-090-5

Haughton, John, *The Silver Lining: Kildonan, a Golden Age of Flying*
    (Finglas Environmental Heritage Project; Dublin, 2003) ISBN-0951850423

Heath, Lady and Wolfe Murray, Stella, *Woman and Flying* (John Long; London, 1929)

Henry, Noel, *From Sophie to Sonia: A History of Women's Athletics* (Vision Print;
    Dublin, 1998) ISBN-0953297101

Jessen, Gene Nora, *The Powder Puff Derby of 1929: The True Story of the
    First Women's Cross-Country Air Race* (Sourcebooks Inc; Illinois, 2002)
    ISBN-978-1570717697

Lomax, Judy, *Women of the Air* (John Murray Ltd; London, 1986)
    ISBN-0-7195-4293-6

Markula, Pirkko (ed.), *Feminist Sport Studies: Sharing Experiences of Joy and Pain*
    (State University of New York Press; Albany, 2005) ISBN-0-7914-6529-2

Millward, Liz, *Women in British Imperial Airspace, 1922-1937* (McGill-Queen's
    University Press; Canada, 2007) ISBN-978-0-7735-3337-0

Naughton, Lindie, *Lady Icarus: The Life of Irish Aviator Lady Mary Heath*
    (Ashfield Press; Dublin, 2004) ISBN-1-901658-38-4

Traynor, Michael, *Iona: Ireland's First Commercial Airline* (Michael Traynor;
    Dublin, 2004) ISBN-0-9549194-0-8

NEWSPAPERS

Limerick Chronicle, 9 December 1897, 3 September 1927
Daily Express, 17 May 1928

DAME NINETTE DE VALOIS

Anderson, Zoe, *The Royal Ballet: 75 Years* (Faber and Faber Ltd; London, 2010)
    ISBN-978-0-571-26090-4

Clarke, Mary, *The Sadler's Wells Ballet: A History and an Appreciation* (A & C Black
    Ltd; London, 1955)

De Valois, Ninette, *Come Dance With Me, A Memoir 1898-1956* (Readers Union;
    London, 1959)

De Valois, Ninette, *Invitation to the Ballet* (John Lane, The Bodley Head Ltd;
    London, 1937)

De Valois, Ninette, *Step by Step* (W.H. Allen & Co. Ltd; London, 1977)
    ISBN-0-491-01598-4

Eliot, Karen, *Dancing Lives: Five Female Dancers from the Ballet D'Action
    to Merce Cunningham* (University of Illinois Press; United States, 2007)
    ISBN-13978-0-252-03250-9

Fleischer, Mary, *Embodied Texts: Symbolist Playwright-Dancer Collaborations*
    (Editions Rodopi; Amsterdam, 2007) ISBN-978-90-420-2285-0

Goodwin, Noel, 'Dame Ninette de Valois (1898-2001)', *Oxford Dictionary of
    National Biography* (Oxford University Press; January 2005), online edition,
    January 2011.

Gottlieb, Robert, *Lives and Letters* (Farrar, Straus and Giroux; New York, 2011)
    ISBN 978-0-374-29882-1

Hoare, Philip, *Noel Coward: A Biography of Noel Coward* (Simon & Schuster;
    New York, 1995) ISBN-0-684-80937-0

Lebrecht, Norman, *Covent Garden The Untold Story: Dispatches from the English Culture
    War, 1945-2000* (Simon & Schuster UK Ltd; London, 2000) ISBN-1-55553-488-0

Sorley Walker, Kathrine, *Ninette de Valois: Idealist Without Illusions*
    (Hamish Hamilton Ltd; London, 1987) ISBN-0-241-12386-0

WEBSITES

www.news.bbc.co.uk/2/hi/entertainment/1209339.stm

DAME KATHLEEN LONSDALE

Authier, André, *Early Days of X-ray Crystallography* (Oxford University Press;
    Oxford, 2013) ISBN-978-0-19-965984-5

Baldwin, Melinda, '*Where are your intelligent mothers to come from?' Marriage and
    Family in the Scientific Career of Dame Kathleen Lonsdale FRS (1903-71)* Notes &
    Records of The Royal Society

Brock, Peter (ed.), *'These Strange Criminals': An Anthology of Prison Memoirs by Conscientious Objectors from the Great War to the Cold War* (University of Toronto Press Incorporated; Toronto, 2004) ISBN-0-8020-8707-8

Hodgkin, Dorothy M. C., 'Kathleen Lonsdale, 28 January – 1 April 1971' *Biographical Memoirs of Fellows of the Royal Society,* Vol.21 (November 1975).

Kass-Simon, G., Farnes, Patricia, Nash, Deborah (eds), *Women of Science: Righting the Record* (Indiana University Press; United States, 1990) ISBN-0-253-20813-0

Lonsdale, Kathleen, *Is Peace Possible?* (Penguin Books Ltd; Middlesex, 1957)

Lonsdale, Kathleen, *Removing the Causes of War,* Swarthmore Lecture (George Allen & Unwin Ltd; London, 1953)

Ogilvie, Marilyn and Harvey, Joy (eds), *The Biographical Dictionary of Women in Science: Pioneering Lives from Ancient Times to the Mid-20th Century* (Routledge; London, 2000) ISBN-0-415-92038-8

Oldfield, Sybil, *Women Humanitarians: A Biographical Dictionary of British Women Active between 1900 and 1950* (Continuum; London, 2001) ISBN-0-8264-4962-X

Rayner-Canham, Marelene and Geoffrey, *Chemistry Was Their Life: Pioneer British Women Chemists, 1880–1949* (Imperial College Press; London, 2008) ISBN-978-1-86094-986-9

Rayner-Canham, Marelene and Geoffrey, *Women in Chemistry: Their Changing Roles from Alchemical Times to the Mid-Twentieth Century* (Chemical Heritage Foundation; Philadelphia, 2001) ISBN-0-941901-27-0

Yount, Lisa, *A to Z of Women in Science and Math* (Facts on File, Revised Edition; York, 2008) ISBN-978-0-8160-6695-7

NEWSPAPERS

The Irish Times, 13 December 2001

WEBSITES

www.3.ul.ie/-childsp/elements/issue4/childs.htm
www.archiveshub.ac.uk/features/03030502.html
www.scripts.iucr.org/cgi-bin/paper?ao8665

Also from The History Press

Irish Women